Functional Beauty

Glenn Parsons and Allen Carlson offer an in[illegible] study of the relationship between function and aesthetic value, breaking with the philosophical tradition of seeing the two as separate.

They begin by developing and defending, in a general way, the concept of Functional Beauty, exploring how the role of function in aesthetic appreciation has been treated by some notable thinkers in the history of aesthetics. They then consider the relationship to Functional Beauty of certain views in current aesthetic thought, especially what they call 'cognitively rich' approaches to the aesthetic appreciation of both art and nature. Turning to work on the nature of function in the philosophy of science, they argue that this line of enquiry can help solve certain philosophical problems that have been raised for the idea that knowledge of function plays an important role in aesthetic appreciation.

Although philosophical discussions of aesthetic appreciation tend to focus largely and sometimes almost exclusively on artworks, the range of aesthetic appreciation is, of course, much larger. Not simply art, but also nature, architecture, and even more mundane, everyday things—cars, tools, clothing, furniture, and sports—are objects of frequent and enthusiastic aesthetic appreciation. Accordingly, in the second half of the book, Parsons and Carlson consider the place and importance of Functional Beauty in the aesthetic appreciation of a broad range of different kinds of things. These chapters explore Functional Beauty in nature and the natural environment, in architecture and the built environment, in everyday artefacts, events, and activities, and finally in art and the artworld. In each case, Parsons and Carlson argue that Functional Beauty illuminates our aesthetic experiences and helps to address various theoretical issues raised by these different objects of appreciation.

Glenn Parsons is Associate Professor of Philosophy at Ryerson University in Toronto, Canada.

Allen Carlson is Professor of Philosophy at the University of Alberta in Edmonton, Canada.

Functional Beauty

Glenn Parsons
and
Allen Carlson

CLARENDON PRESS · OXFORD

OXFORD
UNIVERSITY PRESS

Great Clarendon Street, Oxford OX2 6DP
United Kingdom

Oxford University Press is a department of the University of Oxford. It furthers the University's objective of excellence in research, scholarship, and education by publishing worldwide. Oxford is a registered trademark of Oxford University Press in the UK and in certain other countries

First published 2008
First published in paperback 2012

British Library Cataloguing in Publication Data

Data available

Library of Congress Cataloging in Publication Data

Parsons, Glenn.
Functional beauty / Glenn Parsons and Allen Carlson.
p. cm.
Includes bibliographical references and index.
ISBN 978-0-19-920524-0
1. Aesthetics. I. Carlson, Allen. II. Title.
BH39.P275 2008
111'.85—dc22 2008039109

ISBN 978–0–19–920524–0
ISBN 978–0–19–965931–9 (Pbk)

Printed in the United Kingdom by
Lightning Source UK Ltd., Milton Keynes

This observation extends to tables, chairs, scritoires, chimneys, coaches, sadles, ploughs, and indeed to every work of art; it being an universal rule, that their beauty is chiefly deriv'd from their utility, and from their fitness for that purpose, to which they are destin'd.

David Hume, *A Treatise of Human Nature*

Contents

Preface xi
Acknowledgements xiv

1. Functional Beauty in the Aesthetic Tradition **1**

1.1 Beauty as Fitness in Classical Thought 2
1.2 Beauty and Function in the Seventeenth and Eighteenth Centuries 6
1.3 The Eighteenth-Century Decline: Burke's Counter-Examples 12
1.4 The Eighteenth-Century Decline: Reason and Perception 18
1.5 The Eighteenth-Century Decline: Kant and Beauty 'Apart from Concepts' 21
1.6 The Autonomy of Art 24

2. Functional Beauty in Contemporary Aesthetic Theory **31**

2.1 The Decline of Disinterestedness and the Rise of Cultural Theories of Appreciation 32
2.2 Art, Nature, and Afunctionality 37
2.3 Architecture and Functionalism 42
2.4 The Problem of Translation 45
2.5 The Problem of Indeterminacy 49
2.6 A Role for Functional Beauty 57

3. Indeterminacy and the Concept of Function **62**

3.1 Intentionalism and Indeterminacy 63
3.2 Naturalizing Function 69
3.3 Artefact Selection and Proper Function 73
3.4 The Problem of Novel Artefacts 80
3.5 Indeterminacy and Functional Beauty 84

4. Function and Form **90**

4.1 Knowledge of Function 91
4.2 The Phenomenology of Functional Beauty 94
4.3 Is 'Looking Fit' an Aesthetic Quality? 100
4.4 Utility and Beauty 103
4.5 The Aesthetics of Dysfunction 107

5. Nature and Environment **111**

5.1 The Appreciation of Living Nature 112
5.2 The Immorality Objection 116
5.3 Function and the Beauty of Organisms 120
5.4 Function in the Landscape 124
5.5 Looking Dysfunctional and Positive Aesthetics 130

6. Architecture and the Built Environment **137**

6.1 The Case for Functional Beauty in Architecture 138
6.2 The Function of a Building: The Problem of Indeterminacy 143
6.3 Functional Beauty: a Bourgeois Aesthetic? 149
6.4 Aesthetic Objections: The Problem of Translation 154
6.5 The Beauty of Ruins 161

7. Artefacts and Everyday Aesthetics **167**

7.1 Five Features of Everyday Aesthetic Objects 168
7.2 The Deweyean Approach to Everyday Aesthetics 172

7.3 The Linguistic Practice Argument 177
7.4 Assessing the Linguistic Practice Argument 182
7.5 Functional Beauty as an Everyday Aesthetic 189

8. The Functions of Art 196

8.1 Functions of Art: An Overview 197
8.2 Intentionalist Theories of Art Function 203
8.3 Causal Role Theories of Art Function 209
8.4 A Selected Effects Theory of Art Function 216
8.5 Functional Beauty and the Appreciation of Art 223

9. Conclusion 228

Bibliography 235
Index 251

Preface

The aim of this book is to argue for the importance, in aesthetic appreciation, of knowledge concerning function. We were led to write it because each of us, in investigating various topics in the aesthetics of nature and the built environment, had become convinced of the importance of function, but found little discussion of it in the literature on philosophical aesthetics. In fact, the last major touchstone in this area remains Kant's discussion in his 1790 treatise on aesthetics and teleology, *The Critique of the Power of Judgement*. But, despite the lack of a recent sustained treatment, we found abundant raw materials for such a treatment lying ready to hand: sophisticated accounts of the role of knowledge in aesthetic appreciation, new interest in the aesthetics of utilitarian artefacts, and, most importantly, an impressive body of philosophical work on the concept of function itself. In this book, we draw on these materials in developing the concept that we call 'Functional Beauty' and in arguing that this concept is an important aspect of our aesthetic experience.

In the first half of the book, we develop and defend, in a general way, the concept of Functional Beauty. We begin our investigation by exploring how the role of function in aesthetic appreciation has been treated by some notable thinkers in the history of aesthetics. Drawing on this aesthetic tradition for guidance, we attempt to articulate the basic notion of Functional Beauty and position it with respect to the ideas and debates of contemporary aesthetics. Accordingly, in Chapters 2 and 4, we consider the relationship to Functional Beauty of certain views in current aesthetic thought, especially what we call 'cognitively rich' approaches to the aesthetic appreciation of both art and nature. However, to do justice to the concept of Functional Beauty, we find it necessary to go beyond purely aesthetic matters. Thus, in Chapter 3, we turn to work on the nature of function in the philosophy of science. This line of inquiry, we argue, can help solve certain philosophical problems that have been raised for the idea that knowledge of function plays an important role in aesthetic appreciation.

Although philosophical discussions of aesthetic appreciation tend to focus largely and sometimes almost exclusively on artworks, the range of aesthetic appreciation is, of course, much larger. Not simply art, but also nature, architecture, and even more mundane, everyday things—cars, tools, clothing, furniture, and sports—are objects of frequent and enthusiastic aesthetic appreciation. Accordingly, in the second half of the book, we consider the place and importance of Functional Beauty in the aesthetic appreciation of a broad range of different kinds of things. In Chapters 5 through 8, we explore Functional Beauty in nature and the natural environment, in architecture and the built environment, in everyday artefacts, events, and activities, and finally in art and the artworld. In each case, we argue that Functional Beauty illuminates our aesthetic experiences and helps to address various theoretical issues raised by these different objects of appreciation.

One issue regarding our terminology needs explanation here. In naming the book's central concept, we have opted to use the word 'beauty', a word that many contemporary philosophers avoid in favour of the term 'aesthetic'. This avoidance of 'beauty' is generally a wise practice because the word is often taken to suggest a somewhat narrower notion than the term 'aesthetic' suggests, referring to one particular kind of aesthetic quality. In keeping with this practice, throughout the book we have generally employed the term 'aesthetic', except when this would result in anachronism. For our concern here is with the wider notion of the aesthetic: our central concept is, really, aesthetic appreciation involving knowledge that concerns function. However, we could not bring ourselves to use such an unlovely name for our central concept, and we found that no alternative phrase caught the sense that we wanted to convey so well as 'Functional Beauty'. If it is borne in mind that, in this one expression, 'Beauty' is used, as philosophers occasionally still use it, to mean 'aesthetic appeal in general', rather than the specific sort of aesthetic appearance it typically suggests, no confusion should result.

Glenn Parsons
Allen Carlson
March 2008

Acknowledgements

Some of the material that appears in this book has been previously presented in different versions and in different places. We acknowledge and thank the editors and the publishers of the following items for the use of this material: Glenn Parsons, 'Natural Functions and the Aesthetic Appreciation of Inorganic Nature', *British Journal of Aesthetics* 44 (2004): 44–56; Glenn Parsons and Allen Carlson, 'New Formalism and the Aesthetic Appreciation of Nature', *Journal of Aesthetics and Art Criticism* 62 (2004): 363–76; and Glenn Parsons, 'The Aesthetic Value of Animals', *Environmental Ethics* 29 (2007): 151–69.

We also acknowledge, and express our appreciation to, Ryerson University's Faculty of Arts, the University of Alberta, and the Social Sciences and Humanities Research Council of Canada for support of this project in the form of grants and teaching release.

We thank our colleagues in our respective universities and in the discipline at large for their interest in and discussion of the ideas contained in this work. Many of these ideas were initially presented at various conferences, and we have benefited from the input that we received from our audiences. Similarly, we have profited from comments by Stephen Davies and by an Oxford University Press anonymous reviewer, both of whom read the entire manuscript and made numerous helpful suggestions. We also thank Kim Chow-Morris, David Ma, and Murat Bac for their help on the points of language usage discussed in Chapter 7.

And, most importantly, we thank and express our gratitude to our families for their support, encouragement, and patience.

1

Functional Beauty in the Aesthetic Tradition

In this book, we argue for the cogency and importance of aesthetic appreciation that accords a central role to knowledge of function. In order to situate our argument in the broader context of philosophical aesthetics, we begin, in this chapter, by documenting a tradition, now obscured, that associated aesthetic pleasure with functionality and related concepts, such as utility. Our aim in describing this tradition and some aspects of its evolution is not to give a full historical treatment of the relationship between the ideas of function and aesthetic appreciation. Such a treatment would be a laudable project, but it is not one within our purview.[1] Nor do we aim to provide a comprehensive history of the aesthetic thought of any given period or thinker. Rather, our focus here is on exhuming some central conceptual clarifications and philosophical criticisms that pertain to the idea that we call 'Functional Beauty' and that will play a role in our arguments later in the book. Accordingly, our treatment of the historical issues will be selective. We will sketch some of the classical and eighteenth-century articulations of these ideas and then focus on four pivotal developments: Edmund Burke's famous critique of function-based theories of beauty; the eighteenth-century reconsideration of the relation of reason and perception; the development of non-conceptual theories of

[1] Some aspects of the relationship are treated briefly in Wladyslaw Tatarkiewicz, 'The Great Theory of Beauty and its Decline', *Journal of Aesthetics and Art Criticism* 31 (1972): 165–80, and eighteenth-century developments are covered in Paul Guyer, 'Beauty and Utility in Eighteenth-Century Aesthetics', *Eighteenth-Century Studies* 35 (2002a): 439–53.

beauty; and the rise of the idea of art as an autonomous sphere of activity. We will move freely between describing these issues in their historical context and assessing them philosophically, with an eye to their importance for a contemporary theory of Functional Beauty.

1.1 Beauty as Fitness in Classical Thought

The basic idea of Functional Beauty is that of a thing's function being integral to its aesthetic character. Expressed slightly differently, the idea is that of a thing's aesthetic qualities emerging from its function or something closely related to its function, such as its purpose, use, or end. This general idea can be developed into a number of specific philosophical doctrines concerning aesthetic appreciation.

One very important philosophical articulation of the idea, for example, is the doctrine of beauty as fitness for function, which we find in classical Greek philosophy. In the *Memorabilia* (370 BCE) of the Greek historian and writer Xenophon, for example, Socrates claims that 'all things are good and beautiful in relation to those purposes for which they are well adapted, bad and ugly in relation to those for which they are ill adapted'.[2] Socrates voices a similar view also in the Platonic dialogue *The Greater Hippias* (390 BCE):

> We say that the whole body is beautifully made, sometimes for running, sometimes for wrestling; and we speak in the same way of all animals. A beautiful horse, or cock, or quail, and all utensils, and means of transport both on land and on sea, merchant vessels and ships of war, and all instruments of music and the arts generally, and, if you like, practices and laws—we apply the word 'beautiful' to practically all these in the same manner; in each case we take as our criterion the natural constitution or the workmanship or the form of enactment, and whatever is useful we call beautiful, and beautiful in that respect in which it is useful and for

[2] Xenophon, *Memorabilia* [approx. 370 BCE], Book III, Chapter 8, Section 7, trans. E. C. Marchant, reprinted in Wladyslaw Tatarkiewicz, *History of Aesthetics* [1970–4] (London: Continuum, 2005), Volume 1, 109–10.

the purpose for which and at the time at which it is useful; and we call ugly that which is useless in all these respects.[3]

A connection between beauty and a function-related concept, purpose, is certainly evident in these passages, but the precise nature of this connection needs clarification in two respects. First, what exactly is the logical form of Socrates' view? What Socrates appears to be giving is a conception of what beauty is: beauty is being well adapted to a purpose, and ugliness, correspondingly, is being poorly adapted to a purpose. This is made clear in Xenophon's *Memorabilia* when Socrates' interlocutor raises an apparent counter-example to his claim: a dung basket that is well designed for its purpose is not thereby beautiful, surely? Holding the line, however, Socrates declares that it *is* beautiful, if 'it is well made for its special work', and says that even a golden shield would be ugly, if it were not well made for its special work.[4] Socrates' comment on the golden shield implies that his view is that being well adapted to, or as we shall say, 'fit for', its purpose is a necessary and sufficient condition for an object to be beautiful. In other words, taking 'function' as a general term that covers function-related concepts such as purpose, end, use, and the like, the position that Socrates articulates is that fitness for a function *is* beauty, and, in fact, is the only kind or variety of beauty. We shall call this the 'strong version' of the theory that beauty is fitness for function. Also present in classical thought is what we will call a 'weak version' of this theory: the view that being fit for function, though not necessary for an object to be beautiful, is sufficient for this. That is, fitness is one kind of beauty among others.[5] On this view, a golden shield might lack

[3] Plato, *Greater Hippias* [approx. 390 BCE], 295d, trans. B. Jowett, in K. Aschenbrenner and A. Isenberg (eds), *Aesthetic Theories: Studies in the Philosophy of Art* (Englewood Cliffs, NJ: Prentice-Hall, 1965), 3–17; the quotation is on page 10. The authorship of the *Greater Hippias* is uncertain, although it is commonly attributed to Plato.

[4] Xenophon, *Memorabilia*, Book III, Chapter 8, Section 7, in Tatarkiewicz, *History of Aesthetics*, Volume 1, 109–10. In another Socratic text by Xenophon, Socrates considers similar claims concerning the beauty of his bulging eyes and nose, well-adapted as they are for seeing and sniffing; see *Symposium*, [approx. 360 BCE] Chapter 5, Sections 5–6, ed. and trans. A. J. Bowen (Warminster: Aris and Phillips, 1998), 65–7.

[5] See Tatarkiewicz, 'The Great Theory of Beauty', 171.

the sort of beauty that consists in fitness for its purpose, and yet be beautiful in virtue of its other aspects, such as its dazzling colour, or its visually interesting shape.[6]

Socrates' position that beauty is being well adapted to some end also requires clarification concerning its relevance to 'beauty' in the sense that we understand the term in aesthetic theory today. 'Beauty', of course, has several senses. In aesthetic contexts, it has a relatively specific meaning, referring to a quality of the visual or auditory appearance of an object, namely, its capacity to provide certain kinds of pleasant perceptual experiences.[7] But, in other contexts, 'beauty' has a wider sense that does not refer to perceptual appearances, but to goodness or excellence in general, as when a clever stock trade or an angler's prized catch is celebrated as a 'real beauty'. The Greek term cognate with 'beauty'—*kalon*—was routinely used in this latter sense, and Socrates seems to verge on this non-aesthetic sense in saying that things are beautiful when they are well adapted for their purposes. For this reason, Socrates' view is sometimes disregarded in histories of aesthetics.[8] However, later thinkers have taken Socrates' view as a claim about beauty in the narrower, aesthetic sense as well, and it is this interpretation of the view that concerns us here.[9] On this reading, the view is that an object's being well adapted to its purpose provides that object with that certain kind of pleasing perceptual appearance we call 'beautiful'. This view would be based on the assumption that an item that is well adapted to serving its purpose *looks* well adapted to that

[6] An intermediate view would be that apparent utility is necessary for beauty, though not sufficient. A version of this view is discussed in Guyer, 'Beauty and Utility'.

[7] This gloss is not meant to be an adequate philosophical definition, but only to mark out, roughly, the scope of the narrower 'aesthetic' sense of 'beauty'. See the discussion by Jennifer Anne McMahon, 'Beauty', in Berys Gaut and Dominic Lopes (eds), *The Routledge Companion to Aesthetics* (London: Routledge, 2001), 227–38. Eighteenth-century conceptions are reviewed in Jerome Stolnitz, '"Beauty": Some Stages in the History of an Idea', *Journal of the History of Ideas* 22 (1961a): 185–204. We will return to this topic in Chapter 4, and again in Chapter 7.

[8] See, for example, Monroe Beardsley, *Aesthetics: From Classical Greece to the Present* (New York: Macmillan, 1966), 42.

[9] Tatarkiewicz places the idea of fitness as beauty within the tradition of thought on the narrow, aesthetic sense of 'beauty'; see 'The Great Theory of Beauty', 171.

purpose. Thus, on this interpretation of Socrates' view, it is not *being* fit for function that constitutes beauty, but rather *looking* fit for function. A shield could actually be well suited for warfare, for example, but would be beautiful, in the aesthetic sense, only if its shape and composition cause it to *appear* properly formed for warfare.

When developed in the way specified, the idea of beauty as fitness for function is one important way of articulating the more general idea of Functional Beauty. As we will see, it is by no means the only way of expressing that general idea. However, it has been the most influential historically. Consideration of the doctrine of beauty as fitness for function is also useful insofar as it brings out vividly an important objection that apparently can be mounted against any specific development of the idea of Functional Beauty. This objection involves the relation between the function of an object and its look or appearance. In the specific case of the doctrine of beauty as fitness for function, the objection rejects the assumption that, in some cases at least, an object that is fit for its function *looks* fit for its function. In rejecting this assumption, one might concede that objects can *be* well adapted to their functions and that we can *know* they are well adapted to their functions, but still deny that they can *look* well adapted to their functions. One might deny this on the grounds that adaptedness to function is something that lies outside of, or beyond, our perception of the object, being instead a matter for judgement about the object that is, like all judgement, carried out by the intellect rather than the senses. We can know that an object is well adapted, but this is not something that we can *see*, in the way that we can see its shape or colour. This objection thus calls into question whether our response to an item's being fit for its function can be properly called an experience of beauty, in the aesthetic sense, at all.

This objection makes plain that the general idea of Functional Beauty raises deep questions concerning the nature of, and relationship between, beauty and perception. As we will see in Section 4 of this chapter, these issues have come to play a central role in the history of the concept.

1.2 Beauty and Function in the Seventeenth and Eighteenth Centuries

In spite of their appearance in classical philosophy, versions of the notion of Functional Beauty, such as the idea of beauty as fitness for function, have not been central in the Western tradition of thought on the nature of beauty. That tradition has been dominated by other conceptions, notably the idea that beauty consists in a certain sort of proportion amongst the parts of an object. Yet, taken together, views involving function represent an important and persistent minority view on the nature of beauty.[10]

One example of a philosophical climate amenable to Functional Beauty is seventeenth-century Continental Rationalism. In this tradition, we find judgements of beauty treated, along with perceptual judgements in general, as clear but confused judgements of perfection. To say that something is beautiful, on this general view, is to say, on the basis of a vivid or forceful sensory perception, that it is perfect or excellent, but in some way that one is unable to specify precisely. Leibniz, for instance, notes that artists 'correctly know what is done properly and what is done poorly, though they are often unable to explain their judgements and reply to questioning by saying that the things that displease them lack an unknown something'.[11] As Paul Guyer points out, for at least some objects, the end that constitutes their perfection is the fulfilment of a function of some sort. In these cases, judgements of beauty can be understood, on the rationalists' model, as judgements that the object appears, in perception, to be perfectly fit for its function. Thus a beautiful canon, on this view, is beautiful to the extent that it strikes one as looking perfectly suited to artillery warfare, without it being clear precisely why, or on what grounds, it is perfect.[12]

[10] See Tatarkiewicz, 'Great Theory of Beauty', 171.

[11] G. W. Leibniz, 'Meditations on Knowledge, Truth, and Ideas' [1684], in *Philosophical Essays*, trans. R. Ariew and D. Garber (Indianapolis, IN: Hackett, 1989), 24.

[12] Guyer, 'Beauty and Utility', 445.

Rationalist philosophers, of course, focused upon reason as the paradigm mental activity, and, consequently, tended to view sensory perception not as a fundamentally different kind of activity, but rather as a low-grade form of reasoning. This viewpoint is illustrated famously by the German philosopher Alexander Baumgarten's definition of 'aesthetics' as the science of sensory knowledge.[13] This refusal to sharply separate reason from sense perception somewhat addresses the objection to the idea of Functional Beauty raised at the end of the previous section. For the aesthetic is not here construed as a matter of mere looking as opposed to thinking; consequently aesthetic pleasure in fitness, which seems to involve thinking, can thus be countenanced. For the rationalists, then, the connection between beauty and fitness was a relatively comfortable one. For the British empiricists that followed them, however, this connection was more problematic. Their struggles with Functional Beauty are particularly important since it was their work, in large part, that ultimately established aesthetics as a distinct philosophical discipline in the eighteenth century. We will explore this struggle, and its ultimate resolution, in the following sections, but before doing so it is worth emphasizing the persistence of the theory of beauty as fitness even into this tumultuous period. For, despite the radical changes that the empiricists wrought in aesthetic theory during the eighteenth century, the traditional conception of beauty as fitness for function can be found, with surprising frequency, in the writings of this period.[14]

It is vigorously defended by Bishop Berkeley, for example, in his theological dialogue *Alciphron* (1732).[15] In this dialogue, Berkeley's

[13] Alexander Gottlieb Baumgarten, *Reflections on Poetry* [1735] and *Aesthetica* [1750]. See especially Section 1 of the latter volume.

[14] For an overview of the role of utility in the aesthetic theory of this period, see Guyer, 'Beauty and Utility'.

[15] George Berkeley, *Alciphron, or the Minute Philosopher* [1732], reprinted in David Berman (ed.), *Alciphron or the Minute Philosopher in Focus* (London: Routledge, 1993). The relevant sections are Dialogue 3, Sections 3–9.

protagonist Euphranor accepts the common view of beauty as a pleasing proportion, but argues that the proportion possessed by an object is itself dependent upon its fitness for its purpose. The dialogue proceeds:

> *Euphranor*: ... Could the chair you sit on, think you, be reckoned well proportioned or handsome, if it had not such a height, breadth, wideness, and was not so far reclined as to afford a convenient seat?
>
> *Alciphron*: It could not.
>
> *Euphranor*: The beauty, therefore, or symmetry of a chair cannot be apprehended but by knowing its use, and comparing its figure with that use; which cannot be done by the eye alone, but is the effect of judgement.[16]

Although Euphranor's view accords proportion a pivotal role in beauty, his conclusion is that the fitness of things, 'their aptitude and subordination to [some] end', is 'at bottom, that which makes them please and charm'.[17] Furthermore, Berkeley's discussion seems to amount to a defence of the strong view of beauty as fitness, since he leaves little scope for the perception of beauty without regard to fitness: the beauty of a chair 'cannot be apprehended' without knowledge of its function, and the reference of its form to that function.

In this, however, Berkeley's view is unusual, and the weak theory is more commonly found among eighteenth-century writers. A case in point is the aesthetic theory offered by Hume in his *Treatise of Human Nature* (1739–40).[18] For Hume, the feeling of beauty arises when we perceive an object that we know to serve a useful purpose, or that raises in us an idea of utility. Hume extends this idea to 'tables, chairs, scritoires, chimneys, coaches, sadles, ploughs, and indeed ... every work of art', adding 'it being an universal rule,

[16] Berkeley, *Alciphron*, Dialogue 3, Section 8, 67. [17] Ibid., Section 9, 71.

[18] David Hume, *A Treatise of Human Nature* [1739–40], ed. L. A. Selby-Bigge (Oxford: Oxford University Press, 1960).

that their beauty is chiefly derived from their utility, and from their fitness for that purpose, to which they are destined'.[19] Here Hume puts an important twist on the theory of beauty as fitness, since he takes beauty to be produced not by an object's appearing fit for its function per se, but by the object's conveying the idea of some benefit or utility, through appearing fit for its function. Thus he speaks of beauty occurring in objects in virtue of 'their fitness *for the use of man*', and stresses that the beautiful pleases by its 'tendency to produce an end *that is agreeable*'.[20] Hume's approach to Functional Beauty, then, is somewhat more narrow than that of the theory of beauty as fitness, which takes beauty to consist in an object's appearing fit for its function.[21] Objects have Functional Beauty, or beauty that involves their function, on Hume's account, only insofar as their function is a useful one. Thus, objects that appear fit for a function that is bereft of utility or a function that leads away from human happiness, such as torture devices, for example, could be beautiful on the more traditional 'beauty as fitness' theory, but not on Hume's 'beauty as utility' theory.[22]

This alteration in the idea of Functional Beauty generates a difficulty, however. On the theory of beauty as fitness, the beauty of an item can be apprehended by any observer cognizant of its function. To the extent that the object appears fit for the function, it is found beautiful. For Hume, however, beauty arises not out of the object's fitness to its function, but ultimately out of its appearing

[19] Hume, *Treatise*, Book II, Part II, Section V, 364. Some have argued that Hume's notion of beauty as utility plays an important role in his famous discussion of the justification of judgements of beauty in 'Of the Standard of Taste'; see, for example, Carolyn Korsmeyer, 'Hume and the Foundations of Taste', *Journal of Aesthetics and Art Criticism* 35 (1976): 201–15, and Peter Kivy, *The Seventh Sense: Francis Hutcheson and Eighteenth-Century British Aesthetics*, 2nd edn (Oxford: Oxford University Press, 2003).

[20] Hume, *Treatise*, Book III, Part III, Section I, 577 (our emphasis).

[21] This point is made by Walter J. Hipple, Jr, *The Beautiful, the Sublime, and the Picturesque in Eighteenth-Century British Aesthetic Theory* (Carbondale, IL: The Southern Illinois University Press, 1957), 41.

[22] See ibid. Note that the formulation found in the *Greater Hippias*, cited above, refers to 'the useful'; indeed, later in that dialogue, Socrates denies beauty to 'any things useful for working some evil'; see *Greater Hippias*, 296c. We return to the issue of such 'deviant' functions in Chapter 6, Section 3.

useful. If something appears useful, then it is found beautiful. But useful to whom? Certainly not the observer: our neighbour's fine house may be no good to us, but beautiful nonetheless.[23] To address this issue, Hume invokes an additional element in our perception of beauty: sympathy with others. When combined with utility, sympathy yields the feeling of beauty even in cases where the object indicates no benefit to the observer:

> Thus the conveniency of a house, the fertility of a field, the strength of a horse, the capacity, security, and swift-sailing of a vessel, form the principal beauty of these several objects. Here the object which is denominated beautiful pleases only by its tendency to produce a certain effect. The effect is the pleasure or advantage of some other person. Now the pleasure of a stranger, for whom we have no friendship, pleases us only by sympathy. To this principle, therefore, is owing the beauty, which we find in every thing that is useful.[24]

For Hume, then, objects that appear able to serve some need or desire bring us pleasure insofar as, through sympathizing with others, we feel a vicarious pleasure in the satisfaction, or potential satisfaction, of that need or desire.

As mentioned, Hume's account differs from Berkeley's in invoking only a *weak* version of the idea that beauty is utility. Thus, utility is not the only source of beauty, which 'be sometimes derived from the mere species and appearance of the objects; sometimes from sympathy, and an idea of their utility'.[25] Hume believes, that is, that aspects of an object unrelated to its function, such as its mere colour or shape, for example, can also make it beautiful. This variety of beauty arises in us naturally due to our constitution, without the influence of any thought or judgement concerning the object, such as thought about its fitness for its

[23] Hume also cites a case where 'the fortifications of a city belonging to an enemy are esteemed beautiful upon account of their strength, though we could wish that they were entirely destroyed'; see *Treatise*, Book III, Part III, Section I, 586–7. In this case, the apparent strength of the city walls pleases us, though it does not serve, but actually thwarts, our aims.

[24] Ibid., Book III, Part III, Section I, 576.

[25] Ibid., Book III, Part III, Section V, 617.

purpose, for example. Hume's account of beauty, however, places the emphasis upon the other variety of beauty, that involving the utility of objects. He famously notes that it 'is evident, that nothing renders a field more agreeable than its fertility, and that scarce any advantages of ornament or situation will be able to equal this beauty'.[26] But, despite this emphasis, Hume's admission of an additional species of beauty leaves his view closer to the weak conception of Functional Beauty than to the strong.[27]

Despite these differences, however, the point we wish to emphasize is the common appeal, among eighteenth-century theorists with otherwise very different approaches, to some version of the notion of Functional Beauty. And the influence of theories relating beauty to function extends well beyond Hume and Berkeley to many other theorists of the period. The first chapter of William Hogarth's *Analysis of Beauty* (1753) is titled 'Of Fitness' and argues that 'the bulks and proportions of objects are govern'd by fitness and propriety'.[28] Alexander Gerard's *Essay on Taste* (1759) maintains a similar role for utility, and Adam Smith critiques but also develops Hume's thoughts on the beauty of utility in his *Theory of Moral Sentiments* (1759).[29] Indeed, far from being seen as a fringe view, Functional Beauty was viewed by many theorists as a plainly valid idea. Archibald Alison, for instance, finds the claim that 'pleasing or agreeable Forms receive beauty from their Fitness' to be 'too

[26] Hume, *Treatise*, Book II, Part II, Section V, 364.

[27] For a comparison of Berkeley and Hume, see J. O. Urmson, 'Berkeley on Beauty', in Berman, *Alciphron in Focus* (London: Routledge, 1993), 179–84. There are many other important differences in their aesthetic views. Most prominently, whereas Hume regards beauty as the object of an inner sense, Berkeley views the role of fitness in beauty as demonstrating that beauty is a rational, not a perceptual matter, 'an object, not of the eye, but of the mind'; see *Alciphron*, Section 8, in Berman, *Alciphron in Focus*, 67.

[28] William Hogarth, *Analysis of Beauty* [1753], ed. R. Paulson (New Haven, CN: Yale, 1997), 25.

[29] Adam Smith, *The Theory of Moral Sentiments* [1759], in *The Glasgow Edition of the Works and Correspondence of Adam Smith*, Volume I, ed. D. D. Raphael and A. L. Macfie (Indianapolis, IN: Liberty Fund, 1982). Much earlier, Hobbes also endorses the utility view, claiming that 'pulchrum' refers to 'that which by some apparent signs promises good'; see Thomas Hobbes, *Leviathan or the Matter, Form, and Power of a Commonwealth Ecclesiastical and Civil* [1651], Part 1, Chapter VI (Hamilton, Canada: McMaster University Archive of the History of Economic Thought, 1999), 33.

obvious to require any illustration'.[30] Similarly, for Smith, it is 'so very obvious that nobody has overlooked it'.[31] The tradition of analysing 'beauty', in its aesthetic sense, in terms of fitness, utility, and related concepts, was in fact thriving well into the eighteenth century's 'golden age' of aesthetic theory.

One theoretical feature of this tradition, which surely explains something of its tenacity and persuasiveness, is worth remarking on: its *comprehensiveness*, or its applicability to a broad range of objects. As the above quotations from Hume reveal, theorists of the eighteenth century moved easily, in their discussions of beauty, from artefacts, such as tools, furniture, and buildings, to artworks, to examples from nature, such as landscapes and human and animal form. Those quotations also suggest that this was facilitated, in part, by the appeal to Functional Beauty. Beauty, so understood, became a concept broad enough to apply to objects in each of these different domains. We take this kind of comprehensiveness to be a prima facie virtue in an aesthetic theory. For people seem to engage in aesthetic appreciation, and use aesthetic terminology, not only with respect to the arts but in their intercourse with nature and the highly utilitarian environment of everyday life as well. Thus, all else being equal, a conception of the aesthetic that can illuminate these different domains, and reveal connections among them, possesses an advantage over theories that do not. As we shall see, as the tradition of Functional Beauty begins to decline, this comprehensiveness becomes increasingly difficult to discern in theoretical treatments of the aesthetic.

1.3 The Eighteenth-Century Decline: Burke's Counter-Examples

Despite the importance of Functional Beauty in aesthetic theory during the eighteenth century, this period also witnessed increasing

[30] Archibald Alison, *Essays on the Nature and Principles of Taste*, Essay II, Chapter IV, Section II, Part II (Dublin: P. Byrne et al., 1790), 319.

[31] Smith, *Theory of Moral Sentiments*, Part IV, Chapter 1, Paragraph 1, 179.

criticism of the theory of beauty as fitness, in both its strong and weak forms. The most well-known example of this criticism is a set of famous counter-examples to the theory of beauty as fitness offered by Edmund Burke in his influential treatise *A Philosophical Enquiry into the Origin of our Ideas of the Sublime and Beautiful* (1757).[32] With respect to the strong version of the theory, the view that looking fit is a necessary and sufficient condition for beauty, Burke writes that 'I never in my life chanced to see a peacock fly; and yet before, very long before, I considered any aptitude in his form for the aërial life, I was struck with the extreme beauty which raises that bird above many of the best flying fowls in the world'.[33] Even to a casual observer the peacock is beautiful, but for all such an observer knows, its form may be ill-suited to its ends, such as flying. Broadening the point, Burke continues:

> many things are very beautiful, in which it is impossible to discern any idea of use. And I appeal to the first and most natural feelings of mankind, whether on beholding a beautiful eye, or a well-fashioned mouth, or a well-turned leg, any ideas of their being well fitted for seeing, eating, or running, ever present themselves. What idea of use is it that flowers excite, the most beautiful part of the vegetable world?[34]

Since objects can appear beautiful without appearing fit or well-suited to some use, the strong version of the theory is false: looking fit is not necessary for beauty. But, according to Burke, the weaker theory, that looking fit is a sufficient, though not necessary, condition for beauty (that is, that looking fit represents one kind of beauty among others) is also false. 'For,' Burke writes, 'on that principle, the wedge-like snout of a swine, with its tough cartilage at the end, the little sunk eyes, and the whole make of the head, so well adapted to its offices of digging and rooting, would

[32] Edmund Burke, *A Philosophical Enquiry into the Origin of our Ideas of the Sublime and Beautiful* [1757], ed. James T. Boulton (London: Routledge and Kegan Paul, 1958).

[33] Ibid., Part III, Section VI, 106. Note that Burke often talks of beauty as utility, but by this merely means fitness: 'It is said that the idea of utility, or of a part's being well adapted to answer its end, is the cause of beauty'; see Part III, Section VI, 104.

[34] Ibid., 107.

be extremely beautiful.'[35] Hence fitness and beauty, though they may often occur together, are not 'any way dependent on each other'.[36]

As the previous section has indicated, Burke's complete rejection of the idea of Functional Beauty was unorthodox in eighteenth-century British thought. However, it was not unique. For example, Francis Hutcheson offers counter-examples similar to Burke's.[37] In his rebuttal of Berkeley's theory of beauty as utility, Hutcheson co-opts Berkeley's own examples of doors and chairs, arguing that 'in these very things similitude of parts is regarded, where unlike parts would be equally useful'.[38] He asks his readers to imagine two chairs: one with four identical legs, and one with four mismatched legs of equal length, one turned in, one turned out, and so on. The chair with the four matching legs, Hutcheson claims, would have more beauty than the chair with irregular legs, although the irregular legs would render the chair equally fit for sitting. This example indicates that fitness is not necessary for beauty, since the additional beauty of the more regular chair involves no increased fitness. He also suggests that fitness is not sufficient to confer beauty either, citing a door that, instead of being rectangular, is coffin-shaped (that is, wider at the top than at the bottom). Of such a door, Hutcheson says that it 'would bear a more manifest Aptitude to the human Shape, than that which Artists require', and yet clearly such a door would be viewed as *less* beautiful than the traditional, less functionally apt, door.[39] Thus, like Burke, Hutcheson finds no logical connection between beauty and looking fit for function.

In fact, Burke and Hutcheson's counter-examples were not wholly original; the pig-snout, for instance, clearly echoes the

[35] Burke, *Philosophical Enquiry*, Part III, Section VI, 105. [36] Ibid., 107.

[37] Francis Hutcheson, *An Inquiry into the Original of our Ideas of Beauty and Virtue; in Two Treatises*, 4th edn [1738] Treatise I, Section V, Part I (Glasgow: Robert and Andrew Foulis, 1772). In addition to the counter-examples of Burke and Hutcheson, note the following remark in John Donaldson's *The Elements of Beauty* [1780]: the 'toad is as fit for the purposes of its nature as a turtle-dove'; quoted in Stolnitz, 'Beauty', 197.

[38] Hutcheson, *Inquiry*, Treatise I, Section V, Part I, 41.

[39] Ibid. Hutcheson's counter-examples are discussed by Guyer, 'Beauty and Utility'.

dung-basket of Xenophon's *Memorabilia* (370 BCE) and also Socrates' bulging eyes and large nostrils, so well-suited to seeing and smelling, which he rather cheekily insists are beautiful in Xenophon's *Symposium* (360 BCE).[40] Yet the eighteenth-century examples, particularly Burke's, do highlight the implausibility of the idea of beauty as fitness in a particularly forceful way, and foreshadow a coming change in the direction of aesthetic thought.

But do such counter-examples refute the theory of beauty as fitness? Some have thought so.[41] They do seem to show that the strong claim is false. That is, they show that fitness is not the only species of beauty, or that objects can be beautiful in virtue of properties other than their apparent fitness. But with respect to the weaker version of the theory of beauty as fitness, the theory that 'looking fit' is sufficient for beauty, Burke's counter-examples are less convincing. It is worth noting that some of his other counter-examples strike the modern reader as especially implausible. Burke writes, for example: 'How well fitted is the wolf for running and leaping! how admirably is the lion armed for battle! but will any one therefore call ... the wolf, and the lion, beautiful animals?'[42] Since these animals are for us, if not for Burke, generally viewed as paradigms of the beautiful, they are not even putative counter-examples to the weak theory. The pig's snout, though, does seem to be a case where, prima facie, we would decline to apply the term 'beautiful', although the object does 'look fit for its function'.[43]

[40] Xenophon, *Symposium*, Chapter 5, Sections 5–6, 65–7.

[41] Guyer, 'Beauty and Utility', 445, suggests that the Burke/Hutcheson counter-examples were not answered by eighteenth-century defenders of the view that fitness is a sufficient condition for beauty, and that the relationship of beauty to fitness was ultimately resolved in a different way by Kant (see Section 5 of this chapter). George Landow expresses a similar view in his study of John Ruskin's aesthetics, writing that 'whatever way Hume and others intended the notion of utility to be taken, in these terms the swine would have been beautiful. And swine are not beautiful'; see Landow, *The Aesthetic and Critical Theories of John Ruskin* (Princeton, NJ: Princeton University Press, 1971), 98.

[42] Burke, *Philosophical Enquiry*, Part III, Section VI, 105–6.

[43] Note that it is far from clear, despite what Burke says, that the pig's snout is a paradigm of apparent fitness (for further consideration of this issue, see Chapter 4, Section 2). In the present discussion, however, we will follow him in this assumption.

But there are at least two possible explanations for this. One is that the object has no beauty at all; the other is that some of its aspects are beautiful, while others are not, such that, overall, it fails to merit the summary description 'beautiful'. In more modern terms, the latter explanation is that the object has some aesthetic qualities, but not enough to merit the overall assessment 'beautiful'. So if we admit that beauty comes in a variety of different species, we ought not to conclude, from Burke's example, that apparent fitness is not sufficient for beauty. For, like the dung basket whose odour and colour repulse us, the pig's snout may displease us with its texture, dirty appearance, and foul smell, but nonetheless contain *a* beauty, albeit one that is obscured, in its aptness of form to function.

This was pointed out by one of Burke's early critics, Archibald Alison. 'That Fitness is not the only source of Beauty in Forms,' Alison concedes, 'is sufficiently obvious.'[44] But in response to Burke's example of the pig, Alison argues that we fail to call pigs 'beautiful' because they lack those varieties of beauty that strike us immediately, and furthermore display unpleasing qualities associated with their 'instincts, their characters, and their modes of life'.[45] Here Alison seems to allude to morally problematic traits of animals, as well as displeasing sensory elements of their appearance, such as filthiness or foul smell. Since these qualities dominate our encounters with these creatures, 'in general we never consider the animals in the light of this Fitness of their construction'.[46] But once we put aside these initial adverse responses, and actually attend to the fitness of the creature's form, Alison affirms that we will see beauty in it:

> To say at first, that the head of the Swine was a beautiful Form, might perhaps expose the person who affected it to ridicule; but if the admirable Fitness of its construction, for the necessities of the animal, are explained, there is no person who will not feel from this view of it, an Emotion of Beauty.[47]

[44] Alison, *Essays*, Essay II, Chapter IV, Section II, Part II, 317.
[45] Ibid., 318. [46] Ibid. [47] Ibid.

It is possible to reply to Alison's account, however, by arguing that, even if there are multiple species of beauty, a pig's snout simply has none of them. In other words, one might insist that it is not simply that the snout has little beauty, or a beauty that is obscured for us; rather, it is that the snout has *no beauty at all.* If so, one might conclude that Burke was correct in saying that the term 'beauty' is not applicable to the pig snout, for it is not applicable *even if* we focus attention on the relation of its form to its function. This line of thought does not seem to us obviously correct, though perhaps more could be said in its favour. However, even if it is correct, its significance is undermined by more general developments in eighteenth-century aesthetics.

One of the main movements of the period, and a movement to which Burke himself contributed, was the shift away from the traditional focus on beauty and towards the broader notion of the 'pleasures of the imagination', or what we would call the 'aesthetic' pleasures.[48] Thus, even if, contrary to Alison's insistence, 'beauty' is not applicable to the snout's aptness to its function, the phrase 'aesthetically pleasing' might well be. Burke's own aesthetic theory manifests the movement towards a wider concept of the 'aesthetic' in his inclusion of the sublime as an aesthetic category distinct from the beautiful. By taking the narrower concept of beauty to exhaustively cover the remaining 'aesthetic pleasures', however, Burke also resists this movement to some extent. But once the focus on beauty, with its narrower connotations, becomes displaced in favour of the broader notion of aesthetic pleasure, as it ultimately does, it becomes much easier to admit the aesthetic status of 'looking fit'. This is evident in Burke's contemporary Hutcheson, who, despite being every bit as critical of the association between fitness and *beauty* as Burke was, nonetheless appeared to classify apparent fitness as one of the pleasures of the imagination (that is, an aesthetic pleasure, in our terminology).[49] Thus, even if Burke's

[48] On this point, see Stolnitz, 'Beauty'.

[49] This interpretation of Hutcheson's later views on fitness is given in Kivy, *The Seventh Sense*, 93–5.

pig shows that 'looking fit' is not a species of *beauty*, this does not entail that looking fit is not an *aesthetic quality*. This is the theory that is of interest to contemporary aesthetics and the one we will be concerned with defending in later chapters.

1.4 The Eighteenth-Century Decline: Reason and Perception

For the moment, however, we need to examine another dimension of the eighteenth-century critique of the traditional theory of beauty as fitness. For beneath counter-examples such as Burke's lies a deeper reason why empiricist aestheticians resisted the idea that looking fit produces an aesthetic pleasure, one that harkens back to the objection concerning the imperceptibility of fitness that was raised at the end of the first section of this chapter. For empiricist philosophers, in contrast to the view taken by rationalists, reason and perception were fundamentally different mental processes: whereas reason operates volitionally and non-instantaneously, perception occurs instantly, whether we will it or not. One of the key tenets of the empiricist aestheticians was that the experience of beauty, or what we might call the aesthetic response, is something akin to a perceptual experience, which takes place immediately and independently of any exercise of reason. Given this conception of the aesthetic response, it becomes implausible to think that aesthetic experience could involve characteristics such as function, utility, and the like, which are characteristics that we grasp through the use of reason.[50]

This line of thought is clear in Hutcheson, who considers beauty to be perceived by a special internal sense, and who declares that the pleasure of beauty 'is different from any Knowledge of Principles, Proportions, Causes, or of the Usefulness of the Object; we are struck at the first with the Beauty'.[51] And, though he rejected

[50] See Guyer, 'Beauty and Utility'.

[51] Hutcheson, *Inquiry*, Treatise I, Section I, Part XII, 10.

Hutcheson's idea of an inner sense of beauty, Burke stresses the same point. Contrasting our rational understanding of the aptness of an item's form to its function, or its 'looking functional' to us, with our perceptual awareness of its beauty, he asks:

> How different is the satisfaction of an anatomist, who discovers the use of the muscles and of the skin, the excellent contrivance of the one for the various movements of the body, and the wonderful texture of the other, at once a general covering, and at once a general outlet as well as inlet; how different is this from the affection which possesses an ordinary man at the sight of a delicate smooth skin, and all the other parts of beauty which require no investigation to be perceived?[52]

On Burke's view, the aptness of an object's form to a given purpose or function is a matter to be worked out through the operation of reason, or the understanding, whereas its beauty is something to be grasped immediately through perception, as is its colour or size. Hence, Burke would maintain that even if we do take a sort of pleasure in perceiving the fitness of a pig snout for digging, this pleasure does not arise immediately, but involves the exercise of reason. Consequently, it is not pleasure taken in perception per se, but a pleasure derived from rational contemplation. It is not, therefore, the sort of pleasure that we feel in the beautiful.

But are Burke and Hutcheson correct in this? Again, some have thought so.[53] On the one hand, the assumption that aesthetic pleasure is pleasure taken in the perception of an object is widely accepted. It seems true, also, that we can take a purely intellectual delight in an object's utility or functionality: we may delight

[52] Burke, *Philosophical Enquiry*, Part III, Section VII, 108.

[53] David Rogers, for example, suggests that pleasure in the functional is an intellectual, rather than visual pleasure: 'There is no doubt that the quality of functional efficiency and the suitability of part to purpose can form an aesthetic experience analogous to the appreciation of intellectual beauty in a philosophical or mathematical theorem. But visual beauty does not necessarily follow from it. A good watch, for example, needs to be efficient but need not be visually beautiful'; see Rogers, 'Functionalism', in H. Brigstocke (ed.), *Oxford Companion to Western Art* (Oxford: Oxford University Press, 2001), 263–4; the quotation is on 263.

in the discovery of a new mechanism, or be pleased that the object can be used to help satisfy our own desires. And, further, it seems possible to confuse these 'intellectual' pleasures with pleasure taken in sensory perception. On the other hand, however, the fact that aesthetic pleasure is pleasure taken 'immediately' in what we perceive would only entail that the appearance of fitness cannot give aesthetic pleasure if we assume that 'looking fit' cannot be evident in perception. Granting that the function of things often cannot be known a priori, the issue here is whether an understanding of function, once we have it, can alter perception such that we *are* 'struck at the first', to use Hutcheson's phrase, by the object's appearance of fitness, thereby experiencing an *aesthetic* pleasure. Perhaps Hutcheson and Burke would have been inclined to dismiss this possibility in virtue of their general view that sensory perception is a process that, by its very nature, operates independently of thought. Be that as it may, current thought on this question surely favours the opposite position. After the last century's sustained critique of various attempts to set a rigid distinction between theory and observation, the view that perception is wholly independent of thought seems, at best, an over-simplification and at worst a distortion.[54] In Chapter 4, we will consider this issue in greater depth, specifically as it relates to the relation between aesthetic experience and knowledge of function. But for the time being we may note that, although the eighteenth-century empiricist aestheticians' sharp *general* distinction between reason and perception explains some of their resistance to the idea that fitness can produce aesthetic pleasure, it does not constitute compelling grounds for simply rejecting that idea today.

[54] For further discussion of theory-ladenness of perception, as it relates to aesthetics, see Glenn Parsons, 'Theory, Observation, and the Role of Scientific Understanding in the Aesthetic Appreciation of Nature', *Canadian Journal of Philosophy* 36 (2006b): 165–86.

1.5 The Eighteenth-Century Decline: Kant and Beauty 'Apart from Concepts'

There is, however, still another basis on which one might argue that aesthetic pleasure cannot involve considerations of functionality, as it is supposed to do according to the idea of Functional Beauty. Rather than the appeal to the general view that 'cognitive' elements, such as fitness for function, *cannot* figure in sensory perception, one might appeal to the view that they *need not* do so, and argue that the aesthetic response requires precisely this kind of perception: perception that excludes cognitive content. This view moves increasingly to the fore in late eighteenth-century aesthetic theory, and receives perhaps its most influential formulation in Kant's conception of the 'pure judgement of taste' in his *Critique of the Power of Judgement* (1790).[55]

According to Kant, the pure judgement of taste 'affords absolutely no cognition (not even a confused one) of the object'.[56] Such judgements 'in regard to an object with a determinate internal end would... be pure only if the person making the judgment either had no concept of this end or abstracted from it in his judgment'.[57] For Kant, pleasure in the beautiful arises only when the appearance of an object, *independently of the application of any concept to it*, brings about a certain sort of interaction between the mental faculties of imagination and understanding. Although Kant's theory does not require observers to have perceptual experiences without concepts, something that is perhaps not possible according to Kant's own philosophy, it does entail that beauty can never involve, or be grounded in, the application of a concept to the object.[58] Hence

[55] Immanuel Kant, *Critique of the Power of Judgment* [1790], ed. Paul Guyer, trans. Paul Guyer and Eric Matthews (Cambridge: Cambridge University Press, 2000).

[56] Ibid., Section 15, 113. [57] Ibid., Section 16, 115.

[58] On this point, see Malcolm Budd, 'Delight in the Natural World: Kant on the Aesthetic Appreciation of Nature, Part I: Natural Beauty', *British Journal of Aesthetics* 38 (1998): 1–18; reprinted in Malcolm Budd, *The Aesthetic Appreciation of Nature* (Oxford: Oxford University Press, 2002), 24–47; see 29–30.

the very idea of an object's beauty being based on its apparent fitness or utility would seem to be incoherent for Kant.

This requirement that beauty be appreciated 'apart from concepts' renders Kant's theory less hospitable to the association of aesthetic pleasure with apparent fitness than those of his eighteenth-century predecessors. Burke, as we have seen, sharply distinguishes between judgements of beauty and judgements of functionality, but he sees no fundamental incompatibility between them. He maintains that 'we are rational creatures, and in all our works we ought to regard their end and purpose', emphasizing that his hope is 'by no means to persuade people absurdly to neglect the idea of use in works of art'.[59] Delight in utility remains outside the sphere of beauty proper, for Burke, but is nonetheless a legitimate accompaniment to it. For Kant, however, the ideal state for the appreciative mind seems to be precisely to neglect the idea of use.

Surprisingly, however, Kant does not leave things at this; instead he goes on to acknowledge the existence of judgements of beauty that *do* involve considerations of purpose. These he places in his notorious category of 'adherent', or 'dependent' beauty, judgements of which 'presuppose a concept of the end that determines what the thing should be, hence a concept of its perfection'.[60] There is much dispute regarding the manner in which Kant's notion of adherent beauty should be interpreted, but the most prominent interpretations take adherent beauty not to be a version of the theory of beauty as fitness. For example, Guyer's view is that, when Kant says that the beauty of a church is an adherent beauty, he means not that the fitness of a church for worship makes it beautiful, but only that its function as a church *constrains* what sorts of arrangements and designs we are able to appreciate as beautiful in such a building. Beauty itself does not arise from the application

[59] Burke, *Philosophical Enquiry*, Part III, Section VII, 109. See also the third Earl of Shaftesbury (Anthony Ashley Cooper) in *Characteristics of Men, Manners, Opinions, Times* [1711]: 'the same Shapes and Proportions which make Beauty, afford Advantage, by adapting to Activity and Use'; quoted in Guyer, 'Beauty and Utility', 440.

[60] Kant, *Critique of the Power of Judgement*, Section 16, 114.

of a functional concept, in accord with what Kant says concerning the absence of concepts in judgements of beauty generally. Rather, beauty arises from a free play of understanding and imagination in our perception of the object's form. However, as Kant puts it, one 'would be able to add much to a building that would be pleasing in the intuition of it if only it were not supposed to be a church'.[61]

On this interpretation, Kant's concept of adherent beauty shifts the relationship between function and beauty: fitness for function is no longer a *source* of beauty, but only an 'external' constraint upon it; the beauty of the object must be one that leaves it able to carry out its function. In line with this interpretation, Kant characterizes the judgement of adherent beauty as 'restricted' and 'no longer a free and pure judgment of taste'.[62] Rather than contributing positively to aesthetic pleasure, as one of its constituent elements, an awareness of an object's fitness for its function or purpose now serves only to restrict the occurrence of that pleasure.

It is useful to describe this shift in terms of an ambiguity in the phrase 'Functional Beauty'. In one sense, this phrase can refer to beauty that somehow emerges out of, or depends upon, function. In this sense of the term, function is something 'internal' to at least some aspects of a thing's beauty. The tradition of beauty as fitness certainly exploits this sense, holding fitness to be integral to beauty. But, in another sense, 'Functional Beauty' means 'beauty that is functional'. On this reading, the beauty of the object need not involve, or emerge from, its function at all. Rather, the beauty

[61] Kant, *Critique of the Power of Judgement*, Section 16, 115. See Paul Guyer, *Kant and the Claims of Taste*, 2nd edn (Cambridge: Cambridge University Press, 1997), 219–20, as well as Guyer, 'Beauty and Utility'. Most accounts are similar to Guyer's in viewing utility as 'external' to beauty; see for example, Henry Alison, *Kant's Theory of Taste* (Cambridge: Cambridge University Press, 2001), and Budd, *The Aesthetic Appreciation of Nature*. However, 'internal' accounts are advanced in Robert Wicks, 'Dependent Beauty as the Appreciation of Teleological Style', *Journal of Aesthetics and Art Criticism* 55 (1997): 387–400, and Paul Guyer, 'Free and Adherent Beauty: A Modest Proposal', *British Journal of Aesthetics* 42 (2002b): 357–66. Guyer argues that his internalist interpretation supplements, and does not preclude, his original reading.

[62] Kant, *Critique of the Power of Judgement*, Section 16, 115. For a contemporary view along these lines, see Stephen Davies, 'Aesthetic Judgements, Artworks and Functional Beauty', *Philosophical Quarterly* 56 (2006): 224–41.

is functional in that it 'lines up with', or is compatible with, the object's function. For example, the beauty of the vast vault of a cathedral might be functional in this sense, in that its turning our thoughts to ideas such as vastness and eternity aids the cathedral in facilitating religious feeling.[63] Although the term 'Functional Beauty' can still be applied to the Kantian idea, this belies its fundamental alteration of the relationship between function and beauty. Kant's reconceptualization of the idea of Functional Beauty represents a turn away from the tradition of Functional Beauty running from the ancients to the eighteenth century, in which function is integral to beauty itself.

1.6 The Autonomy of Art

Since the eighteenth century, Kant's idea that aesthetic appreciation ought to eschew concepts has exerted great influence. Taking on many different forms, it has helped to keep function and related notions on the margins of aesthetic theory. We see it at work, for example, early in the twentieth century, in Edward Bullough's influential 'psychical distance' view.[64] Towards the middle of that century, we see it again in the popular 'Aesthetic Attitude' theories that attempted to characterize aesthetic appreciation in terms of a special state of mind that refrained from applying the usual concepts to things and events. In Jerome Stolnitz's influential theory of the aesthetic attitude, for example, this non-conceptual aspect was developed through the notion of 'distinterestedness': he defines the aesthetic attitude as a 'disinterested and sympathetic attention to and contemplation of any object of awareness whatever, for its own sake alone'.[65]

[63] On these issues, see Gordon Graham, 'Art and Architecture', *British Journal of Aesthetics* 29 (1989): 248–57, and 'Architecture', in Jerrold Levinson (ed.), *The Oxford Handbook of Aesthetics* (Oxford: Oxford University Press, 2003), 555–71.

[64] See Edward Bullough, '"Psychical Distance" as a Factor in Art and as an Aesthetic Principle', *British Journal of Psychology* 5 (1912): 87–98.

[65] Jerome Stolnitz, *Aesthetics and Philosophy of Art Criticism: A Critical Introduction* (Boston: Houghton Mifflin, 1960), 35.

In earlier aesthetic theories, the concept of disinterestedness was widely used to denote appreciation of an object for 'its own sake', as opposed to appreciation for some personal benefit that the object signifies. Thus, an observer fails to appreciate a painting distinterestedly if she appreciates it for the financial benefit it will bring her when she sells it, rather than the way it looks.[66] Disinterestedness can thus be seen as a way of clarifying the insight, mentioned in Section 1, that aesthetics has to do with perceptual appearances. But 'disinterested', for Stolnitz, means more than 'that we do not look at the object out of concern for any ulterior purpose which it may serve'.[67] It also means that 'we are not trying to use or manipulate the object. There is no purpose governing the experience other than the purpose of just *having* the experience.'[68] In Stolnitz's approach, disinterestedness, and so aesthetic appreciation, is thought to require disengaging ourselves from all utilitarian activities and ways of attending to the object. The aim of adopting the aesthetic attitude, then, is to 'isolate both us and the object from the flow of experience' and to perceive the object as 'divorced from its interrelations with other things'.[69] This entails not only that we are not trying to actually use the object, but that we do not even consider it, or conceptualize it, in light of what it can do, since that would be to pursue the aim of 'understanding' the object, which is, again, a motive ulterior to simply attending to its intrinsic qualities. In what follows, we will distinguish the sense of distinterestedness used by Stolnitz, which involves a deliberate withholding of concepts, from the more traditional sense mentioned above by capitalizing the former, as 'Disinterestedness'.

[66] A standard short account of the development of the concept of disinterestedness is Jerome Stolnitz, 'On the Origins of "Aesthetic Disinterestedness"', *Journal of Aesthetics and Art Criticism* 20 (1961b):131–43.

[67] Stolnitz, *Aesthetics and Philosophy of Art Criticism*, 35.

[68] Ibid.

[69] Ibid., 52. Other elements of Stolnitz's discussion tend in different directions, however; for discussion, see Allen Carlson, 'Appreciating Art and Appreciating Nature', in Salim Kemal and Ivan Gaskell (eds), *Landscape, Natural Beauty and the Arts* (Cambridge: Cambridge University Press 1993), 199–227.

Stolnitz's stark presentation of a Disinterestedness-centred conception of aesthetic experience makes plain how inhospitable aesthetic theory had become to notions such as Functional Beauty. Seemingly, the very attempt to conceptualize an object in terms of its function is now seen as incompatible with adopting the aesthetic attitude. Stolnitz's account also demonstrates how awkwardly the adoption of this 'conceptually thin' attitude fits with daily life, for the sort of disengaged withdrawal from activity that Stolnitz describes is obviously incompatible with many of the practical demands of everyday experience. Even someone engaged in an activity as commonplace as driving a car or cleaning up the living room cannot easily divorce herself from her interrelations with other things, and isolate herself from the flow of experience in the way that Stolnitz's account suggests. The general view that aesthetic appreciation occurs 'apart from concepts' thus produces the rather pressing problem of where it is to take place. Increasingly, the accepted solution to this problem is that aesthetic experience is to take place in a realm apart from practical life altogether, the realm of the fine arts.

Traditionally, what we now refer to as the fine arts—painting, sculpture, music, poetry, and architecture—were not clearly separated from other utilitarian and practical 'arts'. But the eighteenth century produced the modern notion of the fine arts as a somewhat unified and relatively autonomous set of practices.[70] In later aesthetic theory, this autonomous realm becomes the natural place to situate the conceptually thin brand of experience that is the essence of aesthetic appreciation. This tendency is evident, for instance, in the thinking of twentieth-century formalists, such as Clive Bell. Echoing Kant's view that aesthetic judgement is not based on the application of concepts, formalists argue that attention should be directed towards the 'pure form' of objects: immediately

[70] See the seminal article by Paul Oskar Kristeller, 'The Modern System of the Arts: A Study in the History of Aesthetics I, and II', *Journal of the History of Ideas* 12 and 13 (1951–2): 496–527 and 17–46, as well as Larry Shiner, *The Invention of Art: A Cultural History* (Chicago, IL: University of Chicago Press, 2001).

perceptible visual elements such as arrangements of shapes, colours, and lines. But unlike Kant and most of his predecessors, who take the paradigm objects of the 'judgement of taste' to be natural objects, formalists proceed to associate aesthetic appreciation paradigmatically, if not exclusively, with art. Formalists find an especial affinity between aesthetic appreciation and those artworks, such as post-impressionist paintings, that invite a severing of the link between the object of appreciation and the 'flow of experience'. Thus, in Bell's work, Kant's view of the aesthetic as 'apart from concepts' is applied to art via the precept that a work's representational or cultural meaning must be bracketed in aesthetic appreciation. In this approach, art serves as a place apart from the concerns of everyday life, a place where things can be approached 'apart from concepts', and so as the primary locus for aesthetic experience. Bell, for example, famously claims that 'Art transports us from the world of man's activity to a world of aesthetic exaltation. For a moment we are shut off from human interests ... we are lifted above the stream of life.'[71] As Noël Carroll puts it, in Bell's Formalism the notion of such a separation apparently takes on a more central role than in previous theories of art, becoming not merely a feature of art, but instead the very point and value of art itself.[72]

In this sense, later views, such as Bell's Formalism, through their development of the idea of art as a realm autonomous from 'real life', entail an even more radical disconnection between aesthetic appreciation and function than Kant's view. For they seem to abandon even the limited space for functional considerations that Kant carves out with his category of adherent beauty. No longer is it necessary for an object's form to 'line up with' its function when we appreciate beauty. For, in the world of art, objects slip altogether the bonds imposed by the functional exigencies of daily life. And, as the aesthetic retreats into this realm, discussions of function disappear from aesthetic theory altogether. The result

[71] Clive Bell, *Art* [1913] (New York: G. Putnam's Sons, 1958), 27.

[72] See Noël Carroll, 'Beauty and the Genealogy of Art Theory', *Philosophical Forum* 22 (1991): 307–34.

is a stark opposition between 'two worlds': the non-functional world of art and aesthetic appreciation, and the quotidian world of function, use, and 'daily life'.[73]

Although this opposition is often driven by a view of aesthetic appreciation as, to some degree, occurring 'apart from concepts', once established it seemingly takes on a life of its own. Consider Expressionism, perhaps the most influential position in early twentieth-century aesthetics besides Formalism. In Expressionism, the rhetoric of an opposition between 'two worlds', which was so common in Formalism, was explicitly resisted. On the contrary, expressionists claimed to see the aesthetic as pervasive in, and highly relevant to, everyday life.[74] Indeed, some expressionists held that art was capable of reforming people on some fundamental level, and thereby improving, if not saving, society.

In expressionist writings one occasionally does find explicit associations between function-related concepts and aesthetic appreciation. For instance, in his theory of beauty, Benedetto Croce defines beauty in terms of expression, by which he means a particular mental process that results in a clear, distinct, and particular idea. For Croce, as for most expressionists, the expression of emotion is not merely an externalization of inner feeling, but a particular way of externalizing inner feeling, whereby that feeling is refined and clarified. According to Croce, objects that stimulate such a process in us are beautiful. For functional objects, Croce thinks that this happens when the object appears suited to, or expressive of, its function. As he says, an object will be 'the instrument of aesthetic intuitions' if it is 'perfectly adapted to its practical purpose'.[75] Applied to functional things, Croce's view in

[73] Monroe Beardsley, though not an aesthetic attitude theorist, also views artworks as somewhat detached from the real world, referring to them as 'objects *manqués*', entities that lack something in a way that 'keeps them from being quite real'; see Monroe Beardsley, *Aesthetics: Problems in the Philosophy of Criticism* (New York: Harcourt Brace, 1958), 529.

[74] A point made by Paul Guyer, 'History of Modern Aesthetics', in Levinson (ed.), *The Oxford Handbook of Aesthetics*, 25–60.

[75] Benedetto Croce, *Aesthetic: As Science of Expression and General Linguistic* [1909], trans. Douglas Ainslie (New York: Macmillan, 1922), 102. Other philosophers with expressionist

fact amounts to what we have identified as the strong version of the idea of Functional Beauty: appearing functional is necessary and sufficient for a functional object to be beautiful. As he says: 'a garment can only be beautiful because it is exactly suitable to a given person in given conditions'.[76] Croce's attempt to give function a place in the theory of beauty had little influence, however, partly because of his implausible insistence that there is no beauty beyond expression.[77]

Speaking more generally, Expressionism ultimately failed to do much to illuminate the connection between aesthetic pleasure and function. The reason for this, perhaps, is that expressionists, like formalists, focused discussion of aesthetic experience squarely upon art, which they consistently characterized as dissociated from practical or utilitarian considerations.[78] The most well known example of this is R. G. Collingwood's distinction between art and craft. For Collingwood, 'art proper' differs from mere craft in that art

leanings hold similar views. E. F. Carritt, for instance, contends that 'the shape and size which fit a thing exactly to serve our purpose usually become expressive of the desire which the thing helps us to satisfy and of that satisfaction'; see E. F. Carritt, *What is Beauty? A First Introduction to the Subject and to Modern Theories* (Oxford: Oxford University Press, 1932), 108. Along similar lines, John Hospers argues that: 'we enjoy not merely the shining black and silver of the streamlined automobile ... but rather these surfaces and forms as expressing certain life-values, and adapted to certain life-purposes. The design of the streamlined automobile seems to express speed, efficiency, ease, power (all of them values from life, dependent upon our knowledge from everyday experience of what an automobile is and does)' (*Meaning and Truth in the Arts* (Chapel Hill, NC: University of North Carolina Press, 1946), 13).

However, even within the context of the beauty of expression, function is but one of a myriad of 'life values' that objects can express. In the wider context, therefore, Functional Beauty usually played a minor role within the theories of these writers. George Santayana, for instance, allows that utility can enter into our perception of beauty through a process of association between certain features and practical advantage. Nonetheless, for Santayana the principle that objects may be expressive of their function or utility 'is not fundamental, but an auxiliary one; the expression of utility modifies effect, but does not constitute it'. The fitness of objects may 'lend them some added charm', as he puts it, but it is 'foreign to the stronger and more primitive aesthetic values', those of aesthetic surface and form; see Santayana, *The Sense of Beauty* [1896] (New York: Collier, 1961), 150–2.

[76] Croce, *Aesthetic*, 102.

[77] See Curt Ducasse, *The Philosophy of Art* [1929] (New York: Dover, 1966) Chapter 3, especially Section 6, 54–5.

[78] John Dewey is perhaps an exception here; see *Art as Experience* [1934] (New York: Capricorn Books, 1958). We consider Dewey's and related positions in Chapter 7, Section 2.

proper is not made to serve a pre-existing aim or end; rather, the artwork emerges gradually in the artist's spontaneous expression of her emotions. Though Collingwood has some insightful things to say about craft, his aesthetic theory emphasizes our appreciation of the sort of making that he calls 'art proper'; indeed, he even seems to take 'aesthetic experience' to be synonymous with 'artistic activity', understood as the making of art proper.[79] But this treatment virtually rules out any serious consideration of the aesthetic appreciation of functional objects, which generally *are* produced to serve some pre-existing aim. Failing to be expressive, in Collingwood's sense, such objects are left in the realm of mere craft. So, for all that the expressionists urged a more intimate connection between aesthetic experience and the 'stream of life', they, like other theorists, tended to be beguiled by the traditional idea of art as a kind of aesthetic experience 'preserve'—a realm sundered from the world of practical affairs.[80]

Indeed, the idea of art as a separate sphere that provides the paradigmatic setting for aesthetic experience is one of the most deeply entrenched ideas in aesthetics. As we shall see, even the recent decline of the Disinterested-centred conception of aesthetic experience, which in part motivates and reinforces this idea, has done little to diminish its appeal. This ongoing relegation of aesthetic experience to the apparently functionless world of art, however, represents only one challenge facing a revival of the tradition of Functional Beauty. For a more complete picture, therefore, we turn next to a consideration of the place of Functional Beauty in contemporary aesthetic theory.

[79] R. G. Collingwood, *The Principles of Art* [1938] (Oxford: Oxford University Press, 1958); see especially Book I, Chapter II, and 275.

[80] Croce, for example, declares: 'Art is independent both of science and of the useful and the moral', insisting that art cannot involve practical activity—that is, operation of the will—at all. 'The true artist... finds himself big with his theme, he knows not how; he feels the moment of birth drawing near, but he cannot will it or not will it'; see Croce, *Aesthetic*, 51.

2

Functional Beauty in Contemporary Aesthetic Theory

In the previous chapter, we outlined some facets of the historical development, in the classical period and in the seventeenth and eighteenth centuries, of the notion of looking fit for function as a form of beauty. This notion was the most prominent way of articulating the more general idea that we call Functional Beauty: a thing's function being integral to its aesthetic qualities, or a thing's aesthetic qualities emerging from its function or something closely related to its function, such as its purpose, use, or end. We also sketched the decline of this notion, which we attributed in part to a relegation of aesthetic experience to the 'world' of art, a realm that exists apart from the practical, utilitarian concerns of normal life. This relegation, in turn, springs from the idea that aesthetic appreciation must be Disinterested in the sense of eschewing conceptualization of the object of appreciation. In this chapter, we assess the place of Functional Beauty in contemporary aesthetic theory. From one point of view, it might be expected that Functional Beauty would have made a comeback of sorts, given that the influence of the concept of Disinterestedness has waned significantly in the second half of the twentieth century. As we will describe, however, the resultant changes in aesthetic theory have not reinvigorated discussions of Functional Beauty. On the contrary, Functional Beauty seems to have been further marginalized.

We shall argue that this is due to two factors. The first is a continued focus, in aesthetic theory, upon two apparently afunctional realms: the world of art, and, more recently, nature, especially wilderness. The second factor contributing to the neglect of Functional Beauty is a set of conceptual problems that has surfaced in attempts to apply notions akin to Functional Beauty in architecture.

2.1 The Decline of Disinterestedness and the Rise of Cultural Theories of Appreciation

Despite its enormous influence, the concept of Disinterestedness, understood as a kind of non-conceptual approach to the object of aesthetic appreciation, has been increasingly challenged in recent aesthetic theory. The latter part of the last century witnessed a growing scepticism about applying this concept to the appreciation of art, as well as increasing doubt concerning its role in aesthetic appreciation generally. Most famously, George Dickie argued explicitly that 'Aesthetic Attitude' accounts, such as that of Stolnitz, which characterize aesthetic experience in terms of a special 'disengaged' psychological state or attitude, are vacuous because no such psychological state or attitude exists.[1] Other writers simply ignored Disinterestedness, taking aesthetic theory in new and different directions. For example, Frank Sibley's influential writings on aesthetic properties, beginning with his important essay 'Aesthetic Concepts' (1959), shunned the traditional emphasis on Disinterestedness, treating instead the logic of aesthetic concepts and aesthetic judgements.[2] Likewise, philosophers such as Nelson Goodman, Arthur Danto, and Kendall Walton

[1] Dickie's initial and best-known version of this line of thought is George Dickie, 'The Myth of the Aesthetic Attitude', *American Philosophical Quarterly* 1 (1964): 56–65.

[2] Frank Sibley, 'Aesthetic Concepts', *Philosophical Review* 68 (1959a): 421–50. Sibley further pursues the logic of aesthetic concepts in 'Aesthetic and Nonaesthetic', *Philosophical Review* 74 (1965): 135–59, as well as in other essays. Sibley's movement away from any interest in Disinterestedness and related ideas is evidenced by his collected papers, *Approach to Aesthetics: Collected Papers on Philosophical Aesthetics*,

moved beyond the narrow confines of Disinterested appreciation by arguing, in different ways, that the aesthetic judgements that we pass on artworks are not based on their sensory appearance alone, but are conditioned by our beliefs about matters such as the works' history, genre, and style, and thus that appropriate appreciation involves possessing such beliefs.[3] Feminist and Marxist critics attacked the Disinterestedness tradition more directly, decrying what they saw as the ideological function of a conception of the aesthetic that involves denying, or at least ignoring, the material and ethical implications of art making and art appreciation.[4]

In addition to such theoretical developments, perhaps the central reason for this backlash against the idea of Disinterestedness was its inability to do justice to the richness and variety of the arts. Instead of recognizing the arts as evolving, diverse, and historically and socially informed practices, Disinterestedness-centred aesthetic theories tended to foist upon all art forms a unitary and rather rigid model of appreciation. In this sense, as Dickie puts it, Disinterestedness, in its emphasis on the rejection of conceptualization, 'misleads aesthetic theory'.[5] As we noted in Chapter 1, according to Stolnitz, Disinterestedness requires that we 'isolate both us and the object from the flow of experience' and perceive

ed. John Benson, Betty Redfern, and Jeremy Roxbee Cox (Oxford: Oxford University Press, 2001), which includes his sixteen principal articles and has no treatment of concepts such as Disinterestedness or the aesthetic attitude. The closest he comes to addressing this topic is his critical discussion of Vincent Tomas's notion of 'aesthetic vision', in 'Aesthetics and the Look of Things', *The Journal of Philosophy* 56 (1959b): 905–15.

[3] Nelson Goodman, *Languages of Art* (Indianapolis, IN: Bobbs-Merrill, 1968); Kendall Walton, 'Categories of Art', *Philosophical Review* 79 (1970): 334–67; Arthur Danto, *The Transfiguration of the Commonplace: A Philosophy of Art* (Cambridge, MA: Harvard University Press, 1981).

[4] See, for example, Terry Eagleton, *The Ideology of the Aesthetic* (Oxford: Blackwell, 1990); David Novitz, *The Boundaries of Art* (Christchurch, New Zealand: Cybereditions, 2001); and the essays collected in Hilda Hein and Carolyn Korsmeyer, *Aesthetics in Feminist Perspective* (Bloomington, IN: Indiana University Press, 1993), and Margaret Brand and Carolyn Korsmeyer (eds), *Feminism and Tradition in Aesthetics* (University Park, PA: Pennsylvania State University Press, 1995).

[5] Dickie, 'The Myth of the Aesthetic Attitude', 61.

the object as 'divorced from its interrelations with other things'.[6] But though some artworks are compatible with this model, being intended primarily for 'disengaged' appreciation, many are not. Overtly social, religious, or political artworks, for example, cannot be easily assimilated to this mode of appreciation: such works seem to require that one consider their ulterior purpose.[7] Even in the case of those artworks, such as non-representational paintings, that appear most compatible with Disinterested appreciation in principle, the inadequacy of this conception becomes manifest in the increasingly central role played by art history and art theory in the actual appreciation of such works.[8] The more that the idea of the appreciation of artworks requiring disengagement from the concepts of the everyday world was called into question, the more it became plain that such appreciation involves engagement with the concepts of another, different, world: the so-called 'artworld'.[9]

This new emphasis on the importance of the social context of art is reflected in the rise of what Noël Carroll calls 'cultural' theories of art and art appreciation, which represent a direct response to the deficiencies of the Disinterestedness-centred approach.[10] The best-known example of such a theory is Dickie's Institutional Theory of art, which states that an object becomes an artwork, not in virtue of possessing any specific intrinsic quality, but rather by obtaining a

[6] Jerome Stolnitz, *Aesthetics and Philosophy of Art Criticism: A Critical Introduction* (Boston, MA: Houghton Mifflin, 1960), 52.

[7] See, for example, Arnold Berleant, *Art and Engagement* (Philadelphia, PA: Temple University Press, 1991), and Noël Carroll, 'Beauty and the Genealogy of Art Theory', *Philosophical Forum* 22 (1991): 307–34.

[8] See Danto, *The Transfiguration of the Commonplace.*

[9] The notion of the artworld is initially presented in Arthur Danto, 'The Artworld', *Journal of Philosophy* 61 (1964): 571–84.

[10] Carroll characterizes cultural theories as ones that 'supply the wherewithal to ground aesthetic judgments of art objectively by basing such judgments on the cultural practice and forms—such as artistic genres, styles and movements—in which and through which artworks are created and disseminated'. See Noël Carroll, 'On Being Moved By Nature: Between Religion and Natural History', in S. Kemal and I. Gaskell (eds), *Landscape, Natural Beauty and the Arts* (Cambridge: Cambridge University Press, 1993), 244–66; the quotation is on 255. On this point, also see Allen Carlson, 'Nature, Aesthetic Judgment, and Objectivity', *Journal of Aesthetics and Art Criticism* 40 (1981): 15–27, especially 18.

certain sort of status within the social community of artists, critics, and appreciators known as the 'artworld'.[11] On this view, just as an object's status as an artwork is a matter of the social conventions of the artworld and how they are applied, so too is the issue of how artworks should be appreciated. Dickie says, for example, that our appreciation of art is to be guided by 'conventional distinctions as to which of [the artwork's] aspects are properly appreciated and criticized and which are not'.[12] In short, cultural theories of art, such as Dickie's, represent an explicit theoretical recognition of the long-standing de facto relation of art to a social and historical context, a fact so long suppressed by aesthetic theory's emphasis upon Disinterestedness. One broad way to characterize the difference between Disinterestedness-centred and cultural accounts is in terms of the role accorded by each to knowledge concerning the object of appreciation. Whereas the former require the observer to bracket, or neglect, rather than attend to, concepts and facts that apply to the object of appreciation, cultural accounts reject this requirement. Consequently, they may be characterized as *cognitively rich* theories of appreciation, insofar as they take knowledge about the object of appreciation to be an essential component of its appropriate identification and appreciation.

Seen in this way, it becomes apparent how the move away from the Disinterestedness-centred conception of appreciation and towards a cultural approach clears the way for a return to the idea of Functional Beauty, since cultural approaches allow belief about the object of appreciation a central place in aesthetic appreciation.

[11] George Dickie, *Art and the Aesthetic: An Institutional Analysis* (Ithaca, NY: Cornell University Press, 1974). Other well known cultural theories of art do not necessarily involve institutions, but rather emphasize historical, narrative, functional, and other culture-based aspects of art objects; see, for example, Jerrold Levinson, 'Defining Art Historically', *British Journal of Aesthetics* 19 (1979): 232–50; George Dickie, *The Art Circle* (New York: Haven Publications, 1984); Noël Carroll, 'Art, Practice and Narrative', *The Monist* 71 (1988): 140–56 and 'Identifying Art', in Robert J. Yanal (ed.), *Institutions of Art: Reconsiderations of George Dickie's Philosophy* (University Park, PA: Pennsylvania State University Press, 1994), 3–38; Stephen Davies, *Definitions of Art* (Ithaca, NY: Cornell University Press, 1991); and Robert Stecker, *Artworks: Definitions, Meaning, Value* (University Park, PA: Pennsylvania State University Press, 1997a).

[12] Dickie, *Art and the Aesthetic*, 199.

The stage is thereby set for an awareness of function to enter into, and somehow shape, our aesthetic experiences. However, the shift towards cultural theories of appreciation, in fact, has done surprisingly little to reinvigorate the notion of Functional Beauty. We think that one major reason for this is that art has continued to be conceptualized in non-functional terms. Although cultural theories of art and art appreciation demand that appreciation incorporate an understanding of the artwork's place in the historical and theoretical context of the artworld, a persistent separation of the artworld from 'the everyday world' has effectively maintained the exclusion of utilitarian functionality from this context.[13]

This continuing separation of art from the everyday world is revealed in the fact that as the functionality of an artwork becomes more prominent and difficult to ignore, its status or value as art seems to decline. Nicholas Wolterstorff notes this phenomenon in the lack of attention and status accorded to memorial and commemorative sculpture. The intended purpose of such art, he points out, is 'precisely not contemplative engagement with its aesthetic qualities'; rather, such art 'comes into its own when it functions as a memorial'.[14] But Wolterstorff points out that we tend to regard these as degraded or 'impure' forms of art. For example, the discussion of many such commemorative works, like the much debated Vietnam War Memorial in Washington, DC, is typically focused on social and political issues rather than on aesthetic or artistic ones. Having been created for a purpose, or with some social or political aim in mind, such works remain, in terms of Collingwood's distinction, forms of craft rather than art proper.[15] Art proper, art in the pure and fullest sense, remains that

[13] On this point, see Stephen Davies, 'Aesthetic Judgements, Artworks and Functional Beauty', *Philosophical Quarterly* 56 (2006): 224–41, especially 228.

[14] Nicholas Wolterstorff, 'Why Philosophy of Art Cannot Handle Kissing, Touching, and Crying', *Journal of Aesthetics and Art Criticism* 61 (2003): 17–27; the quotation is on 26. For further discussion, see Chapter 8, Section 5.

[15] Commemorative sculpture would seem to be an example of what Collingwood calls 'magical art', that is, art that has the end of arousing, but not immediately discharging,

which is created freely and spontaneously, involving only artistic, rather than utilitarian, aims.

2.2 Art, Nature, and Afunctionality

As we described in the previous chapter, recent aesthetic theory has focused largely on the artwork as the object of aesthetic appreciation. Nonetheless, in the latter part of the twentieth century, there has also been increasing discussion of the aesthetics of nature. However, in light of the dominance of cultural theories of aesthetic appreciation, the formulation of an adequate account of the aesthetic appreciation of nature has faced certain difficulties. As noted, cultural theories of art, such as Dickie's Institutional Theory, hold that artworks are social objects and, consequently, that knowledge of the social conventions of the artworld guides and shapes art appreciation. Given this emphasis on social conventions, it seems doubtful that an analogous approach could be applied to the appreciation of non-art objects, such as natural objects. Dickie writes that, in contrast to artworks:

> Natural objects lack [an] 'inner life' because they are not embedded in the matrix of conventions in which works of art are ... One characteristic of a natural object is as properly a candidate for appreciation as any other of its characteristics; none of its characteristics enjoys the conventionally engendered status which the aesthetic aspects of works of art possess.[16]

This apparent asymmetry between the appreciation of artworks and natural objects emerges also in other cognitively rich accounts of aesthetic appreciation. Kendall Walton's theory of the aesthetic appreciation of art, for instance, appeals to knowledge of a work's artistic genre or style as necessary for its appropriate aesthetic

certain emotions. See R. G. Collingwood, *The Principles of Art* [1938] (Oxford: Oxford University Press, 1958), 66f.

[16] Dickie, *Art and the Aesthetic*, 199. Cf. Robert Stecker, 'The Correct and the Appropriate in the Appreciation of Nature', *British Journal of Aesthetics* 37 (1997b): 393–402: 'There is a "natural" way to delimit aesthetically (artistically) relevant knowledge of art that we have seen is simply absent with regard to nature' (398).

appreciation. In the case of natural objects, however, Walton at least initially denied the existence of analogous constraints.[17]

The prominent role of artworld social conventions in the dominant cultural theories of aesthetic appreciation has prompted some theorists interested in aesthetic appreciation in other domains, such as nature or everyday life, to develop distinct aesthetic theories. In the case of nature, some follow Walton's initial suggestion that the appreciation of nature, unlike art appreciation, is not governed by anything analogous to artworld conventions or strictures. Developing a line of thought that goes back at least to Hegel's aesthetics, such theorists characterize the aesthetic appreciation of nature as possessing a freedom and subjectivity not found in the appreciation of art.[18] Other writers, in contrast, maintain a more unitary theoretical picture by arguing that, in order to be appreciated, nature must be regarded as if it were art.[19] On this approach, aesthetically appreciating natural things requires pretending that they are the products of intentional design. The theoretical unity achieved by this position, however, is a strained one, since the guiding principle of cultural theories of art, namely, that objects ought to be appreciated as the sorts of objects that they are, is applied only in the case of art.

However, the aesthetic theories of the appreciation of nature that have achieved the most prominence in the late twentieth century are those that apply this guiding insight of cultural theories to both nature and art. These theories maintain the cognitively rich character of cultural theories of art by claiming that all objects should be appreciated as the sorts of objects that they are, while recognizing that natural objects are different from works of art.

[17] Walton, 'Categories of Art'. For an attempt to apply a framework like Walton's to nature, see Carlson, 'Nature, Aesthetic Judgment, and Objectivity'.

[18] John Andrew Fisher, 'What the Hills Are Alive With: In Defense of the Sounds of Nature', *Journal of Aesthetics and Art Criticism* 56 (1998): 167–79; Malcolm Budd, *The Aesthetic Appreciation of Nature* (Oxford: Oxford University Press, 2002). For further discussion of this tradition, see Glenn Parsons, 'Freedom and Objectivity in the Aesthetic Appreciation of Nature', *British Journal of Aesthetics* 46 (2006a): 17–37.

[19] See, for example, Anthony Savile, *The Test of Time* (Oxford: Oxford University Press, 1982). Also note the discussion of this position in Davies, *Definitions of Art*, and Budd, *The Aesthetic Appreciation of Nature*, 90–4.

Thus, they reject the artworld as the appropriate context within which to appreciate natural objects. The best known of such accounts is the 'Natural Environmental Model', which holds that the knowledge about nature that guides and shapes our aesthetic appreciation of natural things ought to come from the branch of inquiry that, on the whole, best reveals the nature of natural objects: the natural sciences. As one of us puts it elsewhere:

> our appreciation of nature is aesthetic and is analogous to that of art in both its nature and its structure. The significant difference is that while in art appreciation ... the knowledge given by art criticism and art history is relevant, in nature appreciation ... the knowledge is that provided by natural history—by science. But this difference is not unexpected; nature is not art.[20]

This view is sometimes called 'Scientific Cognitivism' to mark its relationship to cognitively rich approaches to art appreciation while emphasizing the role of scientific knowledge in the appropriate aesthetic appreciation of nature.[21]

Since, unlike some other recent accounts of the aesthetic appreciation of nature, views such as Scientific Cognitivism are cognitively

[20] Allen Carlson, 'Nature and Positive Aesthetics', *Environmental Ethics* 6 (1984): 5–34; the quotation is on 27–8.

[21] The 'Natural Environmental Model' is originally sketched in Allen Carlson, 'Appreciation and the Natural Environment', *Journal of Aesthetics and Art Criticism* 37 (1979): 267–76. The label 'Scientific Cognitivism' is used by Glenn Parsons, 'Nature Appreciation, Science, and Positive Aesthetics', *British Journal of Aesthetics* 42 (2002): 279–95. In addition to Carlson and Parsons, the view is defended in Holmes Rolston, 'Does Aesthetic Appreciation of Nature Need to be Science Based?', *British Journal of Aesthetics* 35 (1995): 374–86; Marcia Eaton, 'Fact and Fiction in the Aesthetic Appreciation of Nature', *Journal of Aesthetics and Art Criticism* 56 (1998): 149–56; and Patricia Matthews, 'Scientific Knowledge and the Aesthetic Appreciation of Nature', *Journal of Aesthetics and Art Criticism* 60 (2002): 37–48. It is also akin to the tradition of nature appreciation that includes individuals such as John Muir and Aldo Leopold. On the latter, see J. Baird Callicott, 'The Land Aesthetic', in C. K. Chapple (ed.), *Ecological Prospects: Scientific, Religious, and Aesthetic Perspectives* (Albany, NY: State University of New York Press, 1994), 169–83. A number of articles discussing Scientific Cognitivism are contained in Allen Carlson and Arnold Berleant (eds), *The Aesthetics of Natural Environments* (Peterborough, Canada: Broadview Press, 2004). For a recent defence of the position, see Allen Carlson, 'The Requirements for an Adequate Aesthetics of Nature', *Environmental Philosophy* 4 (2007): 1–12. For an overview of current work in the entire field of the aesthetics of nature, see Glenn Parsons, *Aesthetics and Nature* (London: Continuum, 2008).

rich, one might expect the concept of function to make an appearance in this sort of approach. But here, too, functionality has found little application. In this case, however, reservations about functionality have somewhat deeper roots than they have in the case of art, since here the reservations involve scruples concerning the very applicability of teleological concepts such as function, purpose, and the like to the physical world. Critics of the concept of function first point out that functionality is a prima facie anthropomorphic concept: a functional object is apparently one whose existence, nature, and character is to be understood in light of the cognitive states of its designer, in particular, the designer's intentions. Second, they note that the extension of teleological concepts, such as functionality, to the study of the natural world has produced only lamentable results.

Aristotelian natural philosophy, for instance, explained the nature of physical phenomena in a manner analogous to the way in which the features of human artefacts were explained: by reference to 'final causes', goals, or ends that those physical phenomena were to serve.[22] As Aristotle points out, this seems quite sensible insofar as it appears highly unlikely that 'blind' physical laws alone can produce the highly regular phenomena found throughout nature.[23] Only with much effort were seventeenth-century thinkers able to pry the physical sciences away from teleological explanation, invoking instead causal explanation in terms of 'blind' physical laws. In the biological sciences, however, it long remained unclear how the occurrence of highly adaptive, obviously functional traits could be explained in these terms. The sheer improbability of extant materialist explanations for these phenomena gave rise to the eighteenth-century tradition of Natural Theology, and its centrepiece, the teleological argument for the existence of God.

[22] For a succinct discussion, see Steven Shapin, *The Scientific Revolution* (Chicago, IL: University of Chicago Press, 1996).

[23] Aristotle, *Physics* [approx. 350 BCE]; see, for example, Aristotle's arguments at 199a in *The Basic Works of Aristotle*, ed. Richard Mckeon, trans. R. P. Hardie and R. K. Gale (New York: Random House, 1941), 249–50.

This line of thought was sufficiently strong that as prominent a scientific thinker as Charles Lyell showed no compunction in appealing to the special creation of species by God.[24] Yet, once again, the notion that the biological world must be understood in terms of the goals of a designing intellect proved a dead end for empirical inquiry, coming to an end with Darwin's proposal of a potential naturalistic explanation for adaptedness.[25]

The unimpressive track record of teleological concepts in natural science makes it obvious why, for many philosophers and scientists, as Larry Wright puts it, 'wherever it appeared, the smoke of teleological terminology implied the fire of sloppy thinking'.[26] For them, lapses into teleological talk signalled a lazy anthropomorphism that, at best, obscured true causal explanations and, at worst, manifested a confused return to metaphysical speculation, natural theology, backward causation, or some other atavistic notion. Given this general philosophical scepticism concerning function in nature, thinkers insisting upon a role for science in the aesthetic appreciation of nature have turned elsewhere, focusing instead on non-teleological descriptions that eschew mention of functions, ends, and the like: for instance, descriptions based upon historical narratives and natural laws.[27]

When we couple this avoidance of teleological descriptions of the natural world with persisting attitudes concerning the isolation of the 'artworld', we can begin to see why the wane of the influence of Disinterestedness in aesthetic theorizing has not resulted in a

[24] Charles Lyell, *Principles of Geology* [1830]. On Lyell's belief in special creation, see Ernst Mayr, *Towards a New Philosophy of Biology* (Cambridge, MA: Harvard University Press, 1988), 171–2.

[25] In physiology, the teleological approaches that had persisted in the vitalist tradition met a similar fate in the early twentieth century. For discussion, see Ernst Mayr, 'Teleological and Telonomic: A New Analysis', *Boston Studies in the Philosophy of Science* 14 (1974): 91–117, and Ernst Mayr, 'The Multiple Meanings of Teleological', in Mayr, *Towards a New Philosophy of Biology*, 38–66.

[26] Larry Wright, 'The Case against Teleological Reductionism', *British Journal for the Philosophy of Science* 19 (1968): 211–23; the quotation is on 211.

[27] Note, for example, the characterization of Scientific Cognitivism in Allen Carlson, 'Appreciating Art and Appreciating Nature', in Kemal and Gaskell (eds), *Landscape, Natural Beauty and the Arts*, 199–227.

renaissance for Functional Beauty for either art or nature, even though it opened up the possibility for one. On the contrary, aesthetics has remained largely focused upon what it views as the *non*-functional paradigms of 'pure' art and 'purely mechanical' nature. For neither kind of object has the concept of function been thought to play a significant role, since, as one of us recently put it, it seems that 'neither pristine nature nor pure art have, as such, a purpose or a function'.[28] Although we will argue that we should not, after all, accept this statement, it is certainly representative of philosophers' continuing reluctance to apply the concept of function to either artworks or natural things.

2.3 Architecture and Functionalism

Our explanation of the ongoing neglect of Functional Beauty, however, remains incomplete. For it tells us only that the objects considered by aesthetic theory have been viewed as non-functional; it does not tell us why aesthetic theory has also failed to consider objects that clearly *are* functional, such as tools, dwellings, and other everyday artefacts. Some authors see the lack of consideration given to functionality as simply due to a focus upon non-functional things as paradigmatic aesthetic objects.[29] On this view, recent aesthetics has been so obsessed with art that it has simply never got around to developing any interest in functional things. However, although we think there is much truth in this allegation, we also believe that it cannot be the whole story. As we shall see, there are also serious theoretical difficulties with the very notion of Functional Beauty itself. These too have played a role in the reluctance of philosophers to consider the significance of function in aesthetic appreciation.

[28] Allen Carlson, *Aesthetics and the Environment: The Appreciation of Nature, Art and Architecture* (London: Routledge, 2000), 134.

[29] See, for example, Yuriko Saito, 'Everyday Aesthetics', *Philosophy and Literature* 25 (2001): 87–95, as well as some of the essays in Arnold Berleant, *Aesthetics and Environment: Variations on a Theme* (Aldershot, UK: Ashgate, 2005).

These theoretical difficulties have emerged most clearly in discussions dealing with the aesthetics of architecture, where the most sustained efforts have been made to apply notions related to Functional Beauty. As is well known, a number of prominent architectural movements have been characterized in terms of various notions of functionality. Most notably, the term 'Functionalism' has been employed in connection with the work of architects such as Louis Sullivan, Frank Lloyd Wright, Adolf Loos, Le Corbusier, Walter Gropius, Ludwig Mies van der Rohe, and others.[30] Here the basic idea concerned attention to function in designing art-like architectural structures. It was often articulated with the slogan 'Form Follows Function', which is typically attributed to Sullivan. One of Sullivan's stronger statements of the idea is found in 'The Tall Office Building Artistically Considered' (1896), wherein he insists that 'the shape, form, outward expression, design or whatever we may choose, of the tall office building should in the very nature of things follow the functions of the building'.[31] He generalizes the idea as follows:

> when native instinct and sensibility shall govern the exercise of our beloved art; when the known law, the respected law, shall be that form ever follows function; then it may be proclaimed that we are on the high-road to a natural and satisfying art, an architecture that will soon become a fine art in the true, best sense of the word, an art that will live because it will be of the people, for the people, and by the people.[32]

Following Sullivan's impassioned call for Functionalism in architecture, the idea of form following function as a normative theory of design was applied not only to imposing architectural structures such as the tall office building, but also to somewhat less grand

[30] See Edward R. De Zurko, *Origins of Functionalist Theory* (New York: Columbia University Press, 1957) for an extensive historical account of the relationship between form and function as understood by architectural theorists. Also of interest is Maurice Lageux, 'Reconfiguring Four Key "isms" Commonly Used in Architectural Theory', *British Journal of Aesthetics* 39 (1999): 179–88.

[31] Louis Sullivan, 'The Tall Office Building Artistically Considered', in *Kindergarten Chats and Other Writings* [1918] (New York: Dover, 1979), 202–13; the quotation is on 208.

[32] Ibid.

buildings as well as to other kinds of objects. Thus, Le Corbusier famously described the house as 'a machine for living', and Bauhaus artists and artisans designed furniture and appliances in light of what were considered functionalist principles. Throughout the nineteen-twenties and thirties, Functionalism in this sense was not simply a popular idea; it developed into the movement that would become known as 'International Modernism' or simply 'Modernism'. The general idea seemed to be that in order to be beautiful, architectural structures, other buildings, and designed objects in general not only must simply and clearly fit or 'follow' the use or end for which they are intended, but also must avoid ornamentation and similar decorative additions, and be 'sincere', 'authentic', or 'honest'.

As these remarks suggest, the term 'Functionalism', when used to indicate a normative theory of design or as a description of particular architectural movements, is, in different ways, both broader and narrower in scope than the idea of Functional Beauty, which we outlined in the previous chapter. It is broader in the sense that Functionalism in architecture is often expressed, not as an aesthetic thesis, but simply as a thesis about good or valuable architecture. As such, Functionalist claims in architectural theory sometimes seem to deal with much more than aesthetic appreciation, which is the sole focus of the general idea of Functional Beauty, as we have characterized it. Also, functionalist positions in architectural and design theory are often narrower in scope than this general idea, since they often involve commitments to the desirability of specific aesthetic or design characteristics, such as universality and simplicity, as well as specific and controversial claims about what the functions of buildings actually are or ought to be and about how those functions are related to aesthetic appearance. Functionalist claims in architecture, to the extent that they deal with aesthetic appreciation, are best seen as specific developments of the general idea of Functional Beauty. We do not further consider these specific versions of the idea of Functional Beauty here, although we will revisit some of the issues that they raise in Chapter 6.

Rather than get lost in the intricacies of these views, in the remainder of this chapter we will focus instead on the *general* idea of Functional Beauty as it applies to architecture, namely: the idea that function is integral to the aesthetic character of architectural works. This is roughly the view that Roger Scruton, in his groundbreaking volume *The Aesthetics of Architecture* (1979), calls 'aesthetic functionalism': the view that 'true beauty in architecture consists in the adapting of form to function'.[33] Scruton also articulates two important reservations about this idea. These reservations help to explain the ongoing neglect of Functional Beauty and constitute serious problems that must be faced by any attempt to re-establish it as useful concept in aesthetic theory.

2.4 The Problem of Translation

Scruton's two reservations about Functional Beauty can be explained by distinguishing between two distinct aspects of a theory of the aesthetic: psychological and normative.[34] The psychological aspect pertains to the conditions under which observers perceive an object as possessing an aesthetic quality. The normative aspect of a theory of the aesthetic, in contrast, pertains to the conditions under which an attribution of an aesthetic quality to an object can be said to be more correct or appropriate than some conflicting judgement. In other words, the psychological aspect describes the

[33] Roger Scruton, *The Aesthetics of Architecture* (London: Methuen and Company, 1979), 6. Note, however, that the aesthetic Functionalism discussed by Scruton is what we have called a 'strong view', holding that a particular relation of form to function is both sufficient *and necessary* for beauty. Our concern in the coming chapters will be to articulate and defend a weak view of Functional Beauty, on which some relation of form to function is sufficient, but not necessary, for beauty or some aesthetic quality. Various views about the relationships between function and architecture are also discussed in: Allen Carlson, 'Reconsidering the Aesthetics of Architecture', *Journal of Aesthetic Education* 20 (1986): 21–7; Allen Carlson, 'Existence, Location, and Function: The Appreciation of Architecture', in M. Mitias (ed.), *Philosophy and Architecture* (Amsterdam: Editions Rodopi, 1994), 141–64; and Allen Carlson, 'The Aesthetic Appreciation of Everyday Architecture', in M. Mitias (ed.), *Architecture and Civilization* (Amsterdam: Editions Rodopi, 1999), 207–21.

[34] The distinction that we have in mind mirrors one drawn by Kendall Walton in 'Categories of Art'.

occurrence of aesthetic responses, whereas the normative aspect describes which of these responses are correct or appropriate. Each of the problems raised by Scruton for a theory of Functional Beauty can be related to one of these aspects.

The first problem for the notion of Functional Beauty, which we will call the 'Problem of Translation', relates to its psychological aspect. In the case of the notion of Functional Beauty, the psychological aspect of the theory involves the claim that an awareness of an object's function, and so of the fit of its form to that function, can alter the aesthetic qualities that we perceive the object to have. The problem is that it is unclear how awareness of, and attention to, a non-aesthetic function can *alter* or *influence* aesthetic judgement. We can bring out this worry by emphasizing again an apparent truism about the aesthetic that we noted in Chapter 1: the idea that aesthetic pleasure is pleasure taken in an object's perceptual appearance per se—that is, a disinterested pleasure. Thus, for example, looking at a bountiful field of corn may excite pleasure in an observer, but if that pleasure is the gratification of her desire for a good harvest (and, hence, for financial success) rather than pleasure in the way it looks per se, then it is not *aesthetic* pleasure. Only if the pleasure is taken in the appearance of the field, for its own sake, is it aesthetic pleasure. So, whatever precisely it means, the claim that something is functionally beautiful must mean that the function of the object is somehow present in, or 'translates into', the look or sound of the object. For, when things are functionally beautiful, it is not that we see beauty, and then assess how well that beauty fits with function.[35] If things are functionally beautiful, then knowing the function is what allows observers to see the beauty in the first place. So, somehow, knowing the function of the object must change the way the object looks to us. But how this could be, it is insisted, is unclear.

[35] In terms of the distinction that we drew in Chapter 1, Section 5, this would be a case of things having 'beauty that is functional', not of their being functionally beautiful.

This problem echoes the fundamental objection to Functional Beauty that we introduced in Chapter 1, Section 1: What does function have to do with what we can see or hear? In Chapter 1, Section 4, we remarked that eighteenth-century theorists, such as Burke, advance this sort of objection on the grounds that sense perception operates independently of reasoning or judgement. But one need not hold any such general view concerning the limits of sense perception to doubt that knowledge of function can affect aesthetic appearance. Scruton raises such doubts simply by noting that 'it is not clear how any particular "function" is to be translated into architectural "form"'.[36] He illustrates with the example of the strainer arch, an architectural element used to hold up walls. Imagine that we consider a particular strainer arch and ask: is this arch functionally beautiful? The traditional theory of beauty as fitness for function holds that it is functionally beautiful if it looks fit for its function. But what would that look consist in? If something looks fit for its function, then presumably it must lack any visible defect that would keep it from performing its job. A strainer arch with a large crack in it, for example, would surely not look fit. But, beyond this, what does it mean to say that the arch looks fit for holding up the walls? To press the point, if we wanted to make a particular arch *more* functionally beautiful, to have its appearance look more fit for its function, how would we go about that? There do not seem to be obvious answers here. Proponents of specific conceptions of Functional Beauty have a number of other ways of expressing the idea that the function of an object can somehow translate into its appearance: they sometimes say, following Sullivan's slogan, that 'its form follows its function', for instance. Other common locutions include 'form expresses function', 'form realizes function', and variations thereof. But these are metaphors that have little more content than the notion of 'looking fit' itself. 'Does the form of the strainer arch', Scruton asks, 'follow or express its function more perfectly than

[36] Scruton, *The Aesthetics of Architecture*, 40.

would a stretch of scaffolding? If so, why?'[37] To press the point again, if we wanted to create an arch that would *better* follow, express, realize (or whatever) its function, how would we go about that? Scruton's point is that there are not readily apparent answers to these questions. The Problem of Translation, in short, is that a central thought in the concept of Functional Beauty, the idea that function can be somehow 'translated' into the perceptual form of the object, is vague and unclear.

The Problem of Translation presents a serious difficulty for Functional Beauty because unless the problem can be addressed, when we talk about something being functionally beautiful, we have no distinct notion of what we are talking about. This is regrettable in itself, but it also raises the suspicion that, when we talk of 'Functional Beauty', we may not be talking about *aesthetic* appreciation at all. Recall again the truism that aesthetic pleasure is pleasure taken in the perceptual experience of an object per se. If we do not know what we are saying when we say 'X is functionally beautiful', perhaps what we are actually describing is pleasure taken, not in X's perceptual appearance per se, but in some gratification of our needs and desires that X's appearance indicates for us. As we noted in discussing the idea of beauty as 'looking fit' in Chapter 1, the word 'beauty' has many non-aesthetic uses. Perhaps saying that our house is functionally beautiful is not a way of saying that its *look* is pleasing, but only a way of expressing our satisfaction in the fact that it is comfortable, or a sound investment. If this is correct, then Functional Beauty is a thoroughly confused, and confusing, concept that does not, in fact, fall within the purview of aesthetics at all.

In regard to functionalist doctrines in architecture, this sceptical worry is particularly pressing. For there it takes on an important political dimension, given the use made of the specific takes on the notion of Functional Beauty by some architectural movements. For example, in the twentieth century, many architects agitated

[37] Scruton, *The Aesthetics of Architecture*, 41.

for the rejection of older building styles, and their attendant social arrangements, under the banner of slogans such as Sullivan's 'Form Follows Function' and the like. Critics of these movements have long suspected that these slogans lack a clear meaning and have served to obfuscate, rather than advance, architectural theory.

The Problem of Translation, however, is by no means restricted to architecture: it can be raised for any functional object, including everyday artefacts, such as cars and knives. What exactly can it mean to say that a particular knife has a form that is more fit for cutting, or that 'realizes' or 'follows' this function better than the form of some other knife? The Problem of Translation, in sum, presents a challenge for Functional Beauty that is both serious and wide-ranging, a challenge that any defence of the notion, including the present one, must meet.

2.5 The Problem of Indeterminacy

The second problem that Scruton raises for the idea of Functional Beauty is what we will call the 'Problem of Indeterminacy'. This problem is that the term 'function' itself is, as Scruton puts it, 'fundamentally, and perhaps irremediably, obscure'.[38] As an example of this, consider the debate over the Four Seasons Centre, an opera house that opened in Toronto, Canada, in 2006. One of the more common architectural criticisms was that the structure is awkwardly situated relative to the street: it seems somehow to squat nervously on the corner, failing to 'connect with' the surrounding environment. Defenders of the structure have, of course, dismissed such aesthetic judgements as misguided. This aesthetic dispute turns on a profound difference in opinion as to the function of the Four Seasons Centre. One might assume that the function of an

[38] Scruton, *The Aesthetics of Architecture*, 40. See also Gordon Graham, 'Art and Architecture', *British Journal of Aesthetics* 29 (1989): 248–57, especially 256. The problem is articulated for natural things by Malcolm Budd: 'the natural function of a bodily part, the arm, for example, can be manifold, and the part can be well suited to perform some, but not all, its functions'; see *The Aesthetic Appreciation of Nature*, 38.

opera house is to provide a quiet and convenient locale for opera productions. But the aforementioned critics clearly have something very different in mind. The architectural critic Christopher Hume recently compared the Four Seasons Centre to the new opera house in Oslo, Norway, of which he writes:

> Norwegians understood that such a project must address more than the narrow spectrum of opera lovers. ... It will ... change the city and how it's perceived locally and internationally. It ... serves the specific needs of connecting the site to the larger community while dealing with the psychological demands of a city that wants to redefine itself. Indeed, it functions as both an object building as well as part of the landscape. This aspect can be seen most obviously in the roof, a remarkable feature that slopes up from Oslo Fjord to the top of the house, and which will be entirely accessible. That means visitors will be able to wander up seven or eight storeys to enjoy the view, sunbathe or skateboard.[39]

Hume, it seems, has the notion that an opera house has a certain wide-ranging function, a function that includes providing suntanning areas, but also, and more notably, serving wider needs of the community, and indeed of the surrounding architecture. If you conceptualize the Four Seasons Centre as a thing with *that* function, then it may well appear to you as a cold, huddled, and weak thing, failing to extend and open up in the way that it should: in short, not functionally beautiful at all but functionally ugly. If, on the other hand, you incline to the view that beaches are for sunbathing and opera houses are for, well, opera, then you will probably have a very different aesthetic response to it. Cases like this one seem to illustrate Scruton's conclusion that the function of a building is 'something indeterminate'.[40] But if the function of a building is indeterminate, then whatever aesthetic character it possesses in light of its function is also indeterminate.

[39] Christopher Hume, 'The Opera House We Didn't Build', *Toronto Star*, 16 September 2006.

[40] Scruton, *The Aesthetics of Architecture*, 40. Scruton's examples are the Centre Pompidou in Paris as well as 4 Carlton House Terrace and the Roundhouse Theatre, both in London, England.

Scruton does not elaborate much on the upshot of this difficulty, but its importance can be clarified using the distinction between the psychological and normative aspects of an aesthetic theory, introduced in the previous section. For it does not appear that the indeterminacy of function, in itself, rules out the *psychological* claim that awareness of, and attention to, function is involved in some aesthetic judgements. However, it does raise difficulties for the *normative* claim that some judgements of Functional Beauty are more correct or appropriate judgements, since it appears to imply that aesthetic judgement involving function is a relative matter, in which conflicting judgements are equally correct, or appropriate. Here a comparison with the appreciation of art is instructive. Imagine that, as some philosophers have argued, the aesthetic qualities that we perceive an artwork to have depend upon the 'category' or 'genre' to which we take it to belong.[41] On this view, if one reads *Don Quixote* (1605) as a twentieth-century novel, rather than as a seventeenth-century novel, one will have a different aesthetic response to it.[42] One may find certain passages ironic, in contrast to the typical reader who, reading it as a seventeenth-century text, observes no such effect. In this case, our intuitions are that the latter judgement is a more appropriate or correct aesthetic judgement than the former, because 'seventeenth-century text' is clearly the proper category in which to place the work. For, after all, *Don Quixote is* a seventeenth-century work. But if one held that, for any given work, all, or at least many, incompatible artistic categories are equally legitimate, then the grounds for such a normative ranking of aesthetic judgements would vanish. And Scruton's point about the indeterminacy of function seems to entail that this is precisely the situation with respect to Functional Beauty, for the various functions proposed for an object like the Four Seasons Centre all seem more or less

[41] See, for example, Walton, 'Categories of Art'.

[42] This example is adapted from Jorge Luis Borges's famous story 'Pierre Menard, Author of the *Quixote*', in *Labyrinths: Selected Stories & Other Writings*, ed. D. A. Yates and J. E. Irby (New York: New Directions Publishing, 1964), 36–44.

equally legitimate. As a result, no aesthetic judgement based upon a particular function seems any more correct or appropriate than another. Judgement of Functional Beauty, in other words, lacks a normative dimension.

The Four Seasons Centre example not only illustrates the scope and extent of dispute concerning the function of architectural works. It also makes plain why many philosophers have been inclined to simply dismiss Functional Beauty as a hopelessly muddled notion. For what criteria could possible settle such a dispute? With no shortage of possible functions for a building, one side picks the function that favours its interests, or its values, and its opponents some other. And so, once again, as in consideration of the Problem of Translation, the worry emerges that what seem, on the surface, to be aesthetic disputes will turn out to be political or economic struggles over what buildings ought to be used for.[43]

In assessing the importance of this functionally based relativism for the general idea of Functional Beauty, there are two important issues to consider. The first is its scope, or the precise contexts in which it arises, and the second is the extent to which such relativism, where it does arise, is a problem. With regard to the first issue, the problem would seem to be most pressing in the case of architecture, and especially in the case of buildings, which often have a great range of functions. If we look at everyday artefacts, this surfeit of functions seems to be drastically reduced, if not to disappear altogether. Rafael De Clercq, for example, acknowledges that 'there may be no simple "yes" or "no" answer to the question of whether a given aesthetic adjective applies to a multifunctional item', but holds that this is a peculiarity of artefacts with multiple primary functions, where a primary function is one that makes the object the kind or sort of thing it is.[44] His

[43] See, for example, Lewis Mumford, 'The Case Against "Modern Architecture"', in Lewis Mumford, *Highway and the City* (Westport, CT: Greenwood Publishing Group, 1953). As noted, we will return to some of these issues in Chapter 6.

[44] Rafael De Clercq, 'The Aesthetic Peculiarity of Multifunctional Artefacts', *British Journal of Aesthetics* 45 (2005): 412–25; the quotation is on 425. De Clercq's discussion is

examples of such artefacts include such things as sofa beds, clock radios, and washer-dryers. But many, arguably most, artefacts are *not* multi-functional in this sense, but rather are dedicated to a single function: wristwatches are for telling the time, corkscrews are for opening wine bottles, and so forth. Thus the relativity of Functional Beauty, even if endemic in architecture, seems to be an oddity in the realm of everyday artefacts. For as a matter of fact, we all *do* agree, almost all of the time, on the function of everyday artefacts. If we were sizing up the Functional Beauty of a stove, for instance, it would be bizarre for someone to say that it is not functionally beautiful because, having a glass door, it looks like a most ungainly safe.

Although there is, in general, much agreement about function in the realm of everyday objects, two points yet need to be stressed. First, even if there is agreement about the function of an artefact, this does not obviate the philosophical problem of selecting one function as the 'correct' one, unless there is some *reason* we can give against alternative suggestions, however bizarre we may find them. Normative standards concerning some sort of assessment do not arise merely because, as a matter of fact, people happen to agree in their assessments. If everyone in town happens to like vanilla ice cream, rather than chocolate, that does not mean that there is, therefore, a normatively justified choice as to the best flavour of ice cream. That there is no such normatively superior alternative will become apparent the minute a chocolate lover happens along. Second, even in the realm of artefacts with a single obvious function we often find that, as Edward Winters puts it, an object has 'outstripped any restrictive conception of "the function" for which it was designed'.[45] A wristwatch *is* for telling the time, but

more general, concerning the thesis that 'beautiful' is a 'sortal-relative' term, and more specifically the claim that 'multifunctional artefacts are unique in allowing the following to occur: for some x there are sortal nouns "S" and "S*" such that x is a beautiful S, and S*, but not a beautiful S*'; see 413.

[45] Edward Winters, 'Architecture', in Berys Gaut and Dominic McIver Lopes (eds), *The Routledge Companion to Aesthetics* (London: Routledge, 2001), 519–30; the quotation is on 527.

it can do much else besides: display one's wealth or social status, serve as a fashion accessory, remind one of a previous owner, keep one's wrist from getting suntanned, and so on. Each of these would be what De Clercq calls a 'secondary function': 'an optional characteristic that does not make [the object] the kind of thing it is'.[46] And such functions fall outside the scope of De Clercq's discussion, since he simply defines 'multifunctional artefact' as an artefact with more than one *primary* function. De Clercq provides no reason for this exclusion, but there ought to be one, since there is nothing in the nature of a 'secondary' function, as opposed to a primary one, that obviously renders it unable to serve as, in De Clercq's words, 'a standard or criterion or ideal of beauty for the entities falling under it'.[47] In fact, secondary functions do so serve. To use one of De Clercq's examples, a common secondary function of perfume bottles is 'symbolizing the qualities of the person wearing the substance'.[48] But this could easily constitute 'a standard or criterion or ideal of beauty': we can imagine a perfume bottle that dispensed perfume poorly but elegantly symbolized the wearer's personality (perhaps it is fragile and transparent). Indeed, 'secondary' functions can ground aesthetic judgements even when they are not intended at all, as when an old perfume bottle is used as a bud vase and found, serendipitously, to be beautiful as a bud vase.[49] Thus, the scope of the relativism emerging from the indeterminacy of function is perhaps wider than it might initially appear to be.

Even if it is true that the Problem of Indeterminacy is a significant theoretical problem for functional things in general, however, one might still ask why the aesthetic relativism it generates should be viewed as a 'threat' or a 'problem' for the notion

[46] De Clercq, 'The Aesthetic Peculiarity of Multifunctional Artefacts', 412.

[47] Ibid., 413. [48] Ibid., 412.

[49] De Clercq may be assuming, for the purposes of his discussion, that there is something wrong with aesthetically appreciating objects in light of such serendipitous secondary functions, or perhaps he thinks that these are not really functions at all. But for a defence of Functional Beauty, such grounds for narrowing the discussion need to be established; they cannot simply be assumed at the outset.

of Functional Beauty. Why not simply accept that the aesthetic character of architecture, or everyday objects, is relative? In fact, exactly this conclusion is explicitly articulated by Socrates in the original explication of the idea of beauty as fitness. Socrates is asked whether he means to say that 'the same things are both beautiful and ugly'. 'Of course', he replies, 'and both good and bad. For what is good for hunger is often bad for fever, and what is good for fever bad for hunger; what is beautiful for running is often ugly for wrestling, and what is beautiful for wrestling ugly for running'.[50] There is nothing new, then, in the notion that Functional Beauty brings relativity in its train. Also, in developing views on the aesthetics of functional objects, a number of philosophers have suggested that any theory of the aesthetics of such objects must contain a significant element of relativity.

Consider, for example, Yuriko Saito's description of the aesthetic appreciation of everyday artefacts as taking place in the absence of appreciative conventions, and thus as 'making us the creator of its aesthetic object'.[51] Saito gives the example of aesthetically appreciating a baseball game, in which we select, from a great number of possibilities, certain features to appreciate, such as the cheers of the fans, the smell of hot dogs, and the heat of the sun beating down on our necks. Saito's conception of appreciators creating the object of their aesthetic experience, however, renders a normative dimension for such appreciation elusive: it becomes difficult to see how aesthetic responses to the everyday might be critiqued as more or less appropriate, or how any meaningful critical discourse might be developed in regard to it. In the example alluded to above, for instance, it is hard to see how a dispute over the aesthetic merits of a baseball game could ever be resolved, when each of two observers has selected different

[50] Xenophon, *Memorabilia* [approx. 370 BCE], Book III, Chapter 8, Section 7, trans. E. C. Marchant, in Wladyslaw Tatarkiewicz, *History of Aesthetics* [1970–4] (London: Continuum, 2005), Volume 1, 109–10.

[51] Saito, 'Everyday Aesthetics', 89.

elements to appreciate. This feature of Saito's account is evident in her shifting between the phrase 'aesthetic appreciation', with its connotation of an object possessing a more or less determinate aesthetic character that we may succeed or fail in appreciating, and the less committal 'aesthetic experience', with more emphasis on the latter phrase.[52]

Views such as Saito's provide insight into the distinctive nature of everyday things, including functional objects, as objects of aesthetic attention. However, their emphasis on relativity also imposes upon them a fundamental limitation. Saito, for example, is not alone in lamenting the lack of philosophical scrutiny given to the aesthetics of everyday objects.[53] But, given her own account, the reason for this neglect is not hard to see. If conflicting aesthetic judgements of everyday things are not better or worse, if they cannot be disputed or adjudicated, it would seem that discourse concerning the aesthetic value of those things can allow little place for criticism, constructive dialogue, or education. This problem is compounded by the fact that influential conceptions of the aesthetics of art and of nature typically do possess a strong normative dimension and do make room for these notions. In fact, much of the philosophical interest in these areas stems precisely from the applicability of these notions. In comparison with these domains, aesthetic appreciation of the everyday, as it is characterized by thinkers such as Saito, seems unlikely to be developed or sophisticated enough to lend itself to articulation or theoretical analysis.

In short, a functionally based relativism concerning Functional Beauty would diminish the seriousness of the aesthetics of the everyday, setting it apart from the aesthetic value of both art and nature, and in doing so justify its ongoing neglect by aestheticians. For these reasons, together with the scope of such relativism, which is larger than it may first appear, we see the indeterminacy

[52] Saito, 'Everyday Aesthetics', 91. [53] Ibid., 94.

of function as a major problem for the concept of Functional Beauty, and so a position to be accepted only as a last resort. Along with the Problem of Translation, then, the Problem of Indeterminacy presents a challenge for Functional Beauty that must be addressed.

2.6 A Role for Functional Beauty

The twentieth-century developments in aesthetic theory described in this chapter have produced a context in which, despite both a decline of the influence of Disinterestedness and a focus on Functionalism in architecture and design, the notion of Functional Beauty remains on the margins of mainstream aesthetic theory. Why ought this to concern us? This situation is, perhaps, regrettable in its own right, given the intrinsic interest of the idea of Functional Beauty. In addition, this situation is related to two other issues regarding current work in aesthetics: lack of comprehensiveness and lack of unity.

First, as we have already noted in Chapter 1, Section 2, comprehensiveness is a virtue in an aesthetic theory. All else being equal, an aesthetic theory is better to the extent that it can illuminate as wide a range of our aesthetic practices as possible. Many contemporary aesthetic theories, despite their other strengths, lack this virtue in that they continue to neglect, and fail to facilitate attention to, the aesthetic appreciation of *utilitarian* artefacts. If anything, the development of cultural theories of art appreciation, on the one hand, and Scientific Cognitivism regarding nature appreciation, on the other, appears to have further marginalized the appreciation of functional artefacts, given that these theories have little applicability to those artefacts, leaving them stranded in the 'never-never land' between the artworld and the natural world.[54] And yet, despite not being discussed in current aesthetic theory, functional artefacts,

[54] Carlson, *Aesthetics and the Environment*, 133.

from tools and machines to clothing and kitchen implements, continue to occupy a central and important place in our aesthetic attention. We may not want to accord these items a status equal to that of art, but that our contemporary aesthetic theory fails to include them seems to us a flaw.

This point is reinforced by the fact, emphasized in the previous chapter, that eighteenth-century theoreticians, such as Hume, employed a concept of Functional Beauty to analyse aesthetic experience not only of art and nature, but of a diverse assortment of utilitarian objects including tools, weapons, equipment, furniture, and buildings. That the lack of comprehensiveness of contemporary aesthetic theory is indeed a flaw is also supported, perhaps, by the observation that in many non-Western cultures aesthetic appreciation focuses on a broad range of objects, including functional artefacts. These cultures either lack the conceptions of 'pure' art and nature that the West has used to corral aesthetic experience, or else have not privileged these conceptions to the extent that we have done.[55] This further suggests that the 'ghettoization' of aesthetic experience within the artworld is not a necessary development, but rather a situation that could be remedied through the extension of a more broadly applicable concept, such as Functional Beauty.

A second drawback of current aesthetic theory is its lack of unity across the principal domains that it does cover: nature and art. For, although aesthetic theories of nature and art have both turned to cognitively rich conceptions of aesthetic appreciation, these accounts have diverged in radical ways. Theorists who accept Scientific Cognitivism, for example, have tended to see the appreciation of art and of nature as differing in important respects, and they have taken pains to clearly distinguish them. The motivation here has been the perceived importance of clear ontological

[55] See, for example, Saito, 'Everyday Aesthetics', 88; Crispin Sartwell, 'Aesthetics of the Everyday', in Jerrold Levinson (ed.), *The Oxford Handbook of Aesthetics* (Oxford: Oxford University Press, 2003), 761–70, especially 765; and Berleant, *Aesthetics and Environment*, 108.

differences between artworks, understood as social artefacts defined by their relations with the artworld, on the one hand, and natural objects, understood as physical things governed by natural laws, on the other. Although not sympathetic to this divergence, Arnold Berleant succinctly captures the point by noting that 'such distinctive objects seem to require different accounts of their creation and meaning'.[56] These different accounts translate, even within the same over-arching cognitively rich framework, into quite different ways of appreciating artworks and natural objects. This approach is prominent in a contrast, drawn previously by one of us, between the 'order appreciation' characteristic of nature and the 'design appreciation' paradigmatically associated with art.[57] The most vivid illustration of this radical difference, however, is the claim that nature differs fundamentally from art in being universally, and perhaps necessarily, aesthetically good. Recent defences of this view, often referred to as 'Positive Aesthetics', have appealed to the distinct character of natural objects and the corresponding distinctness of the knowledge involved in their aesthetic appreciation. Some point to scientists' use of aesthetic criteria for theory selection, some towards the absence of a designer for nature, and others towards the existence of a distinctive ecological role played, and expressed, by every entity in the natural environment.[58]

In one sense, the recognition of differences between art and nature as aesthetic objects is a positive development, given the prevailing tendency to casually apply aesthetic theories developed for one to the other. However, it has also created a problematic fragmentation and polarization in aesthetic theory. Recent critiques of the sharp distinction between nature and culture,

[56] Arnold Berleant, *The Aesthetics of Environment* (Philadelphia, PA: Temple University Press, 1992), 164.

[57] See Carlson, 'Appreciating Art and Appreciating Nature'.

[58] See Carlson, 'Nature and Positive Aesthetics'; Holmes Rolston, *Environmental Ethics: Duties to and Values in the Natural World* (Philadelphia, PA: Temple University Press, 1988), Chapter 6; Eugene Hargrove, *Foundations of Environmental Ethics* (Englewood Cliffs, NJ: Prentice Hall, 1989), Chapter 6; and Yuriko Saito, 'The Aesthetics of Unscenic Nature', *Journal of Aesthetics and Art Criticism* 56 (1998): 101–11.

as well as criticisms of the idea of Positive Aesthetics suggest that there may be more important commonalties in the aesthetic appreciation of art and nature than is sometimes recognized.[59] Furthermore, the idea that the aesthetics of nature and art are categorically different seems to be belied, ultimately, by our actual practice. For example, we freely move between aesthetically appreciating natural objects and artworks as well as the functional artefacts in our homes. Indeed, it is arguable that the central concern of the aesthetics of domestic settings is the proper alignment and integration of these varying elements. Such integration would be puzzling, if not impossible, if the aesthetic character possessed by each were a completely distinct species. At the very least, it seems that we should only accept a radical difference as a view of last resort. If an account is able to draw illuminating connections between the aesthetic appreciation of these different objects, this speaks in its favour. As we will argue, Functional Beauty provides, in the notion of function, a feature that, being found not only in both art and nature but also in everyday things, can serve to illuminate connections and commonalties in what are often taken to be radically disparate aesthetic objects.

In sum, we think that current treatments of aesthetic experience, as insightful as they are, often lack comprehensiveness and unity. These qualities should certainly not be pursued at all costs—it may be that, given the nature of the subject matter, a theory having these qualities to a very high degree is not feasible. It is also probably true that these virtues have been over-emphasized in some traditions in philosophical aesthetics. Nonetheless, they remain theoretical virtues. And it seems to us that reintroducing the idea of Functional Beauty may go some distance towards achieving them. This, along with the intrinsic interest of the idea itself, motivates us to undertake a reappraisal of that moribund tradition

[59] See, for example, Janna Thompson, 'Aesthetics and the Value of Nature', *Environmental Ethics* 17 (1995): 291–305.

that makes functionality a central aspect of aesthetic appreciation. Although the contemporary, cognitively rich approach to aesthetic appreciation has not yet been developed in a way redolent of this tradition, we will attempt to show, in the following chapters, how it might be.

3

Indeterminacy and the Concept of Function

The aim of the remainder of this book is to sketch, in broad outline, a theory of Functional Beauty and to draw out some of its implications. However, before such a theory can be made plausible, a good deal of groundwork is required since, as we have seen, the notion of function has been critiqued for being too limited in applicability, for being too far removed from perception to be relevant to aesthetic experience, and even for being, as Scruton puts it, 'fundamentally, and perhaps irremediably, obscure'.[1] A vindication of Functional Beauty, therefore, will require some clarification of this concept. In this chapter, we begin this clarification by addressing the Problem of Indeterminacy.

We trace the problem concerning the indeterminacy of function to an intuitive and widely held view concerning the functions of artefacts: that they are ultimately a matter of human intentions towards artefacts. We will argue, however, that the indeterminacy of function is not merely a consequence of this view, but also a symptom of its failure to provide a cogent analysis of the functions of artefacts. A better view, we suggest, can be gleaned from what may seem an unusual source: the philosophy of science. It is in this field that the concept of function has been considered in greatest depth, and the understanding of the concept that has emerged in

[1] Roger Scruton, *The Aesthetics of Architecture* (London: Methuen and Company, 1979), 40.

this field may also be extended to the realm of artefacts. Doing so, we will claim, not only provides us with a better conception of artefact functions, but also dispels much of the indeterminacy and obscurity thought to characterize the notion of function itself. By applying some of the insights of this work to the case of artefacts, we show that the concept of function is not too nebulous and vague to serve as the cornerstone of a theory of Functional Beauty.

3.1 Intentionalism and Indeterminacy

Function, and teleological concepts more generally, have been extensively investigated in recent philosophy, especially in the philosophy of biology. However, function, as applied specifically to artefacts, has not been so widely studied.[2] Part of the reason for this is that philosophers have assumed that functional talk about artefacts is comparatively straightforward in the sense that artefacts have functions in virtue of human intentions concerning their use. It is this prima facie conceptual connection between function and intention, after all, that makes functional talk in biology as philosophically interesting as it is, raising suspicions of disguised anthropomorphism, latent theism, and the like. To the extent that your typical philosopher might pause to reflect on functional talk as applied to artefacts, then, she might offer something like the following analysis:

(1) X has function F if and only if a human agent has intended that it perform F.

This is the basic idea underlying what we can call *intentionalist approaches* to understanding artefact function.

But this basic idea, of course, is unsatisfactorily vague as stated. It is tempting to refine the view by specifying a particular sort of

[2] An exception is Randall Dipert, *Artifacts, Art Works, and Agency* (Philadelphia, PA: Temple University Press, 1993); see also the references below.

agent, and here the artefact's designer comes first to mind. For some artefacts, it clearly seems to be the designer whose intentions correspond to the item's function. The fountain pen, for example, has the function of allowing smooth uninterrupted writing, and this, presumably, is what its inventor or inventors intended it to do. Thus, we could refine (1) to yield:

> (2) X has function F if and only if the designer of X has intended that it perform F.

But unfortunately, not all artefact functions correspond to the intentions of designers in this way. Pipe cleaners, for instance, were designed to clean smoking pipes, but today their function is to serve as a material for children's crafts.[3] It seems that it is the manufacturers of present-day pipe cleaners whose intentions give rise to *this* function. In still other cases, it is the intentions of neither the designers nor the manufacturers, but the users of an artefact that seem to correspond to its function. This is often the case with architectural works, which typically outlive their designers and builders. Edward Winters offers the example of the Plaza Major of Madrid, which was originally designed and built as a royal courtyard by the Spanish Habsburg ruler Philip II (1556–98). It is a paradigmatic example of how the nature and the function of structures can change over time. Today, people speak of its function as housing a range of civic activities: dining, festivals, markets, and so on.[4] Or consider the heavily fortified flak towers built in Vienna by the Nazis during the Second World War.

[3] This example is from Beth Preston, 'Why is a Wing Like a Spoon? A Pluralist Theory of Function', *Journal of Philosophy* 115 (1998): 215–54; see 241.

[4] Edward Winters, 'Architecture', in Berys Gaut and Dominic McIver Lopes (eds), *The Routledge Companion to Aesthetics* (London: Routledge, 2001), 519–30; see especially 526–27. The Plaza Major (Plaza Mayor) is the most famous square in Madrid. It was built as a courtyard flanked by royal apartments and other residences. Since its construction, it has been re-modelled by several different architects and hosted activities as varied as religious pageants, public executions, bullfights, and soccer games. Today, lined with traditional shops and cafes, it is primarily a market place, as well as a major tourist attraction; see Jesús Escobar, *The Plaza Mayor and the Shaping of Baroque Madrid* (Cambridge: Cambridge University Press, 2004).

Since their walls were so thick that they could not be manageably destroyed, these towers were left standing. Today they are used in a variety of ways: one provides a climbing wall, another is the screen for an outdoor cinema, and another functions as an aquarium. It seems natural to refer to these uses as the current functions of the towers, though they were certainly not intended to do any such things by their nefarious creators.

A reasonably precise version of an intention-based theory of function talk concerning artefacts, then, will need to be more complex than (2), perhaps along the lines of

> (3) X has function F if and only if S is a designer or maker or user of X and S has intended that it perform F.

This analysis will capture all of the cases of function mentioned above, and will, in general, do justice to the rich complexity and multiplicity of artefact function. It does so in virtue of its being a highly disjunctive analysis, of course. But, on reflection, it really ought not to surprise us that a theory of artefact functions based on human intentions towards artefacts turns out not to be neat or straightforward. Human intentions towards artefacts, after all, are not neat or straightforward.[5]

However, a theory of artefact function ought to capture not only the complexity and multiplicity of functional talk about artefacts, but another feature as well. This feature is that, in many cases, one function in this multiplicity stands out as the *proper function* of the

[5] In fact, an intentionalist theory will need to be more complex still, for, in some cases, things have the function of Fing without there being specific intentions that they F on the part of anyone at all. Christopher Boorse offers the example of yeast having the function of converting sugar to carbon dioxide and alcohol in the brewing process. Well into the history of brewing, it was discovered that this is actually the function of yeast in the brewing process, which entails that yeast had this function before anyone intended that it do this specific thing (since no one knew, before the discovery, that yeast did this). To address this, an intentionalist theory will need to add a category of functions that can arise indirectly from more general intentions, such that, as Boorse puts it, 'intentions about parts are unnecessary given intentions about the whole'. See Christopher Boorse, 'Wright on Functions', *Philosophical Review* 85 (1976): 70–86, especially 80f; the quotation is on 73. Also relevant is Philip Kitcher, 'Function and Design', *Midwest Studies in Philosophy* 18 (1994): 379–97.

object. The most basic idea behind the notion of a proper function is the idea that it is the function that belongs to the object itself.[6] Proper functions are often contrasted with 'accidental functions': in the course of a gun battle, a belt buckle might happen to deflect a bullet, thereby functioning as a shield.[7] But that would not be the proper function of the belt buckle, the function that belongs to the object itself. Rather, this function has been imposed upon the buckle, as it were, by chance and circumstance. This difference is reflected in the fact that we prefer to say that the belt buckle has *functioned as* a bullet shield, on this particular occasion, rather than that it *has the function of* shielding us from bullets. This grammatical shift seems to signal our tacit recognition that some functions 'belong' to the object itself in a way that others do not.

Moreover, proper functions can also be contrasted with functions that are imposed in other ways. The intentions of users of an artefact, for example, may bestow a multiplicity of functions on an object, as analysis (3) holds, but these functions do not thereby become proper functions of the object. Consider an object such as a frying pan. A frying pan can have many functions: it can function as a weapon, as a paperweight, or perhaps, with some inventive modification, a satellite dish. But even if it has these other functions, the proper function of a frying pan is not any of these things. It is providing a portable hot surface for cooking. Our intuitive tendency to distinguish proper functions from 'garden

[6] This basic articulation of the notion is the one used by Millikan in her influential presentation; see Ruth Millikan, *Language, Thought, and Other Biological Categories: New Foundations for Realism* (Cambridge, MA: MIT Press, 1984). Millikan also takes proper functions to ground the possibility of objects malfunctioning. The idea of proper function can be characterized in a number of other ways as well. Some describe the proper function of a thing as what the thing is 'supposed to do', as opposed to merely something it happens to do, while others describe it with the phrase 'the function of X', as opposed to 'a function of X'; see Larry Wright, 'Functions', *Philosophical Review* 82 (1973): 139–68, especially 141. Also, proper function is sometimes said to be 'standardly ascribed' to the object, whereas other functions are ascribed less frequently, or in idiosyncratic contexts; see Pieter E. Vermaas and Wybo N. Houkes, 'Ascribing Functions to Technical Artefacts: A Challenge to Etiological Accounts of Functions', *British Journal for the Philosophy of Science* 54 (2003): 261–89, especially 265.

[7] This example is drawn from Wright, 'Functions'; see 147.

variety' functions, or functions *simpliciter*, is a well-entrenched feature of talk about artefact function. Consequently, a satisfactory analysis of artefact function ought to be able to account for, and explain, this tendency.[8]

Intentionalist theories of artefact function, however, face serious difficulties here. For in various cases, it seems that intentions of *different* agents correspond to the proper function of the object: in the case of fountain pens, the designer, in that of pipe cleaners, the manufacturers, and in the case of the Plaza Major, the current or recent users. This entails that, if an intentionalist theory is the true theory of artefact function, and hence is capable of differentiating proper functions from functions *simpliciter*, there is something shared by the intentions of these different particular agents, in these particular cases. In other words, for an intention-based theory to account for the existence of *proper* functions, it must provide a qualitative description of the peculiar sort of intention that suffices to bestow a *proper* function, as opposed to a function *simpliciter*. In other words, analysis (3) must be supplemented with:

> (4) X has proper function F if and only if S is the designer/maker/user of X and S has intended that X perform F, where the intention in question is of kind K.

However, as an argument by Beth Preston suggests, it is hard to see a qualitative characterization of intention that would render (4) true.[9] Preston points out some prominent features of the intentions of artefact designers that, at first glance, may seem to 'line up with' an artefact's proper function. For example, it is true that designers often have intentions towards the artefact that are more creative and innovative than the intentions that others have for that artefact: the intentions of the creator(s) of the fountain pen,

[8] Thus Vermaas and Houkes make drawing the distinction between proper and accidental functions one of their four desiderata for a theory of artefact function; see Vermaas and Houkes, 'Ascribing Functions to Technical Artefacts', 265.

[9] Beth Preston, 'Of Marigold Beer: A Reply to Vermaas and Houkes', *British Journal for the Philosophy of Science* 54 (2003): 601–12.

presumably, were much more creative and innovative than Jones's intention to use it as a paperweight, for instance. The intentionalist might suggest, on this basis, that intention gives rise to proper function, as opposed to function *simpliciter*, when it is sufficiently creative. But, as Preston points out, this is not necessarily the case. Although some clever individual's inspired use of a frying pan as a satellite dish would be very creative, that would not change its proper function, which remains providing a portable hot surface for cooking. Another possibility that Preston mentions is that intentions might generate a proper function when they involve a sufficient modification of the object. But even if a clever individual modifies his frying pan, coating it with some foreign substance and removing the handle, that still does not change its proper function, which remains providing a portable hot surface for cooking. In short, as Preston puts it, 'the intentions of users do not appear to differ from the intentions of designers in any relevant way'.[10] More generally, for any kind of intention that lines up with an artefact's proper function in some cases, we can imagine cases where agents have that same sort of intention, but the object does not have the corresponding proper function. This means that an intentionalist theory will leave our identification of some functions as proper functions, rather than merely functions *simpliciter*, completely inexplicable. The importance of this practice, something admitted even by intentionalist theorists, renders this a devastating criticism of the intentionalist approach.

Preston's argument is not entirely conclusive, however. As she notes, it remains conceivable that the intentionalist might eventually succeed in providing a qualitative characterization of the peculiar sort of intention that gives rise to proper functions. However, the line of thought that Preston advances is compelling and, as we will show in Section 3 of this chapter, it can be reinforced by considering some recent serious attempts to articulate an intentionalist theory. For the moment, however, we want only

[10] Preston, 'Of Marigold Beer', 608.

to focus on the failure of intentionalist theories to date, and the significance of this for the Problem of Indeterminacy. That problem stems from a lack of clarity over how to determine 'the function' of a complex artefact, such as an architectural work. The intentionalist view of artefact function, which we suspect is tacitly assumed by many philosophers, directly leads to this difficulty, entailing, as it does, that we have no account of why, or on what basis, certain artefact functions can be singled out as proper functions. Intentionalism, in other words, leaves the idea of '*the* function' of the object an indeterminate, even meaningless, notion. It therefore underwrites and lends substance to Scruton's claim that the function of an artefact is a 'fundamentally, and perhaps irremediably, obscure' notion.

3.2 Naturalizing Function

In the previous section, we argued that the Problem of Indeterminacy of artefact function is but a symptom of a larger problem in the philosophy of artefacts: the failure to provide an analysis of artefact function that explicates the intuitive distinction between proper functions and functions *simpliciter*. In this section, we show how recent theories of function in the philosophy of biology point the way towards a better theory of artefact function, and a solution to the Problem of Indeterminacy.

Recent analytic philosophy of biology has seen a resurgence of discussion on teleology and related topics.[11] Initially, this discussion emerged from the fact that, despite the reservations of philosophers and physical scientists about applying such 'anthropomorphic' concepts to nature, biologists simply have not abandoned teleological concepts, such as functionality, in the way that physical

[11] For an overview, see Mark Perlman, 'The Modern Philosophical Resurrection of Teleology', *The Monist* 87 (2004): 3–51. Two recent collections on this topic are: Colin Allen, Marc Bekoff, and George Lauder (eds), *Nature's Purposes: Analyses of Function and Design in Biology* (Cambridge, MA: MIT Press, 1998), and Andrew Ariew, Robert Cummins, and Mark Perlman (eds), *Functions: New Essays in the Philosophy of Psychology and Biology* (Oxford: Oxford University Press, 2002).

scientists did in the seventeenth century. The biologist Ernst Mayr describes the motivation for this by saying that 'biologists have insisted that they would lose a great deal, methodologically and heuristically, if they were prevented from using such language'.[12] For example, biological scientists have continued the practice of 'functional explanation': explaining the existence and/or form of biological traits and structures by making reference to their function. This continued use of functional concepts by biologists spurred a prolonged effort by philosophers of science to *naturalize* function and other teleological concepts through the provision of a purely causal, non-intentional analysis. Early efforts in this direction tried to break the connection between functionality and a designing intellect by rejecting the idea that natural things have a function in virtue of their antecedent history. Instead, functionality was understood as a physical property intrinsic to the object itself and/or its contemporaneous or future environment. These early efforts focused on concepts such as feedback from an external goal, non-redundancy, 'useful effects', uniform causal behaviour across a range of environments, and internally self-correcting behaviour.[13]

The most influential analysis of this sort is Robert Cummins's view that 'for something to perform its function is for it to have certain effects on a containing system, which effects contribute to the performance of some activity of, or the maintenance of some condition in, that containing system'.[14] The heart's function of

[12] Ernst Mayr, 'The Multiple Meanings of Teleological', in Ernst Mayr, *Towards a New Philosophy of Biology* (Cambridge, MA: Harvard University Press, 1988), 38–66; the quotation is on 41.

[13] On feedback from an external goal, see Arturo Rosenblueth, Norbert Wiener, and Julian Bigelow, 'Behaviour, Purpose and Teleology', *Philosophy of Science* 10 (1943): 18–24; on non-redundancy, see Morton Beckner, *The Biological Way of Thought* (New York: Columbia University Press, 1959); on 'useful effects', see John Canfield, 'Teleological Explanations in Biology', *British Journal for the Philosophy of Science* 14 (1964): 285–95; on uniform causal behaviour across a range of environments, see Richard Braithwaite, *Scientific Explanation* (Cambridge: Cambridge University Press, 1953); and on internally self-correcting behaviour, see Ernst Nagel, 'The Structure of Teleological Explanations', in Ernest Nagel, *The Structure of Science* (New York: Harcourt, 1961), 401–28.

[14] Robert Cummins, 'Functional Analysis', *Journal of Philosophy* 72 (1975): 741–65; the quotation is on 741. For further discussion of Cummins's analysis, see n. 24 below.

pumping blood can be used to illustrate the approach. According to Cummins, the heart's pumping blood contributes, in a certain kind of way, to the circulatory system's ability to distribute nutrients throughout the body. It does something that is crucial to the circulatory system's ability to distribute nutrients: namely, it pumps blood, and this is just what we mean when we say that the function of the heart is to pump blood.[15] That is, Cummins's analysis identifies a trait or part's having a function with the trait or part in question playing a certain sort of causal role in a larger system of which it is a component. For this reason, these functions are sometimes referred to as *causal role functions*.[16]

Some philosophers have claimed that this sense of function has an important role in branches of biology such as physiology, anatomy, and ecology.[17] One of its limitations, however, is what one commentator calls its apparent promiscuity: it appears that animal parts and traits have a multiplicity of functions in this sense, only a few of which interest biologists.[18] Consider again that the heart, in addition to pumping blood, also does other things, such as make noise. Further, this noise contributes to a capacity of a containing system: the circulatory system's capacity to make noise. On Cummins's account, it would seem that the function of the heart is not only to pump blood, but also to make heart sounds. But even if this is a function in some sense, it is surely not the *proper* function of the heart, which, intuitively, is pumping blood. In other words, Cummins's account, though it may explicate function talk in some biological contexts, does not explain how we draw the distinction between proper functions and other functions.

[15] On this example, see Karen Neander, 'Functions as Selected Effects: The Conceptual Analyst's Defence', *Philosophy of Science* 58 (1991a): 168–84.

[16] The term is due to Neander, ibid. See also her 'The Teleological Notion of "Function"', *Australasian Journal of Philosophy* 69 (1991b): 454–68.

[17] See, for example, Ronald Amundson and George Lauder, 'Function without Purpose: The Uses of Causal Role Function in Evolutionary Biology', *Biology and Philosophy* 9 (1994): 443–69, and Paul Sheldon Davies, *Norms of Nature: Naturalism and the Nature of Functions* (Cambridge, MA: MIT Press, 2001).

[18] Ruth Millikan, 'In Defense of Proper Function', *Philosophy of Science* 56 (1989): 288–302.

Other naturalized theories of function, however, have proven better able to explicate this distinction. The most important of these is what is sometimes called the 'selected effects' theory of functions.[19] Indeed, this theory is usually presented as a theory of *proper* function, rather than function *simpliciter*:

> Trait X has a proper function F if and only if X currently exists because, in the recent past, ancestors of X were successful in enhancing fitness because they performed F, leading to reproduction of the genotype for trait X.[20]

The basic idea behind the theory is simple: the proper function of a particular animal's biological part or trait is an effect of that part or trait that, first, achieves a certain kind of success in relation to its environment: namely, enhancing the fitness of its bearers. Second, this success leads to the spread of the trait, via the reproduction of its bearers and the consequent spread of the genes for the trait. Through its selective success, then, this effect explains the current existence of the part or trait in the animal population. Such an effect, on this theory, is the trait or part's proper function. Thus, the proper function of a heart is to pump blood, since pumping blood is, first of all, what made ancestral hearts successful with respect to their environment. Second, this success caused the spread of hearts, when creatures with hearts lived longer and left more offspring, spreading the genes for hearts. Pumping blood, then, is the effect that explains why our hearts exist today: it is the heart's proper function. Making heart sounds, though also something that ancestor hearts did, does not explain the existence of hearts today, since there was no natural selection for making heart sounds. Therefore, making heart sounds is not a proper function of our hearts.

[19] The label is from Neander, 'Functions as Selected Effects'. The theory has its roots in the seminal etiological analysis of function proposed in Wright, 'Functions'. It has been further developed by other theorists: see, for example, Millikan, *Language, Thought, and Other Biological Categories* and 'In Defense of Proper Functions'; Neander, 'Functions as Selected Effects'; and Peter Godfrey-Smith, 'A Modern History Theory of Functions', *Noûs* 28 (1994): 344–62.

[20] This version is based on Godfrey-Smith, ibid.

The idea of proper functions as selected effects has been applied not only within biology, but also in other areas of philosophy, notably the philosophy of mind and the philosophy of language.[21] For our purposes, the important advance of this idea is that it provides a principled theoretical account of the distinction between proper functions and functions *simpliciter*. This raises the possibility that an analogous approach could provide an account of proper function for artefacts.

3.3 Artefact Selection and Proper Function

In Section 1 of this chapter, we outlined the way in which intentionalist approaches to artefact function lead to a failure to provide an account of proper functions, or, in other words, to an indeterminacy of function. A possible solution to this failure presents itself, however, when we take a somewhat counter-intuitive turn away from human intention, and towards the sort of 'naturalistic' approaches applied to function in biology. In particular, we may hope to avoid this failure by understanding the proper functions of artefacts as selected effects. The hope here is that just as selected effects theories succeed in capturing our intuitive sense that some functions belong properly to animal parts and traits, however many other things they may happen to be used for, an analogous theory could capture our intuitive sense that some functions belong properly to artefacts, however many other things they may happen to be used for.

The theory of selected effects as developed for the biological case, however, cannot simply be applied to artefacts, such as iPods and Volvos. For one thing, although the effects of artefacts might

[21] See, for example, Ruth Millikan, *Language, Thought, and Other Biological Categories*, and *White Queen Psychology and Other Essays for Alice* (Cambridge, MA: MIT Press, 1993), as well as the essays in two recent collections: Denis M. Walsh (ed.), *Naturalism, Evolution and Mind* (Cambridge: Cambridge University Press, 2001), and Graham Macdonald and David Papineau (eds), *Teleosemantics* (Oxford: Oxford University Press, 2006). Macdonald's and Papineau's introduction to the latter volume, 'Teleosemantics: The Programme, Prospects, and Problems', is especially informative.

be said to make them successful with respect to their environment, they are successful in a way that is very different from the way in which biological traits are successful.[22] The success of any of the effects of an iPod does not increase its fitness in the biological sense: that is, it does not raise the probability that it will produce a daughter iPod, which is effectively zero. A different slant on the same point is that, when the effects of artefacts do result in success with respect to the environment, whatever that might mean, this does not cause artefacts to be reproduced in the way biological traits are reproduced, since artefacts do not have genes. In short, the reproduction of artefacts is obviously different from that of organisms, and this means that a selected effects theory of proper function for artefacts must be based upon a type of 'selection' quite different from that which we find in biology.

The most developed attempt to spell out the sort of selection involved here is due to Beth Preston, who draws the analogy explicitly:

> The first step in the biological process is that a new trait arises by mutation or as the by-product of other traits. Alternatively, an existing trait may be used for a new operation. Similarly with artifacts, the first step is the production of a prototype by an inventor or designer, or someone puts an existing artifact to a new use. In biology, if the new trait or use of a trait is successful in its performance, and its success contributes to the reproductive success of its possessor, it thereby ensures its own reproduction as well. Similarly with artifacts, if the new artifact is successful it will be reproduced, initially, perhaps, for use by the inventor or designer, but later for use by other people. In the cultural milieu, this history of reproduction contingent upon success shows up as a history of manufacture and distribution by trade or sale. In the case of new uses of existing artifacts, they begin to be manufactured in whole or in part for the new market.[23]

[22] This point is emphasized by Vermaas and Houkes, 'Ascribing Functions to Technical Artefacts', 263.

[23] Preston, 'Why is a Wing like a Spoon?', 244. The account stems from Millikan's theory of proper function, developed in her *Language, Thought, and Other Biological Categories* (see especially 28). However, Millikan's theory of artefact function is more complex than this.

We propose to gloss Preston's idea here as follows:

> X has a *proper function* F if and only if Xs currently exist because, in the recent past, ancestors of X were successful in meeting some need or want in the marketplace because they performed F, leading to manufacture and distribution of Xs.[24]

On this analysis, the proper function of an artefact is, more or less, an effect that has allowed that artefact to pass muster in the

[24] Preston's theory of artefact function extends beyond this theory of proper function to a theory of function *simpliciter*. Preston suggests that these can be explicated by Cummins's sense of function, which she calls 'system function'. These 'usually are cases where an artefact is used for something unrelated to its proper function, but is not modified for that use'; see Preston, 'Why is a Wing like a Spoon?', 250. She cites, among other examples, using a screwdriver to open paint cans and using twist-ties as cat toys. This part of Preston's theory is not salient for our discussion here, and is logically separable from her theory of artefact proper function. That is, one could reject Preston's theory of functions *simpliciter*, by accepting an intentionalist analysis along the lines of analysis (3), while accepting her view that proper functions are selected effects. In fact, such a position may be more attractive than Preston's more thoroughly 'naturalized' view. For while Cummins's analysis is somewhat 'promiscuous', it does not seem to us capable of capturing all instances of artefact function *simpliciter*.

As Paul Sheldon Davies has recently stressed in *Norms of Nature*, Cummins's original analysis requires that the effect in question not only play some causal role or other, but that it play a causal role that figures in an informative explanation of a capacity of a larger system. On Cummins's account, an explanation of a system's capacity C is informative to the extent that it (i) breaks C down in terms of components that are simpler than C; (ii) breaks C down in terms of components that are different in type from C; and (iii) explains C in terms of a sophisticated interaction among its components (see *Norms of Nature*, 78). To put the point in a less technical way, we could say that Cummins's account preserves a distinction between a thing merely doing X, and its having X as a causal role function. Many cases of artefact function, however, seem to be cases of the former, and not the latter. For instance, when Jones pries a paint can open with a screwdriver, what is the system whose operation is explained? The paint can? Or perhaps Jones, her screwdriver, and her paint can? And what is the capacity of that system—its capacity to remove lids? If so—and there are no obviously better alternatives here—then it is far from clear that any interesting analysis along Cummins's lines is in the offing for these cases. For instance, analysing the system 'Jones, her screwdriver, and her paint can' into the components Jones, her screwdriver, and her paint can is hardly to break the system down in terms of components that are simpler and different in type, and which engage in some sophisticated interaction.

Preston herself acknowledges this point at other places in her discussion. She mentions, for instance, the case where a belt buckle saves someone's life by deflecting a bullet. 'Here', she writes, 'it is hard to imagine what system could be described such that this singular event would come out as a function of the buckle rather than as just a lucky accident'; see Preston, 'Why is a Wing like a Spoon?', 221–2. Yet the same point seems to apply to many of the co-opted functions of artefacts that she wishes to analyse as functions in Cummins's sense, such as using an antique flat-iron as a doorstop, hammering a stake with a rock, or carrying strawberries in a large leaf (ibid., 252).

marketplace. For example, on this theory, the proper function of a particular shovel is to allow the easier movement of loose material, since this is what earlier shovels did that brought about the manufacture and distribution of more shovels, including this particular one. Propping up a broken garage door is not a proper function of a particular shovel, because that effect has done nothing to bring about the manufacture and distribution of shovels in the past, and so does not explain the current existence of shovels today.

Two key concepts in this analysis require further explication. First, what does it mean to say that one artefact is an ancestor of another? Since artefacts are not genetically related, in the sense that organisms are, this phrase must have a different meaning here than in the biological case. We will take an artefact X's ancestors to be those objects that are (1) similar to X and (2) whose success in the marketplace was a causal factor in the production of X. Second, what does it mean to say that an artefact X was 'manufactured and distributed' because of its ability to F? In particular, how many instances of X need to have been made or sold? How long does X need to be manufactured or distributed, due to its ability to F, for it to acquire F as a proper function? We think that there are not clear answers to these questions, because the notion of proper function itself is somewhat vague. Take the example, offered by Preston, of the use of beer as slug bait by gardeners.[25] Intuitively, poisoning slugs is not a proper function of beer. If people start purchasing large quantities for this use, however, such that breweries begin producing beer for this market, we may change our view here, and see it as a proper function of (some) beer. But our intuitions do not dictate any precise sales figure that is required for this.[26]

Note that this theory of the proper functions of artefacts has the same general form as the selected effects theory for biological traits. The basic form of the selected effects theory in the biological case

[25] Preston, 'Of Marigold Beer'.

[26] Note that the very same vagueness characterizes the biological theory of proper functions as selected effects: there is no set number of generations that has to pass before a trait acquires a proper function.

is that a proper function of X is an effect of Xs that, in past cases, was successful with respect to its environment, thereby ultimately bringing about the current existence of Xs. On the present theory for artefacts, the same is true. What is different is, first, the sort of success involved, and, second, the way in which this success explains the current existence of artefacts. An artefact's effect is successful when it meets a market want or need. And this success explains the current existence of the artefact when it leads human agents to manufacture and distribute that artefact.[27]

The key point about the present analysis, for our purposes, is that it lifts proper functions out of the messy realm of human intentions. For, on this analysis, the intentions of particular human agents towards an artefact are not sufficient to confer a proper function upon it. If a clever individual chooses to rig up her frying pan as a satellite dish, this does not mean that it is 'selected' for this effect, in our sense. For this use would not make it the case that frying pans have passed muster in the marketplace because of this effect. Rather, it would still be the case that they have thrived in the marketplace because they provide a portable hot surface for cooking.[28] It is true that human intentions are involved in an artefact's passing muster in the marketplace. After all, it is human agents that make decisions about the reproduction and distribution of artefacts. But, on the present analysis, these intentions are involved only in an indirect way in the object's being selected.[29] More to the point, no *individual's* intentions regarding the object are sufficient to imbue that object with a proper function. The event of manufacture and distribution, as a consequence of meeting market demand, is necessary for proper function.

[27] Historical accounts of development of artefacts that emphasize selective process are found in George Basalla, *The Evolution of Technology* (Cambridge: Cambridge University Press, 1988), and John Ziman (ed.), *Technological Innovation as an Evolutionary Process* (Cambridge: Cambridge University Press, 2000). Ziman's initial essay in the latter volume, 'Evolutionary Models for Technological Change', is especially informative.

[28] This is what Vermaas and Houkes calls the 'broad sense' of artefact selection, as opposed to the narrow sense, in which an individual agent selects an artefact; see Vermaas and Houkes, 'Ascribing Functions to Technical Artefacts', 262.

[29] This point is emphasized in Preston, 'Of Marigold Beer', 611.

This conclusion obviously entails that there is no kind of intention whose possession is sufficient to bestow a proper function on an artefact. In Section 1 of this chapter, we followed Preston in arguing for this claim on the grounds that none of the obvious ways of characterizing such an intention fit the facts about proper function. Yet, as we noted, this argument against the intentionalist approach is not definitive, and must ultimately be made good by examining particular examples of intentionalist theories and their attempts to define such an intention. Having developed the theory of proper functions as selected effects, we are now in a position to reinforce our earlier argument by examining a recent intentionalist theory of artefact function offered by W. N. Houkes and P. E. Vermaas.[30] They gloss their analysis as the view that 'an artefact function is any role played by an artefact in a use plan that is justified and communicated to prospective users'.[31] Since 'use plans' are complex sets of intentions directed towards artefacts, this amounts to an intentionalist approach to artefact function. On this view, the sort of intention that bestows a function on an artefact is an intention to employ it in a reasonable plan for achieving some goal.

Houkes and Vermaas, however, also want their analysis to capture at least something of the distinction between proper function and function *simpliciter*: thus they distinguish between standard plans and alternative plans, such that using beer to quench thirst and become intoxicated is a 'standard' plan, whereas feeding it to slugs to kill them is an 'alternative' plan. As we have argued, and as Houkes and Vermaas themselves insist, drawing this distinction is essential in any theory of artefacts.[32] But how do they then

[30] Wybo N. Houkes and Pieter E. Vermaas, 'Actions versus Functions: A Plea for an Alternative Metaphysics of Artifacts', *The Monist* 87 (2004): 52–71. Preston, in 'Of Marigold Beer', argues that an earlier presentation of their analysis of function fails to draw the distinction between proper functions and functions *simpliciter*.

[31] Houkes and Vermaas, 'Actions versus Functions', 66.

[32] Regarding the distinction between standard and alternative uses of artefacts, Houkes and Vermaas write that it is 'too widespread and intuitively, not to mention legally, important to discard as a figment of unschooled intuition. This is not to say that conceptual analysis or a philosophical reconstruction should leave the prima facie distinction intact... Yet the primary goal should be to conceptualize the distinctions as such'; ibid., 53.

distinguish between 'standard' and 'alternative' use plans? They write:

> Initially, only use of an artifact that is in accordance with an original design or traditional use plan is regarded as standard. Users may, however, develop their own plans for the artifact ... In the course of time, these non-standard plans can be proven successful by actual use and they can be communicated ... Eventually they can be as well-established as the original use plan and use in accordance with them becomes, by our definition, standard use.[33]

On this theory of function, an artefact X has F as its proper function when someone intends to use X to F as part of a standard plan. But a plan that involves using X to F is standard only if X's F-ing was *actually successful*, such that it brought about dissemination of the plan. The distinction between standard and alternative use plans, in other words, is determined by none other than performance in the marketplace.

Of course, this move allows Houkes and Vermaas to use their theory to distinguish proper functions from functions *simpliciter*. Using beer to quench thirst and become intoxicated is a 'standard' plan because, in the course of time, drinking beer has proven successful in quenching thirst and producing intoxication, thus leading to production of beer and the widespread intention to drink it. Feeding beer to slugs to kill them is an 'alternative' plan because doing so has not led to an analogous result. But, plainly, this move also renders Houkes and Vermaas's theory, in the final analysis, a non-intentionalist theory of artefact function, since there is no intention that, in and of itself, is sufficient for the assignment of a proper function. The event of manufacture and distribution, as a consequence of meeting market demand, is necessary for proper function. This result reinforces the conclusion that, unless we are willing to dispense with the notion of proper function altogether, a satisfactory theory of artefact function must include some version of the selected effects theory.

[33] Houkes and Vermaas, 'Actions versus Functions', 63.

3.4 The Problem of Novel Artefacts

So far we have defended the conclusion that only a selected effects theory can explicate the intuitive distinction that we draw between the functions of artefacts *simpliciter* and their proper functions. However, the capacity of selected effects theories to explicate this distinction has been challenged, on the grounds that such theories are unable to explicate that subset of attributions of proper function that apply to novel objects. Vermaas and Houkes lay out this criticism of selected effects theories, providing two examples of the ascription of proper function to 'innovative or atypical' artefacts.[34] The artefacts that figure in these examples are: (1) the teletypewriter, a combination of a telegraph and a typewriter serving as output device that became widely used in the early twentieth century; and (2) the deck of the Victorian-era Britannia Bridge, a novel element in bridge construction consisting of a hollow iron tube that was modelled on ship hulls.

In each of these examples, Vermaas and Houkes see the artefact in question as having a particular proper function at the time of its creation. When invented, the teletypewriter had the proper function of 'transmitting texts', and the proper function of the tube of the Britannia Bridge was 'to make possible railway traffic across a body of water'.[35] However, these attributions of proper function are not accounted for by the selected effects theory, since that theory requires that, if X has a proper function, then, in the recent past, ancestors of X have been 'selected' by market forces. The artefacts in question, however, are said to be novel, and so have no ancestors. They therefore lack a history of selection by market forces, and so cannot have proper functions, according to the selected effects theory. But we do attribute proper functions to these artefacts; hence, it is claimed, the selected effects theory fails to adequately explicate talk of the proper functions of artefacts.

[34] Vermaas and Houkes, 'Ascribing Functions to Technical Artefacts'.

[35] Ibid., 264, 279.

The premise underlying this objection, that selected effects theories of proper function are unable to assign proper functions to truly novel items, is correct.[36] However, it is unclear whether this fact can be parlayed into a substantial objection to selected effects theories of proper function. Preston argues that it cannot, pointing out that any theory of proper function is an attempt to clarify and render consistent a rough and intuitive linguistic practice. It may simply be that no theory can account for *all* of the extant attributions of proper function. The point is a familiar one: the concepts that we attempt to analyse philosophically often have uses that cannot all be captured by a logically consistent analysis. Consequently, the most that we can ask is that a fruitful and consistent analysis capture as much of our intuitive practice as possible.[37] We have already seen that intentionalist theories of proper function for artefacts capture very little of this, being unable to draw any principled distinction between proper functions and functions *simpliciter*. A selected effects theory, in contrast, allows us to draw that distinction in the overwhelming majority of cases. If it does not allow us to draw it in the case of a truly novel artefact, then some such failure in a theory of proper function may be inevitable. Thus, when faced with comparing the overall performance of intentionalist and selected effect theories, the choice, Preston thinks, is clear.[38]

As far as it goes, we think that Preston's response is perfectly sound. However, a somewhat stronger response is possible. For it is not clear to us that there actually are compelling cases of the attribution of proper functions to truly novel artefacts. To begin

[36] This consequence of the analysis has been noted for selected effects theories of biological function; see Godfrey-Smith, 'A Modern History Theory of Functions'.

[37] The attempt to achieve such a match between an analysis and our intuitive practice is typically understood in terms of the well-known philosophical notion of reflective equilibrium. The method was labelled and popularized by John Rawls in *A Theory of Justice* (Cambridge, MA: Harvard University Press, 1971) as a means of balancing principles of justice with moral intuitions, although it was proposed earlier by Nelson Goodman in *Fact, Fiction, and Forecast* (Cambridge, MA: Harvard University Press, 1955) as a method for establishing principles of inductive logic.

[38] As Preston puts it, 'the distinction between proper function and accidental function is central to the phenomenology of artifact production and use in ways that the ascription of proper function to novel artifacts is not'; see Preston, 'Of Marigold Beer', 609.

with, it ought to be emphasized that the artefacts in question must be *truly* novel in order for us to conclude that they lack ancestors, and hence cannot be covered by a selected effects theory. The examples provided by Vermaas and Houkes are problematic in this regard. The teletypewriter, for example, is said to be 'innovative and atypical'. However, a teletypewriter is highly similar to a telegraph: indeed, it *is* a telegraph with an output device attached to it. Hence, according to a selected effects theory, there is no great mystery as to why the teletypewriter, upon its emergence in the early twentieth century, had the proper function of 'transmitting texts'. For the teletypewriter existed, in part, because its ancestors, telegraphs, had been flourishing in the marketplace for a half-century by doing precisely that.

The deck of the Britannia Bridge is a more compelling candidate for a truly novel artefact, or one with no ancestors, since it appears to have borne little similarity to previous bridge decks. However, it remains unclear whether it is a truly novel item since, as Vermaas and Houkes describe the case, it strongly resembles a certain kind of ship hull. If this resemblance is sufficiently strong, it will be possible for a selected effects theory to assign it a proper function, namely, doing whatever it was that its ancestors, certain ship hulls, did that caused them to pass muster in the marketplace. Thus, on such a theory, the proper function of the Britannia Bridge deck would be to, say, withstand water pressure while keeping a ship afloat. Vermaas and Houkes reject this conclusion out of hand, but the basis for this move is unclear. If the resemblance between the deck of the Britannia Bridge and the ship hulls in question is strong enough to make us classify those ship hulls as its ancestors, then the intuitive way to describe this situation would be as an instance of someone cleverly using a ship hull to function as part of bridge. In fact, this would seem to be precisely what made the bridge the noteworthy and unusual thing it was, rather than merely one more engineering innovation.

In order to fashion a compelling instance of a truly novel artefact, one with no ancestors at all, we need to consider an object with no similarity to speak of to *any* extant artefacts. As an example, we could try to imagine a new sort of bridge deck having sufficiently little resemblance to ship hulls, or any other artefacts. But, instead, let us consider a different example: a device such as a can-opener that bears no obvious resemblance to any previous can-openers, containing none of the same sorts of major parts or mechanisms. Further, imagine also that it does not bear any obvious resemblance to any other sort of extant artefact.[39] Such an object seems conceivable, as, say, the product of some incredibly ingenious inventor developing entirely new technological principles. The question then becomes: can we describe this object as having the proper function of opening cans? If so, then a selected effects theory cannot account for all attributions of proper function. It seems clear to us that, intuitively, we would want to describe the object in question as having the function of opening cans. However, it is not clear that our intuitions dictate that this is its *proper* function. As mentioned in Section I of this chapter, the core idea behind a proper function is that of a function belonging to the object itself, as opposed to being imposed upon it by use, context, or happenstance. When we contemplate an artefact that bears no relation whatever to devices that have come before, and that has never been allowed to perform in the marketplace, such as our imaginary can-opener, we simply fail to find any strong intuitions that one of the things the artefact can do is the one that really belongs to the object.

There is no doubt that when we consider a truly novel artefact, such as our fantastic can-opener, we instinctively think of the function intended by its designer first, and, moreover, think of this function as being somehow the primary or most important one. But this is not the same as thinking of it as the item's proper function, and is easily explicable on other grounds. For any *truly* novel artefact will, by definition, work on a novel and hitherto unappreciated set of principles. In the case of our can-opener, for

[39] Perhaps this is what Preston has in mind in mentioning 'a novel prototype can opener'; see Preston, 'Of Marigold Beer', 602.

example, if it does not share any parts or mechanisms with previous can-openers, it must work though some principle that is entirely innovative, at least as applied to opening cans. Perhaps it works through the use of electromagnetism, for example, to open cans in some way never before imagined. But any such causal process is bound to attract our interest in virtue of its sheer novelty and innovation, as any ingenious technological innovation would. It is this quality, rather than any privileged connection of the effect in question with the object itself, that renders the function intended by the designer the primary and most important one in our minds.

The pre-eminence we instinctively accord to the function intended by the designer in such cases of entirely novel artefacts is also unstable in a way that proper functions are not. For example, our novel can-opener's ability to open cans captures our attention because of the new and interesting principles used in achieving that end. But were we to discover that the very same device does something else of even greater interest, curing cancer, say, we would quickly shift our attention to this other function, thinking of *it* as the primary and most important one. And here we would not instinctively say that 'Here is a can-opener that also happens to do something neat: curing cancer!' Rather, we would say: 'This novel device, which we thought to be a can-opener, has, in fact, turned out to be a cancer curing machine!' We would not say the first thing here because there is as yet no basis on which to say that opening cans is a power that 'belongs' to the object in a way that curing cancer does not. Rather, in these cases, our attention to function is driven by our interests merely, and not by any firm intuitions about proper function.

3.5 Indeterminacy and Functional Beauty

How does this analysis of the proper function of artefacts help us to address the Problem of Indeterminacy facing the notion of Functional Beauty? Recall that the Problem of Indeterminacy really manifests itself in two ways. For some objects, such as architectural works, it simply is not clear what the object's function is. For other artefacts, such as everyday mass-produced artefacts, although it seems intuitively obvious what the object's function is, we lack any philosophical grounds for singling out that one as the correct or proper function. This entails an absence of norms for the appraisal of Functional Beauty, making judgement of Functional Beauty relative to some extent. The present account addresses this worry about the function of everyday mass-produced artefacts by justifying our intuitive ascriptions of proper function. We do not need a theory to tell us *that* propping up a garage door is not the 'right' function to use when judging the Functional Beauty of a particular shovel, but we do need a theory to tell us *why* this is the case. This theory does that, and thus serves to defend Functional Beauty from the charge of being thoroughly relativistic. Consequently, this theory helps put the appreciation of Functional Beauty on a par with other forms of aesthetic appreciation.

But this sort of manifestation of the Problem of Indeterminacy, regarding everyday artefacts such as shovels, is the easy case, where dispute over proper function is rare. What we really want to know is how the other manifestation of the problem can be addressed: How does this theory help in the *hard* cases where we lack clear intuitions regarding proper function, such as the case of architectural works? Consider again the opera house example, the Toronto Four Seasons Centre, introduced in Chapter 2, Section 5. What is the building's function? Is it facilitating the performance of opera, or is it changing perceptions of the city, providing a general civic space, and the like? Seen in the light of our theory of proper function, the Problem of Indeterminacy in this example can be reduced to a definite question, namely: What effect of opera houses has been salient in keeping them in existence in their recent past? On our account, to find the *proper* function of the Four Seasons Centre, we need to find that effect of opera houses that, in the recent past, has led them to pass muster in the marketplace and thereby be manufactured.

Of course, answering *this* question may not be easy. Perhaps some may even think it is no easier to answer than the initial question 'What is the function of the Four Seasons Centre?' But we think that would be unduly pessimistic. Certainly, answering our question is not a straightforwardly empirical matter, like deciding the proper function of an animal trait. It will require, perhaps, a division of labour, with contributions from history, economics, architectural criticism, and other social sciences. It is not entirely clear what standards of proof we will demand. But this does not mean it is intractable.

For example, in the Four Seasons case, we suspect that, as initially absurd as some of his claims may sound, Christopher Hume's account of the proper function of the centre is more plausible than the conservative view that its 'real' or 'true' function is merely to house opera.[40] For opera houses nowadays are commonly built with funding from city councils and governments that are directly accountable to the general public. The general public's interest in opera is, it seems to us, sufficiently small that, if this consideration alone determined whether opera houses would be built, they would not be. City councils choose to build opera houses, we suspect, because they see them as doing important things other than slaking the thirst for Verdi, including, quite possibly, some of the sorts of things to which Hume alludes. Perhaps Hume's particular account of the factors that allow opera houses to pass muster in the market is arguable, and a closer study would certainly want to assess these factors more carefully. But, in general terms, it seems plausible to think that he is closer to identifying the proper function of the Four Seasons Centre than his opponents. And, if this is right, then when Hume calls that building a 'generic and inward looking box', he is closer to a correct or appropriate appraisal of its Functional Beauty, or lack thereof, than his opponents.

[40] Christopher Hume, 'The Opera House We Didn't Build', *Toronto Star*, 16 September 2006.

For a second example of how the present analysis can be used to settle vexed disputes concerning function, consider the recent discussion surrounding the aesthetic appreciation of large-scale industrial farming. It has seemed highly plausible to some philosophers, including one of us, to consider the aesthetic value of the sort of high-tech structures and equipment found in these environments (designer silos, programmed irrigation systems, automated machinery, and so on) in light of its function.[41] But just what is the function of the large-scale industrial farm? On the one hand, the function of such a farm seems more or less evident: providing food cheaply, profitably, and on a large scale.[42] On the other hand, some writers have resisted that conclusion. Ned Hettinger, for example, argues that 'modern agriculture is fossil-fuel and fossil-water reliant, it is soil eroding, it is a prime water polluter, and it destroys rural communities'.[43] Hettinger succinctly sums up his take on the function of such built environments by saying that they act as a 'poison delivery system' for surrounding ecosystems.[44] It is *this* function, he asserts, that is the most appropriate to use when we assess the aesthetics of the industrial farm. And considering this function, Hettinger insists, will radically change our aesthetic response to it. In defence of this assertion, however, Hettinger says little more than that 'community or social uses and purposes seem more relevant' for aesthetic and moral appreciation.[45] We here construe Hettinger as allowing something like the traditional version of Functional Beauty as looking fit for function, but disputing the claim that

[41] See, for example, Allen Carlson, 'On Appreciating Agricultural Landscapes', *Journal of Aesthetics and Art Criticism* 43 (1985): 301–12, and Allen Carlson, 'Viljelysmaisemien Esteettinen Arvo Ja Touttavuus' ('Productivity and the Aesthetic Value of Agricultural Landscapes'), in Y. Sepänmaa and L. Heikkilä-Palo (eds), *Pellossa Perihopeat* (*Fields: The Family Silver*) (Helsinki: Maahenki Oy, 2005), 52–61.

[42] See Carlson, 'On Appreciating Agricultural Landscapes', 308–10 .

[43] Ned Hettinger, 'Carlson's Environmental Aesthetics and the Protection of the Environment', *Environmental Ethics* 27 (2005): 57–76; the quotation is on 69.

[44] Ibid., 71.

[45] Ibid.

the proper function of the industrial farm is to produce food cheaply, profitably, and on a large scale.[46] How might this dispute be resolved?

If the present analysis of artefact function is correct, then the proper function of an industrial farm is that effect by means of which its ancestors have passed muster in the marketplace. Even if industrial farms do function, and have functioned, as poison delivery systems, it seems most unlikely that this is their proper function, since it is most unlikely that they have passed muster in the marketplace because of this. This is not to say that producing cheap food on a wide scale is more important than acting as a poison delivery system, or that we ought to downplay, in any way, the latter effect. On the contrary, if Hettinger is right about industrial farming being a poison delivery system, we obviously ought to be gravely concerned about this situation. However, moral objections to industrial farming do not require us to believe, and would not entail, that producing cheap food on a wide scale is not the proper function of the industrial farm, or what the industrial farm is for. To that extent, it seems to us that an evaluation of the Functional Beauty, or lack thereof, of the industrial farm, ought to consider this particular function.

We will consider further these and related cases in Chapter 6. Here we want to stress that these examples demonstrate the general way in which the present analysis of the proper function of artefacts as selected effects can undercut the Problem of Indeterminacy: by making clear the sense in which not all of the many functions of a particular artefact are equal. In doing so, it removes the primary

[46] Hettinger's appeal to 'uses' is reminiscent of David Hume's view, discussed in Chapter 1, Section 2, that things are beautiful, not in virtue of looking fit for function, but in virtue of looking useful, or capable of serving human needs. Perhaps Hettinger's position can be developed along the lines of Hume's view, but since we will return to such views, and the serious difficulties they face, in the next chapter, we here construe Hettinger's comments in relation to the more traditional version of Functional Beauty as looking fit for function.

reason for suspecting that judgements of Functional Beauty must be infected with some sort of thoroughgoing relativism. Even among all the vagaries of architecture, Functional Beauty is a concept that can be deployed clearly and profitably in accounting for our aesthetic experiences.

4

Function and Form

If the line of thought developed in the preceding chapter is on the right track, then, contrary to Roger Scruton's suggestion, there is sense, rather than obscurity and confusion, in speaking of the aesthetic appreciation of an object in light of its function. However, this would be for naught if there were no solution to the other important problem for Functional Beauty that Scruton raises: the Problem of Translation. This is not a matter of determining the function of an object, but rather of understanding how knowledge of that function can play a role in our perception of, and hence our aesthetic appreciation of, that object. As noted in Chapter 2, Section 4, Scruton illustrates this problem with the example of a mundane architectural element, the strainer arch. The function of a strainer arch is to hold up walls. But what does it mean to say that a particular strainer arch is functionally beautiful, so that, for example, it has a form that looks fit for holding up walls? A particular strainer arch might actually *be* fit for holding up walls, having served to hold them up well, and one might *know* that this is the case. But how would this be evident in the perceptual appearance, or the look, of the item? As Scruton puts it, 'it is not clear how any particular "function" is to be translated into architectural "form"'.[1] In short, the problem here is that an idea central to the notion of Functional Beauty, the idea that the function of an object can be somehow 'translated' into its perceptual form, requires a clear, non-metaphorical analysis.

[1] Roger Scruton, *The Aesthetics of Architecture* (London: Methuen and Company, 1979), 40.

This issue has been considered in the literature of philosophical aesthetics, though not in any very systematic way. In this chapter, we attempt to consolidate and extend some of these scattered insights, and to address some lingering concerns about the aesthetic status of fitness and other function-related aesthetic qualities. We propose to frame the issues in the somewhat broader terms afforded by cognitively rich conceptions of aesthetic appreciation. In doing so, we will break the problem into two parts. First, we will outline how, on a cognitively rich conception of aesthetic appreciation, knowledge of function can affect, or translate into, perceptual experience in general. Next, we will describe how such conceptions can explain the translation of knowledge of function into the perceptual experience of aesthetic qualities.

4.1 Knowledge of Function

Cognitively rich accounts of aesthetic appreciation, such as the cultural theories of art discussed in Chapter 2, Section 1, take knowledge about the object of appreciation to be an essential component of its appropriate appreciation. According to these sorts of approaches, knowledge about an object influences our aesthetic appreciation of it through our employing certain groupings, classifications, or 'categories' when we perceive the object. As an example of such an approach, consider Kendall Walton's theory of the aesthetic appreciation of art.[2] Walton's theory is based on a division of perceptual qualities into aesthetic (elegance, for example) and non-aesthetic (redness, for example). Artistic categories embody our knowledge about particular kinds of artworks by specifying the sorts of non-aesthetic perceptual properties that are 'standard', 'variable', and 'contra-standard' for those kinds.[3] The

[2] Kendall Walton, 'Categories of Art', *Philosophical Review* 79 (1970): 334–67. We use Walton's theory as a model here since it is concisely and clearly presented as well as being a well-known account.

[3] Walton, ibid., defines these terms as follows: a non-aesthetic perceptual property N is *standard with respect to a category* C if and only if the absence of N tends to disqualify an

use of these categories, according to Walton, affects the way we perceive the works' non-aesthetic perceptual properties. Standard non-aesthetic perceptual properties are perceived as necessary, variable non-aesthetic perceptual properties may appear unremarkable, and contra-standard non-aesthetic perceptual properties will be perceived as jarring, dissonant, or 'out of place' elements of the work. By employing a category in perceiving an artwork, then, we implicitly impose a kind of structure upon its various perceptual qualities. In other words, our knowledge of the kind of artwork we are viewing, by implicitly designating specific features as either standard, variable, or contra-standard, causes us to *see* a certain sort of order, or lack of order, in the overall array of non-aesthetic perceptual properties possessed by that object. This change in perception may then affect our perception of the object's *aesthetic* qualities: by employing a certain artistic category in perceiving a work, we may come to perceive the work as having different aesthetic qualities from those it otherwise would. For instance, if one views a cubist painting using the category of traditional representational painting, many of its non-aesthetic perceptual properties (for example, containing only geometric shapes) are apt to look contra-standard, and the resulting aesthetic impression may be one of chaos and disorder. But seen in the category of cubist painting, for which possessing only geometrical shapes is a standard property, its particular arrangement of shapes might appear calm and serene instead.

If we consider the issue of the 'translation' of understanding of function into perceptual form along the lines of this sort of cognitively rich account, the issue resolves into a definite question: are there forms of understanding of function, or 'functional categories', that alter the perceptual appearance of non-aesthetic

item being a member of C; a non-aesthetic perceptual property N is *variable with respect to a category* C if and only if the absence or presence of N is irrelevant to an item being a member of C; and a non-aesthetic perceptual property N is *contra-standard with respect to a category* C if and only if the presence of N tends to disqualify an item from being a member of C.

perceptual properties? An affirmative answer to this question would constitute the foundation for a substantial response to the Problem of Translation by specifying, in a non-metaphorical way, how knowledge of function helps to shape perceptual experience.

In approaching the question, we can note that there are at least two meanings that can be attributed to the phrase 'understanding of function'. It could mean understanding of the *identity* of an object's function (what the object's function is) or it could mean understanding of *how*, or in what way, the object performs its function. This distinction is apt to go unnoticed, since for many kinds of familiar functional objects, it is obvious to us how they fulfil their function. For instance, if we are attempting to assess the Functional Beauty of a chair or a hammer, it seems that all we need to learn is that the item is a chair or a hammer: the question of *how* it fulfils its function does not even arise, since all chairs and all hammers work according to the same basic principles, on general designs that are so familiar to us as to be obvious. However, the operation of many functional items is not obvious in this way, and there may be many alternative designs that satisfy the basic function of the item. In these cases, understanding of the identity of the object's function is separable from, and often exists in the absence of, understanding of how it fulfils its function.

Are either, or both, of these sorts of understanding capable of altering the non-aesthetic perceptual properties of functional objects? Cases where the two sorts can be separated, we think, make it apparent how this question ought to be answered. For, in such cases, knowledge of the identity of an object's function seems insufficient to alter the object's perceptual appearance. If one is shown a strange machine, for example, and told that its function is to determine the X-ray diffraction patterns of protein molecules, this revelation alone would likely do little to alter the perceptual appearance of the machine. This is because such knowledge, on its own, would be unlikely to structure our perception differently. It would not allow one to see certain of the machine's parts, or the arrangement thereof, as, for instance, out of place, situated in the correct location, or compactly arranged, because knowing that the object is an 'X-ray diffraction pattern detector' does not entail knowing what non-aesthetic perceptual properties are standard, variable, or contra-standard for such a device. Functional categories that incorporate at least some understanding of *how* the object performs its function, in contrast, often do involve such knowledge, and as such are capable of changing the object's perceptual appearance. An understanding of the basic way in which an X-ray diffraction pattern detector works (emitting X-rays from a power source, focusing them on a sample, feeding images to an attached screen, and so on), for example, could allow an observer to see certain parts, or the arrangement thereof, as standard, variable, or contra-standard. This, in turn, may alter the way that the object *looks*: certain parts of the object, being contra-standard features, may look discordant, or out of place, for example. Thus, cases such as this one, in which knowledge of the identity of the object's function is distinct from knowledge of how the object fulfils that function, make clear that an understanding of function can affect perceptual appearance, but only when it includes understanding of *how* function is carried out, rather than merely *what* it is. Hereafter, then, we will mean this sort of understanding when we employ phrases such as 'knowledge of function', 'understanding of function', and 'functional category'.

4.2 The Phenomenology of Functional Beauty

An account of the sort sketched above provides the foundation for a substantial response to the Problem of Translation by specifying how knowledge of function helps to shape perceptual experience in general. However, it does not provide a complete answer, since what the Problem of Translation calls on us to clarify, ultimately, is how knowledge of function can alter the perception of *aesthetic* qualities. A complete solution, therefore, must also include an account of how our understanding of the function of objects translates into the specific aesthetic qualities that we perceive them as having. We could also say, a little more grandly, that a complete solution requires a phenomenology of Functional Beauty: an account of the way in which function 'shows up' not just in what we experience perceptually, but in the aesthetic qualities that we experience perceptually.

In addressing this portion of the Problem of Translation, we can draw upon a number of accounts that philosophers have given of Functional Beauty, or related notions.[4] While insightful, however, these accounts also suffer from limitations. Most of them seem to be offered as *the* account of the phenomenal character of Functional Beauty, tacitly assuming that knowledge of function affects only one type of aesthetic property. But this assumption is no more warranted than the assumption that our knowledge of an artwork's artistic category affects only one sort of aesthetic property. In the case of an artwork, choice of artistic category can affect several different kinds of aesthetic properties.[5] This seems true also for functional categories. Moreover, these accounts, while capturing something true about the phenomenology of Functional Beauty, often fail to explain how this peculiar kind of translation of knowledge of function into aesthetic experience is possible. We think that these limitations are transcended, and a more comprehensive and satisfactory response to the Problem of Translation is provided, by situating these accounts in a cognitively rich framework for aesthetic appreciation. Thus considered, the issue can be reduced, again, to a definite question: which aesthetic qualities are altered by changes in functional categories, and how are they so altered?

One answer to this question comes from the traditional notion that we introduced in Chapter 1 in connection with classical and eighteenth-century thought: the notion of an object's 'looking fit' for its function. This account can be situated in our framework by thinking of 'looking fit' as an aesthetic quality that things possess

[4] We do not discuss all of these accounts here; in particular we omit those that are so vague as to not clearly specify how function affects aesthetic qualities at all.

[5] See Walton, 'Categories of Art', 343–54.

when the functional category employed to perceive them causes us to see those things as having no contra-standard features at all and as having, to a high degree, certain variable features that are indicative of functionality. As an example, consider the now rather dated aesthetic of the muscle car. The look cultivated in the muscle car is one of looking fast, in virtue of having all of the standard features of a car (inflated tyres, etc.) and also possessing, to a high degree, certain variable features that, though not strictly required for speed, are indicative of it (for example, having a spoiler, or a large engine). Many muscle cars look fit for their function of going fast, in this sense, and in virtue of this, possess that certain pleasing visual quality that we call 'looking fit'. This is a kind of aesthetic quality that can be said to truly 'emerge out' of function, for the same features that we find attractive in a muscle car would surely detract from the appearance of, for instance, a golf cart or a hearse. A spoiler, one suspects, would not contribute to the pleasing visual quality of 'looking fit' in a hearse.

Although discussions of the phenomenology of Functional Beauty in the philosophical tradition have discussed the quality of 'looking fit' in some depth, in some ways this focus has been an unhealthy one. For, in doing this, the tradition has taken 'looking fit' to constitute the whole phenomenology of Functional Beauty, which is an overly narrow view. It has led to a neglect of other, equally valid forms of Functional Beauty. Further, among these various forms, 'looking fit' raises certain special concerns that have led to suspicion of the cogency of the idea of Functional Beauty in general. We will take up these concerns in the following sections, but first we will fill out our account of the phenomenology of Functional Beauty by mentioning two other kinds of aesthetic quality that depend upon knowledge of function.

The first of these kinds includes aesthetic qualities like simplicity, gracefulness, or elegance, as possessed by functional objects. Thus, in the case of the X-ray diffraction pattern detector discussed above, an understanding of the way in which it works may allow an observer to see most or all of the parts of the machine as, for example, standard elements, in turn making it look elegant and streamlined. This kind of analysis is applied by David Best to the functional or purposive movements of athletes engaging in sport:

> A graceful sweep of the left arm may be very effective in a dance, but the same movement may look ugly and absurd as part of a service action in tennis or of a bowler's action in cricket, since it detracts from the ideal of total concentration of effort to achieve the specific task. A specific movement is aesthetically satisfying only if in the context of the action as a whole it is seen as forming a unified structure which is regarded as the most economical and efficient method of achieving the required end.[6]

On Best's analysis, functional entities, including the purposeful motions employed in sports, appear graceful when they are free of features that are 'extraneous' and 'irrelevant' in relation to their function.[7] In terms of the framework described above, this happens when the functional category used to perceive the object causes it to appear as having few contra-standard or variable features, but only standard ones. As an example, consider an elegant-looking stove, perhaps a sleek stainless-steel model. Its elegance can be said to 'emerge' out of its function, in the sense that it is elegant insofar as its visible features (for example, a glass door, a set of burners)

[6] David Best, 'The Aesthetic in Sport', *British Journal of Aesthetics* 14 (1974): 197–213; the quotation is on 205. Cf. Paul Guyer, 'Free and Adherent Beauty: A Modest Proposal', *British Journal of Aesthetics* 42 (2002b): 357–66, especially 365. Francis Hutcheson suggests a similar view with his claim that the bodies of animals manifest unity amidst the variety of their multiple functions, and are thereby beautiful: 'As to the beauty of animals, either in their inward structure, which we come to the knowledge of by experiment and long observation, or their outward form, we shall find vast uniformity among all the species which are known to us, in the structure of those parts, upon which life depends immediately. And how amazing is the unity of mechanism, when we shall find that almost infinite diversity of motions, all their actions in walking, running, flying, swimming; all their serious efforts for self-preservation, all their freakish contortions when they are gay and sportful, in all their various limbs, performed by *one simple contrivance* of a contracting muscle, applied with inconceivable diversities to answer all these ends! Various engines might have obtained the same ends; but then there had been less uniformity, and the beauty of our animal systems, and of particular animals, had been much less, when this surprising unity had been removed from them.' See Francis Hutcheson, *An Inquiry into the Original of our Ideas of Beauty and Virtue; in Two Treatises*, 4th edn [1738], Treatises I, Section II, Part VIII (Glasgow: Robert and Andrew Foulis, 1772), 21–2 (our italics). We will return to the aesthetic appreciation of animals, and their Functional Beauty, in Chapter 5.

[7] Best, 'The Aesthetic in Sport', 204.

are all standard for the functional category in which we perceive it (namely, 'stove'). This becomes apparent when we reflect on the fact that, if we viewed the same object using a different functional category, thinking that it was a safe, for example, it would not look elegant in the same way at all. This is because possessing a glass door and a set of burners on the top surface are standard properties for the category 'stove', but contra-standard properties for the category 'safe'.

Best presents this idea as a rather categorical one, seemingly requiring that a functional object appear perfectly economical and efficient in order to seem 'aesthetically satisfying'. But this claim would be unduly strong: our understanding of the function of some object could cause it to appear *more* aesthetically appealing than it would otherwise without making it look *maximally* so. To adapt one of Best's examples, the arm movement of a child performing a dance may not be the most economical and efficient dancing motion, and so may not appear elegant or graceful. Nonetheless, it may still look *more unified* than it would if considered as part of a tennis serve or bowler's motion. In other words, appearing economical and efficient is a matter of degree, and so are the aesthetic qualities produced by this appearance. In fact, this kind of 'streamlined appearance' is perhaps the most familiar sort of Functional Beauty. It is the basis for a good deal of modernist design, such as that of the 'functionalist' architects and the Bauhaus artists and artisans mentioned in Chapter 2. And it continues to be a staple of the popular furniture and appliances that are associated with 'Scandinavian' design.

There is a third way in which functional categories can affect aesthetic appearance, however, that is somewhat opposed to the foregoing account and that generates a different sort of Functional Beauty. In this case, the object is able to perform its function, but the functional category that we apply in perceiving it causes it to appear as having some features that are contra-standard (that is, as lacking some standard features). In this event, the item, by still looking capable of performing its function, may display a pleasing dissonance in its sensory elements. Although they are manifestly functional, appearing capable of performing their function, such objects also possess perceptual features that are 'at odds with' this manifest functionality. The resulting aesthetic quality might be described as a surprising, vibrant look, or an aesthetically pleasing 'visual tension'.[8]

For instance, consider the large steel cranes that raise massive loads in building construction. We *know* how powerful they are, but seen from a certain distance, at least, they do not *look* powerful, perhaps because they fail to look solid: appearing as hollow structures, they can seem, from a distance, too slight to be moving the massive loads that they do. This effect is enhanced by the tapering of the long vertical arm of the crane as it nears the base, a common feature of these cranes that makes it look as though the long arm might simply snap off at the base. These sorts of visual features are contra-standard features for the functional category 'crane', and so stand out in the overall appearance of cranes, seeming not quite right somehow. And, as a result, these cranes frequently have a sort of surprising, vibrant look or an aesthetically pleasing visual tension. Other examples of this sort of Functional Beauty include furniture and buildings designed in such a way that heavy masses seem to hang suspended implausibly in mid-air. Chairs like Viktor Schreckengost's famous Beverly Hills lawn chair (see front cover) and buildings like Will Alsop's Sharp Centre for Design at the Ontario College of Art and Design in Toronto, Canada, seem to possess this aesthetic quality, to a certain degree.[9] Once again, it is important to stress that the aesthetic quality of

[8] On the aesthetic effects of contra-standard properties in artworks, see Walton, 'Categories of Art', 349–54.

[9] The classic 'Lawn Chair, Beverly Hills Model' was designed by Viktor Schreckengost in 1941 and widely distributed by the Sears Roebuck Company. Its innovative three-quarters S-shaped (without the top line) frame is formed of only two slender pieces of stamped steel and makes the chair appear, when viewed from the side, to hold its occupant without adequate support. The Sharp Centre for Design at the Ontario College of Art and Design in Toronto, Canada, was designed by English architect Will Alsop and completed in 2004. The structure is a steel-framed, black and white, box-shaped enclosure that hovers fifteen storeys above the other buildings at the college. The horizontal slab on which it rests measures 83

visual tension in these objects emerges from our awareness of their function. If we were to learn that what we think is a construction crane is actually a very large wire sculpture or a large radio antenna that never lifted anything, for instance, then it would lose this visual tension. It is because we know what it is that these objects are for and how they are to carry out their functions, that certain of their non-aesthetic perceptual properties stand out, giving them the peculiar sort of aesthetic appearances that they have.

4.3 Is 'Looking Fit' an Aesthetic Quality?

In the preceding section, we argued that the aesthetic quality of looking fit is one way, although certainly not the only way, in which our understanding of an object's function can actually become a part of the content of our perception of the object. However, as we mentioned, philosophers have shown mixed feelings about the idea that looking fit is an aesthetic quality. Scattered among the writings of aestheticians are passages that are supportive of this idea, several of which we noted in Chapter 1. For example, John Hospers, in his discussion of expressive aesthetic qualities, writes that, in aesthetic appreciation, 'we enjoy not merely the shining black and silver of the streamlined automobile ... but rather these surfaces and forms as expressing certain life-values, and adapted to certain life-purposes'.[10] This passage suggests that adaptation to purposes is a legitimate object of aesthetic experience. But other philosophers have questioned whether an object's possession of an appearance that is 'fit' with respect to its function results in it possessing a distinct *aesthetic* quality. Francis Sparshott, for example,

by 31 by 10 metres and is held aloft by 12 thin, 26 metre steel columns. Needless to say, the impression is that of a structure unable to be supported by its underpinnings.

[10] John Hospers, *Meaning and Truth in the Arts* (Chapel Hill, NC: University of North Carolina Press, 1946), 13. See also J. O. Urmson's comments on 'the functional view of aesthetics', in 'What Makes a Situation Aesthetic?', in Joseph Margolis (ed.), *Philosophy Looks at the Arts* (New York: Charles Scribner's Sons, 1962), 13–27, esp. 24, and Horatio Greenough's stipulation that by 'beauty I mean the promise of function' in his *Travels, Observations and Experiences of a Yankee Stonecutter* (New York: Putnam, 1852), 187.

criticizes the idea that buildings that exhibit fitness for function, by displaying their sturdy internal supports, are thereby beautiful:

> there seems ... to be no obvious reason why structural soundness and constructive integrity in fact should be a source of constructive vividness in appearance. If the demand is simply that the supporting members of a building should be left visible, one is at a loss to see what the aesthetic value of this should be.[11]

George Dickie further questions the legitimacy of basing a species of beauty on notions related to fitness, remarking: 'The simple fact is ... that no one, except an occasional philosopher, has ever claimed that utility is a kind of beauty.'[12]

In considering these sceptical claims, we take it as more or less obvious that, generally speaking, people find objects that appear highly fit for their function pleasing.[13] Therefore, the salient issue is whether this pleasure is aesthetic or not. Comments such as those of Sparshott and Dickie suggest that this pleasure is not aesthetic. In favour of this view, it can be noted that, often, the pleasures that we take in things that look fit involve the satisfaction of certain of our desires. Part of what Jones might find pleasing in his fit-looking muscle car, for example, is the fact that it satisfies his desire to drive fast, or to impress women at the beach. Expanding on this point, one might suggest that, in fact, it is this sort of satisfaction that ultimately accounts for *all* of the pleasure that we take in observing things that are fit for their function. The fit look itself may only serve to signal a thing's capacity to satisfy certain desires, thereby engendering our pleasure in the satisfaction, or potential

[11] Francis Sparshott, *The Structure of Aesthetics* (Toronto, Canada: University of Toronto Press, 1963), 68.

[12] George Dickie, *The Century of Taste: The Philosophical Odyssey of Taste in the Eighteenth Century* (Oxford: Oxford University Press, 1996), 38.

[13] There is a complication here regarding objects with morally problematic functions, such as weapons, torture devices, and so on. Hume, for one, appears to have held the view that such objects cannot be viewed as functionally beautiful; see our discussion in Chapter 1, Section 2. We return to this issue in Chapter 6, Section 3. For the purposes of the current discussion, we are content to show that for *some* functional objects, at least, appearing fit for function can produce a change in aesthetic appearance.

satisfaction, of those desires. Jones may find the sight of his muscle car pleasing, for example, not because of the fit look per se, but simply because that look signals that his desires to drive fast and to impress women at the beach will be fulfilled.

As we saw in Chapter 1, just such an account formed the basis of Hume's theory of beauty as utility. Hume generalizes the account, however, noting that not all things that look pleasingly fit for their function indicate that one's desires will be satisfied: Hume cites a case where 'the fortifications of a city belonging to an enemy are esteemed beautiful upon account of their strength, though we could wish that they were entirely destroyed'.[14] In this case, the strength of the city walls pleases us, though it does not gratify, but actually interferes with, our personal desires. Hume accommodates these cases by taking the ultimate source of the beauty of functional things to be their utility in advancing *general* wants and needs of humanity. Thus, we find the enemy fortress attractive, not because it serves our interests, but because it serves the interest of some persons (the enemy), with whom we (perhaps unconsciously) sympathize. For Hume, the fact that all the pleasure we take in things that look fit is, ultimately, a pleasure in their utility, is no sort of difficulty—such pleasure is, he thinks, the essence of one species of beauty.

In contrast to Hume's view, however, many contemporary philosophers would parlay this same point into an objection to the idea of Functional Beauty. On Hume's view, much beauty is produced not by an object's appearing fit for its function per se, but by the object's conveying the idea of some ultimate benefit or utility, through appearing fit for its function. This kind of view concerning the ultimate source of the pleasure that we take in things that look fit seems to make a strong case for the sceptical view that our pleasure in things that look fit is, in fact, a non-aesthetic pleasure. As we discussed in Chapter 1, philosophers traditionally

[14] David Hume, *A Treatise of Human Nature* [1739–40], Book III, Part III, Section I; ed. L. A. Selby-Bigge (Oxford: Oxford University Press, 1960), 586–7.

insist upon distinguishing between aesthetic pleasure, which is distinterested pleasure—pleasure taken in the sensory appearance of things per se, or for their own sake—and pleasure taken in things other than sensory appearance, such as the fulfilment of antecedent desires. This would seem to apply even to the sorts of generalized desires that Hume invokes, ruling them out as sources of *aesthetic* pleasure.[15] If this distinction is sound, and if Hume is correct in saying that the ultimate source of all our pleasure in things that look fit is their utility in advancing human interests, rather than their appearance per se, then 'looking fit' is not an aesthetic quality. Rather, when we speak of something's 'looking fit' as 'Functional Beauty' we are speaking in the loose sense of 'beauty', rather than the aesthetic sense. For, in so speaking, we are describing a pleasure that is not grounded in the look or appearance of the object, but in something else, and 'beauty' means no more than good, or excellent.

4.4 Utility and Beauty

The sceptical view sketched in the previous section represents a kind of resurrection, and extension, of the Problem of Translation, which we tried to vanquish above. For it entails that, even if our knowledge of function can be said to translate into the appearance of things, in making objects truly 'look fit', this has nothing to do with aesthetics. We may find this or that look gratifying, pleasurable, enjoyable, but we do so on grounds other than aesthetic ones. Therefore, 'looking fit' fails to constitute a way in which function 'translates' into our aesthetic experience.

[15] This is the milder sense of 'distinterestedness' that we noted in Chapter 1. As Korsmeyer points out, the desires to which Hume's account of beauty as utility ultimately appeals are not based upon the fulfilment of one's *personal* desires or aims; see Carolyn Korsmeyer, 'Hume and the Foundations of Taste', *Journal of Aesthetics and Art Criticism* 35 (1976): 201–15, especially 208. Nonetheless, they remain pleasures that are not based on the object's appearance in itself, but on the gratification or future gratification of generalized desire.

We think that this sceptical line of thought is a significant one. But it is important to see that, being directed against the specific quality of 'looking fit', it has limited force as an objection against the theory of Functional Beauty as a whole. For, as we have seen in Section 2 of this chapter, Functional Beauty consists in other sorts of aesthetic qualities that, like looking fit, 'arise out of' functional categories. In these cases, it is not at all obvious that the pleasure we take in contemplating objects with these qualities can be attributed to a satisfaction felt in the anticipated gratification of generalized desires. Take, for instance, the case of design objects, such as the Beverly Hills lawn chair, that take on a pleasing visual tension in light of our awareness of their function. In such cases, our pleasure increases as the form is arranged in a way that is contra-standard, relative to that functional category. This increase need not give rise to any increased expectation, on our part, that the object better serves its function, and is therefore likely to lead to gratification of the general desires of humanity. It follows that the pleasure that we take in this visual quality does not depend upon any satisfaction felt in the anticipated gratification of those general desires. Rather, it is a pleasure that we take simply in the object's look per se. This means that, even if the sceptical line of thought were correct in claiming that 'looking fit' is not an aesthetic quality, this alone would be insufficient to vitiate the general notion of Functional Beauty.

However, the sceptical line of thought remains a potential threat to the idea that apparent fitness is a form of Functional Beauty. Can it be answered? The line of thought is based on two premises: first, the idea that aesthetic qualities are characterized by disinterestedness, in the sense of involving a pleasure taken in perceptual appearance for its own sake, and, second, the assumption that the ultimate source of all our pleasure in things that look fit is their utility in advancing human interests, rather than their appearance per se. Although some might wish to quarrel with the first of these premises, we would not. We think that the traditional notion of disinterestedness, when properly interpreted, is well founded and necessary for an acceptable analysis of the aesthetic.[16] The second premise, however, seems dubious.

There is no doubt that those things that look fit for their functions are generally indicative of the advancement of human interests. There is also no doubt that sometimes some of the pleasure we take in these things is precisely a contentment in this advancement, or the promise thereof. But it is not at all clear that *all* our pleasure in things that look fit can be attributed to this source. Responding to Hume's defence of one version of our second premise, Adam Smith argues that 'fitness, this happy contrivance of any production of art, often be more valued, than the very end for which it was intended'.[17] As an example, Smith cites the widespread admiration for timepieces of split-second accuracy. He writes:

> A watch ... that falls behind above two minutes in a day, is despised by one curious in watches. He sells it perhaps for a couple of guineas, and purchases another at fifty, which will not lose above a minute in a fortnight. The sole use of watches however, is to tell us what o'clock it is, and to hinder us from breaking any engagement, or suffering any other inconveniency by our ignorance in that particular point. But the person so nice with regard to this machine, will not always be found either more scrupulously punctual than other men, or more anxiously concerned upon any other account, to know precisely what time of day it is. What interests him is not so much the attainment of this piece of knowledge, as the perfection of the machine which serves to attain it.[18]

[16] As noted in Chapter 1, Section 6, we distinguish between the less controversial concept of disinterestedness and the stronger notion that we have referred to with the capitalised term 'Disinterestedness'. The former concept need not, and ought not to, be interpreted as requiring that one experience the object without applying any concepts to it. For a discussion of the nature of the latter concept, see Allen Carlson 'Appreciating Art and Appreciating Nature', in S. Kemal and I. Gaskell (eds), *Landscape, Natural Beauty and the Arts* (Cambridge: Cambridge University Press, 1993), 199–227, especially 199–205.

[17] Adam Smith, *The Theory of Moral Sentiments* [1759], Part IV, Chapter 1, Para. 3, in *The Glasgow Edition of the Works and Correspondence of Adam Smith*, Volume I, ed. D. D. Raphael and A. L. Macfie (Indianapolis, IN: Liberty Fund, 1982), 179.

[18] Ibid., Part IV, Chapter 1, Para. 5, 180.

The more precise watch is loved better than the one that is less accurate, as attested by the higher price it commands. But in terms of how well the two can satisfy the desires of the owner, there is nothing whatever to choose between them. In our era, Smith's point is even more apparent. The difference in precision between a thirty-dollar quartz watch and a thousand-dollar Swiss watch is to be measured in seconds per year or less, and as such confers no practical advantage whatsoever. Yet far greater pleasure is taken in the more finely wrought watch.[19] 'What pleases these lovers of toys,' Smith writes, 'is not so much the utility, as the aptness of the machines which are fitted to promote it.'[20]

Smith's line of thought demonstrates that the second premise underlying the sceptical take on the status of 'looking fit' as an aesthetic quality is false: it is not the case that the ultimate source of *all* our pleasure in things that look fit is their utility in advancing human interests, rather than their appearance per se. We may, of course, not derive this aesthetic pleasure when we contemplate a particular functional object, delighting instead in the gratification of our desires that the object signals, just as the farmer, by delighting in the pecuniary rewards of his field, rather than the field itself, may fail to engage in aesthetic appreciation. We may each of us consult our own experience to determine the extent to which our delight in functional things is aesthetic. But the above example shows that, however much we actually exercise it, we do possess the capacity to take pleasure in the mere perception of a thing's looking fit. As such, looking fit qualifies as an aesthetic quality.

[19] It is important to consider the watches in this example as regular timepieces, as Smith of course does. Today, many wristwatches possess exceptional and highly specialised features, such as the ability to display the current time in foreign cities, or to operate beneath a hundred metres of water. The delight that many take in these watches, however, is consistent with the second premise of the sceptical view. For, in such cases, one could say that the appreciator is simply experiencing the pleasure that *a true user* of such a device (a diplomat, or a deep-sea diver, say) would derive from these devices. But the greater pleasure taken in one of Smith's two timepieces is not consistent with this assumption, since there is no advantage that *anyone* could gain from such additional precision *in an everyday timepiece.*

[20] Smith, *The Theory of Moral Sentiments*, Part IV, Chapter 1, Para. 6, 180.

4.5 The Aesthetics of Dysfunction

So far, our discussion of the phenomenology of Functional Beauty has dealt only with positive aesthetic qualities. In particular, we have argued that our knowledge of an object's function, by structuring our perception of an object, can cause that object to have certain positive aesthetic qualities, such as elegance and 'looking fit'. But what about the opposite case: objects that appear manifestly *unfit* to perform their function? Can we maintain the parallel claim that the use of functional categories may contribute to such objects appearing displeasing aesthetically, having a *negative* aesthetic quality?

It does seem plausible to think that, often, we are displeased by the appearance of things that are manifestly non-functional. Bicycles missing their seats, cars with flat tyres, houses with missing shingles: all seem displeasing. Furthermore, it seems plausible to think that someone without functional concepts such as 'bicycle', 'car', and so on might not experience this displeasure: it is hard to see why, without an idea of what a bicycle is for, one would find one without a seat displeasing, for example.[21] Moreover, the view that 'looking unfit' is an aesthetically displeasing quality would make sense of a good deal of discussion of the aesthetic value of houses and urban environments, where sites that are 'rundown' or contain unfit-looking objects (derelict cars, for instance) are regarded as eyesores, or aesthetic blights.

As in the case of things looking fit, however, one might take a more sceptical view, arguing that our displeasure with these sorts of dysfunctional things is actually a non-aesthetic displeasure. In support of this view, one could appeal to the notion that things that look unsuited to perform their functions bespeak a thwarting of our desires and needs, and as such will engender in us frustration and

[21] Compare such hypothetical cases with our actual experiences of objects with which we are unfamiliar. For example, most of us have probably been in the situation of being without the relevant functional categories for at least some esoteric kinds of objects, such as power tools or surgical instruments.

displeasure. Such a view needs to be rounded out by an appeal to something like Hume's sympathetic identification with the plans and wants of others: one can understand why Jones becomes frustrated when *his* car looks ready to quit, but why would Jones feel frustrated by the rundown look of some unknown person's vehicle, as he drives through a foreign city? And yet such a sight would be displeasing. But once supplemented in this way, we have a potential non-aesthetic explanation for our disposition to be displeased by things that look unfit for their function. Further, the line of thought underlying this explanation is familiar and widely held. Paul Guyer, in commenting on Kant's notion of adherent beauty, notes the view, pervasive in eighteenth-century thought, that 'the human mind is inherently teleological—that is, it is natural for us to seek purposes and to find them wherever we can, and to be frustrated when we cannot find them where we think we should be able to do so'.[22]

But, as in the case of things that look fit, it seems that, although things that look unfit often produce a practical sort of frustration, in many cases our displeasure at these items outruns this frustration. Consider a car with a flat tyre, which is a displeasing object. Adding to the number of deflated tyres increases our displeasure with the sight of it, though it does nothing to add to the inconvenience or frustration the object causes. Or, imagine a computer whose screen has 'died', rendering the entire device utterly useless. Ripping several buttons from its keyboard, or denting it out of vexation or false hope, would make it no less useful than it already is (since it is already of no use at all) but would certainly make it *look* worse. It does appear, then, that as we can take *aesthetic* pleasure in things that appear fit for their function, we can also take *aesthetic* displeasure in things that appear unfit.

This latter claim, however, may still seem less plausible than the former. This is due to the fact that some functional things

[22] Paul Guyer, 'Beauty and Utility in Eighteenth-Century Aesthetics', *Eighteenth-Century Studies* 35 (2002a): 439–53; the quotation is on 448.

appear to be manifestly unfit for their function without appearing aesthetically poor. Many items of fashion, notoriously, look unfit for their function (for example, ostentatious hats, overly long dresses) but nonetheless are subject to enthusiastic aesthetic appreciation. Also consider ruins. Although they consist of structures that, by definition, look unable to perform their functions, they have been paradigmatic objects of aesthetic appreciation since at least the eighteenth century.

Do these examples show that our parallel thesis is false? It seems to us that they do not, though for interestingly different reasons in each case. We will defer considering ruins until Chapter 6, when the discussion shifts to architecture. Here we will concentrate on the other putative counter-example to our parallel thesis, fashion items. Consider, for example, a pair of very high-heeled women's shoes that provide no covering for the top of the foot, and look most ill-suited for walking. Yet imagine that, despite this, people do not find them functionally ugly; they find them aesthetically good. It seems that, on our view, the proper function of a pair of shoes is to protect the feet during walking. And, seen as such, the high heels described above would look unfit. Yet some observers apparently do not detect functional ugliness in this type of item. How can this be, if looking unfit really is a negative aesthetic quality?

It seems to us that in these cases functional ugliness is not reported because function is not attended to. What admirers of fashion items such as the shoes described above admire is, perhaps, the pleasing shape of the shoe, continuing as it does the curve of the wearer's foot, or its attractive colours, or perhaps not the shoe at all, but the look of the foot or leg that it produces. But when they admire them in this way, they are not really considering the shoes in their actual functional category: that is, as covers to protect the foot during walking. When we appreciate a shoe—like the aforementioned high heel—in its actual functional category, then it does indeed look displeasing. High-heeled shoes that appear unfit for walking, by throwing their wearer off balance, contorting the foot into painful positions, or leaving the foot open and unprotected, have a negative aesthetic quality: looking unfit. This goes unnoticed when we neglect their function, however, especially if the wearer is standing still. This point bristles with feminist implications, but the significance of the example, for our purposes, is only that in our aesthetic appreciation of everyday artefacts we do not always attend solely to Functional Beauty. Sometimes, as in the appreciation of fashion items of this kind, we simply 'bracket' or neglect the item's utilitarian function altogether, appreciating instead its more formal aspects: colour, pattern, shape, and so on. So it is not the case that there are occasions on which these items look unfit, but fail to displease us; rather, on those occasions where they fail to displease us, they do not look unfit at all. We maintain, therefore, that looking unfit for function, where it occurs, is a negative, or displeasing, aesthetic quality.

Our conclusion concerning objects that appear unfit or manifestly unsuited to performing their function broadens further the phenomenology of Functional Beauty that we have sketched in this chapter. Although the aesthetic tradition, insofar as it has treated the influence of function on aesthetic qualities, has largely focused upon 'looking fit', the range of aesthetic qualities that are tied to function is wider. This has important implications for the significance of Functional Beauty, for it suggests that this concept in fact denotes a rich and varied form of aesthetic experience, rather than a narrow and limited one. This conclusion can also be supported, in a different way, by showing how this form of aesthetic experience can be applied to, and used to illuminate, the aesthetics of various different kinds of objects and environments. In the following chapters, we take up this task.

5

Nature and Environment

In the previous chapters, we have sketched a general conception of Functional Beauty and addressed some of the main criticisms that have dogged this idea. In the remainder of the book, we will apply this conception to a range of objects of aesthetic appreciation and show its utility for aesthetic theory.

In this chapter, we will outline some of the ways in which the concept of Functional Beauty can be applied to natural things. We will begin with a somewhat neglected topic in nature aesthetics: the aesthetics of living organisms, and especially animals. In the first section, we will survey some common approaches to the appreciation of living organisms. In the next, we will describe a difficulty facing these approaches, which seems to explain the lack of attention given to the topic by aestheticians. In Section 3, we will argue that a form of appreciation employing Functional Beauty, as we conceive it, can avoid this difficulty.

In the second half of the chapter, we will turn to the aesthetics of natural things other than living organisms, including individual natural objects such as stones and rivers as well as larger natural entities, such as ecosystems and environments. Although this topic has received more attention from philosophers, Functional Beauty has hardly been considered in relation to it. We will argue that Functional Beauty not only has a role to play in this area, but also that deploying the concept here sheds light on a central but controversial thesis in recent discussions of the aesthetics of nature: Positive Aesthetics. In doing so, Functional Beauty provides the basis for a richer conception of nature as an aesthetic object.

5.1 The Appreciation of Living Nature

Despite a recent renaissance of philosophical writing on the beauty of nature, the aesthetic appreciation of living organisms remains a neglected topic. Sustained discussions are rare, and where we do find philosophers and other theorists taking up the topic, we discover a bewildering variety of approaches.[1] In this section, we will survey some of these.

One approach is illustrated by the nineteenth-century critic John Ruskin's theory of the 'Vital Beauty' of living things. According to Ruskin, 'the appearance of felicitous fulfilment of function in living things' utters to us a 'call for sympathy', through which we are prompted to 'look upon those as most lovely which are most happy'.[2] He contends that, 'those forms will be the most beautiful... which exhibit most of power, and seem capable of most quick and joyous sensation'.[3] Thus the vibrant, and hence, one supposes, happy, rose bush is beautiful, whereas the stoic cactus is not.[4] Along similar lines is Hegel's remark that 'the sloth displeases because of its drowsy activity; it drags itself painfully along and its whole manner of life displays its incapacity for quick movement and activity'.[5]

These thinkers seem to consider vitality in frankly moral terms, as an indicator of some laudable disposition, rather than simply as an

[1] To our knowledge, there exists no systematic review of aesthetic practices concerning animals. In fact, the only philosophical work focusing specifically on the topic, of which we are aware, is Holmes Rolston, 'Beauty and the Beast: Aesthetic Experience of Wildlife', in Daniel J. Decker and Gary R. Goff (eds), *Valuing Wildlife: Economic and Social Perspectives* (Boulder, CO: Westview Press, 1987), 187–207. For an overview of Rolston's aesthetics of nature, see Allen Carlson, '"We see beauty now where we could not see it before": Rolston's Aesthetics of Nature', in C. Preston and W. Ouderkirk (eds), *Nature, Value, Duty: Life on Earth with Holmes Rolston, III* (Dordrecht, Holland: Springer, 2006), 103–24.

[2] John Ruskin, *Modern Painters* [1843–60] (London: J. M. Dent & Co., 1907), Volume 2, Chapter 12, 240.

[3] Ibid., 246. Ruskin qualifies this claim, however, because animals can also possess 'typical' beauty, which is independent of their vital beauty.

[4] Ibid., 243–4.

[5] G. W. F. Hegel, *Hegel's Aesthetics: Lectures on Fine Arts* [1835], trans. T. M. Knox (Oxford: Oxford University Press, 1975), Volume I, 130–1.

aesthetic quality. But one might argue that quick and lively animals just do appear more pleasing to the eye. Holmes Rolston suggests, for example, that wild animals contribute to the aesthetic value of wilderness areas though their ability to 'raise the excitement level'.[6] Rolston's view has an important ethical dimension also, however, since he argues, on this basis, for the superiority of our aesthetic experience of wildlife in its natural environment, over that provided by domestic animals and by wildlife constrained in artificial settings, such as zoos.

A related, though less philosophically scrutinized, ground for the appreciation of animals is the exoticism, or sheer strangeness, of living things, a feature manifest in the long traditions of the menagerie, the travelling circus, and the safari.[7] In its most basic form, this kind of appreciation involves simply putting on display an animal that the audience would never have occasion to see, as when the Ringling-Barnum Circus showed nineteenth-century Midwestern Americans a sea elephant by towing it around a circus field on a platform. Animals capable of performing tricks or stunts add an additional incongruity, as when elephants are trained to open wine bottles or monkeys taught to ride ponies. However, an appreciation of the strangeness of animals need not involve such ethically dubious scenarios: witness Diane Michelfelder's discussion of 'how the experience of wildlife in an urban setting receives its aesthetic character in part through the element of being "out-of-place" '.[8] Michelfelder stresses the positive value of the element of surprise and 'wildness' that animals such as coyotes bring to otherwise tame environments.

Another approach involves anthropomorphizing animals to yield what might be viewed as a somewhat 'kitsch' form of animal

[6] Rolston, 'Beauty and the Beast', 189.

[7] On this topic, see George Speaight, *A History of the Circus* (London: Tantivy Press, 1980), 125–8, and Charles Philip Fox and Tom Parkinson, *The Circus in America* (Waukesha, WI: Country Beautiful, 1969), 262–9.

[8] Diane Michelfelder, 'Valuing Wildlife Populations in Urban Environments', *Journal of Social Philosophy* 34 (2003): 79–90; the quotation is on 85. Michelfelder's essay is not concerned with the aesthetics of wildlife per se, but with the broader issue of our moral relations with urban wildlife.

appreciation. This probably occurs on a number of levels, but one basic way involves exploiting certain visual features of animals that act as cues for particular emotional responses. The ethologist Konrad Lorenz suggests that morphological features characteristic of human infants, such as short extremities and a large head, produce an automatic response of sympathy and nurturing.[9] In representations of animals, these features are often highlighted or exaggerated, setting up a certain relationship to the animal as kind of 'quasi-child'. In his essay, 'A Biological Homage to Mickey Mouse' (1980), Stephen J. Gould documents changes in representations of Mickey Mouse over the twentieth century, suggesting that Mickey's features became progressively more 'childlike' in a (possibly unconscious) effort to engender a more positive attitude towards the character.[10]

A more subtly anthropocentric approach focuses on an appreciation of the symbolism associated with particular animals. On this view, we appreciate the eagle, for example, not simply as a natural creature but as an emblem or symbol of freedom.[11] Mark Sagoff develops this view, pointing out the deep association in American history between ideals of the new Republic (courage, innocence, freedom, strength, and the like) and wilderness, including wild animals: 'the paradigm, the symbol, if you will, of freedom has been the wilderness, the deer, the bear, the eagle, a rapid

[9] Konrad Lorenz, 'Part and Parcel in Animal and Human Societies' [1950], in *Studies in Animal and Human Behaviour*, Volume 2, trans. Robert Martin (Cambridge, MA: Harvard University Press, 1971), 115–95. For further discussion of this response, see John Morreall, 'Cuteness', *British Journal of Aesthetics* 31 (1991): 39–47.

[10] Stephen J. Gould, 'A Biological Homage to Mickey Mouse', in *The Panda's Thumb: More Reflections in Natural History* (New York: W.W. Norton & Company, 1980), 95–107. See also Elizabeth A. Lawrence, 'Neoteny in American Perceptions of Animals', in R. J. Hoage (ed.), *Perceptions of Animals in American Culture* (Washington, DC: Smithsonian Institute, 1989), 57–76.

[11] In his empirical study of attitudes towards wildlife, Stephen Kellert defines the 'aesthetic attitude' as one that 'primarily emphasizes the attractiveness or symbolic significance of animals. The major concern is with the artistic merit and beauty of animals, or their allegorical appeal as bearers of some special message'; see Stephen Kellert, 'Perceptions of Animals in America', in Hoage (ed.), *Perceptions of Animals in American Culture*, 5–24; the quotation is on 8.

river'.[12] Furthermore, the very understanding of these ideals is shaped by the use of these particular symbols. According to Sagoff, this cultural function provides a reason for valuing and preserving wild animals:

> A society which values freedom and which makes its forests or the wildlife in them the expressive symbols of freedom will not treat the wildlife in them frivolously, nor discard them without a second thought. If it does, then this act will count as evidence that the society either no longer values freedom or that its paradigms of freedom have changed. They may have changed, for example, from wildlife to motor cars and washing machines. In this case, we can draw the conclusion that the meaning of freedom in that society has itself changed. Accordingly, one way to keep our concept of freedom intact is to respect the objects that express it.[13]

Although Sagoff focuses on cases where animals serve as a generally recognizable cultural emblem of some idea or concept, symbolism might also occur at a more individualistic level. Someone who grew up on a farm, for instance, might find that chickens evoke vivid memories of their happy childhood and, although chickens are not generally symbols of bucolic bliss, for this sort of person they could be.

Finally, we also find evidence of purely formal appreciation of animals, an appreciation based solely on enjoyment of their interesting and appealing shape, colour, and pattern. The art critic Kenneth Clark, for example, celebrates the curves of a horse's body as 'without question the most satisfying piece of formal relationship in nature'.[14] This idea is developed in detail by the philosopher Nick Zangwill, who argues that some animals simply present patterns or motions that we find visually pleasing. Referring to the example of a polar bear swimming underwater, Zangwill writes that 'it is a formally extraordinary *phenomenon*. It might even turn

[12] Mark Sagoff, 'On Preserving the Natural Environment', *Yale Law Journal* 84 (1974): 205–67; the quotation is on 243.

[13] Ibid., 228.

[14] Kenneth Clark, *Animals and Men: the Relationship as Reflected in Western Art from Prehistory to the Present Day* (New York: William Morrow and Company, Inc., 1977), 36.

out to be an artfully choreographed swimmer dressed in a polar bear suit. No matter. It is still a beautiful *spectacle*.'[15]

5.2 The Immorality Objection

Our survey of approaches to appreciating living things has been cursory, and by no means does justice to the full range of approaches or to the nuances of each approach. We will not attempt to develop any of them further, however, since it seems to us that none of them presents a satisfactory direction for developing an account of the aesthetics of organisms. For some of the approaches that we have described, this is apparent insofar as it is unclear whether these approaches are, in fact, concerned with forms of *aesthetic* appreciation at all.[16] But even for those approaches that do seem relevant to aesthetic appreciation, there is a larger difficulty to consider. The difficulty is that aesthetic appreciation, when applied to beings such as animals, is morally problematic.

This objection is perhaps more familiar from consideration of the aesthetics of persons, also a neglected topic in contemporary aesthetics.[17] Feminists, for example, have argued that one of the most pervasive forms of female oppression has been the treatment of women as aesthetic objects (that is, as objects of visual pleasure for men).[18] This line of thought seizes on the fact that aesthetic

[15] Nick Zangwill, 'Formal Natural Beauty', *Proceedings of the Aristotelian Society* 101 (2001a): 209–24; reprinted in *The Metaphysics of Beauty* (Ithaca, NY: Cornell University Press, 2001b), 112–26; the quotation is on 116.

[16] A different but related difficulty with an aesthetics of living things is the potential confusion of moral and aesthetic responses. On this issue, see Glenn Parsons, 'The Aesthetic Value of Animals', *Environmental Ethics* 27 (2007): 151–69.

[17] An earlier consideration of this issue is Ducasse's 'The Art of Personal Beauty', Chapter VII of Curt Ducasse, *Art, the Critics, and You* [1944] (Indianapolis, IN: Bobbs-Merrill, 1955), 151–78. Discussion of it remains rare, but is increasing: see, for example, Carol Gould, 'Glamour as an Aesthetic Property of Persons', *Journal of Aesthetics and Art Criticism* 63 (2005): 237–47. There is a brief consideration of the aesthetics of persons in Nick Zangwill, 'Beauty', in Jerrold Levinson (ed.), *Oxford Handbook of Aesthetics* (Oxford: Oxford University Press, 2003), 325–43, especially 336–9; see also Mary Devereaux, 'The Ugly', *American Society for Aesthetics Newsletter* 24/3 (2005), 1–2.

[18] Perhaps the best-known development of this line of thought is Naomi Wolf's *The Beauty Myth* (New York: Doubleday, 1992).

appreciation appears to focus on the most superficial and least important aspect of a person: namely, the sensory qualities that she or he presents to our perceptual faculties. In addition to being largely beyond the person's control, these qualities apparently pertain only to his or her 'surface'. Since women, indeed all persons, are intellectual, moral, and emotional beings, autonomous agents with a rich range of plans, priorities, and projects, to *aesthetically* appreciate them can seem a shallow and 'dehumanizing' means of relating to them. This problem does not arise for artworks, which, however valuable to us, remain inanimate objects lacking the richer aspects of persons. But it does arise, if not for all living organisms, then at least for certain animals. For certain animals, as many philosophers have argued, are moral patients, if not moral agents.[19] Indeed, one might argue that recognition of the moral status of animals has been one of the most significant achievements of contemporary ethics. In this light, a theory of the aesthetic appreciation of animals may seem as ill conceived, retrograde, and tasteless as a theory of catcalls and wolf whistles. Though largely unstated, this worry concerning the shallowness, and hence inappropriateness, of applying aesthetic discourse to animals represents a significant obstacle to any aesthetics of animals and, perhaps, accounts for the ongoing neglect of the topic itself. We will call it the 'immorality objection'.

This problem about the aesthetics of animals is not one that can be easily dismissed. In response to it, one might simply insist upon a firm distinction between aesthetic and moral value. One might say, for instance, that the aesthetic excellence of a person, or an animal, is independent of whatever morally relevant qualities it possesses. Although the discussion of aesthetic appreciation may raise uncomfortable questions, and present opportunities for oppression, ignoring it does not make it go away, or reduce its theoretical interest for its own sake. While there may be some

[19] On the moral agent/moral patient distinction, see Tom Regan, *The Case for Animal Rights* (Berkeley, CA: University of California Press, 1983), 151–6.

truth in this position, it is also overly simplistic and not very helpful in this context. For, in general, ethical considerations *do* shape and guide what is 'of theoretical interest'. No one thinks, for instance, that the pleasures that sadistic individuals derive from torturing puppies or destroying the environment are worthy of theoretical scrutiny 'for their own sake'. If so, then, we need a reason why we should attend to a way of relating to animals that seems ethically problematic. In the case of art, it is easier to brush aside this general problem, since the effect of art on human relations is a fraught issue: a morally bad book is still just a book, and it is notoriously difficult to connect reading immoral books to committing immoral acts. In the case of appreciating other living beings, however, this move is unavailable, since treating another being as an object of aesthetic appreciation is itself a kind of morally evaluable action.

More importantly, none of the common approaches to appreciating animals helps in, or even offers much hope for, evading the immorality problem. The underlying reason for this is that none of them take *the nature of animals* to figure, in any significant way, in their aesthetic value. This is most obvious in the case of the formalist approach, since on that view only facts about the 'sensuous surface' of animals (their shape, colour, and so forth) come into play. Indeed, Zangwill goes so far as to explicitly say that, so far as aesthetic appreciation goes, it does not even matter if the creature really is a living creature at all. On some of the other approaches mentioned, aspects of the animal beyond its sensory surface are involved, but these turn out to be primarily aspects of the animal's relation to some human-centred standard or narrative, rather than aspects of the animal per se. For instance, the 'exoticism' of a sea elephant is not so much a matter of its look as it is a matter of the limited experience of Midwestern audiences. As well, the appreciation of animals in proportion to their 'vitality' involves construing animals in light of the familiar standard according to which being active is good and being inactive is not. But this is a standard with less applicability to a mammal like the sloth, for whom each sudden movement risks detection by predatory raptors, than to the English middle classes.

This inappropriate framing of animals in terms of human standards and concerns occurs just as blatantly in the anthropomorphic and symbolist approaches. Regarding the former, in describing the delightful appeal of the familiar cast of Disney characters, Gould concludes that 'the magic kingdom trades on a biological illusion—our ability to abstract and our propensity to transfer inappropriately to other animals the fitting responses we make to changing form in the growth of our own bodies.'[20] In other words, we generate specific responses to animals by purposefully assigning to them, or exaggerating, traits shared with human infants.[21] Something similar can be said about the idea of approaching animals as symbols as well. For to appreciate the eagle as a symbol of freedom, for example, is to appreciate it in light of its place in an anthropocentric, and usually arbitrary, system of cultural symbolism. Since eagles are no more free, one supposes, than are crows or sparrows, appreciating them as symbols of freedom has little to do with eagles. Rather, it has to do with a particular constellation of associations prevalent in a given culture.

In sum, these forms of appreciation fail to provide a robust response to the charge that aesthetically appreciating animals involves relating to them in a shallow, and hence morally inappropriate, manner. This is so even for those forms of appreciation, such as the ones defended by Rolston, Michelfelder, and Sagoff, that are explicitly intended to serve as grounds for the preservation of wild animals. This prompts one to ask whether it is possible, in fact, for the aesthetic value of an animal to bear some significant relation to the nature of the animal itself. That is: is the aesthetic

[20] Gould, 'Homage to Mickey Mouse', 104.

[21] As morality tales for children, anthropomorphic representations seem unobjectionable enough, although the broader implications of this practice may sometimes be problematic. Marcia Eaton argues that the representation of deer in *Bambi* affected deer management policies for the worse, through its effect on public opinion; see Marcia Eaton, 'Fact and Fiction in the Aesthetic Appreciation of Nature', *Journal of Aesthetics and Art Criticism* 56 (1998): 149–56.

appreciation of animals *necessarily* superficial, and therefore open to the immorality objection? We suggest that one way to give the nature of animals a role in their aesthetic value is to look at aesthetic value in a different way, one that focuses on the notion of function.

5.3 Function and the Beauty of Organisms

Functional Beauty, as we have developed it, is a concept that can be applied widely to living organisms, since many of the parts and traits of living creatures can be said to have functions in the sense that those forms have been naturally selected in virtue of performing certain tasks.[22] When living creatures are functionally beautiful, certain of their aesthetic qualities emerge out of, or depend upon, these functions. This is most apparent in the case of the aesthetic quality that we refer to as 'looking fit'.[23] Consider the cheetah, for example. One of the aesthetic qualities of this creature consists in the way that its body parts appear 'built for speed'. Virtually every visible feature or part of the cheetah is manifestly geared to that end: its long legs bespeak a formidable stride, its non-retractable claws reveal its gripping and steering ability, its narrow body and small head bespeak an aerodynamic movement, and so forth. This manifest fitness gives the cheetah's appearance a certain form of Functional Beauty: that pleasing visual quality

[22] Some of the literature introduced in Chapter 3 considers the application of 'function', in this sense, to the traits of animals. Two representative treatments are Karen Neander, 'The Teleological Notion of "Function"', *Australasian Journal of Philosophy* 69 (1991b): 454–68; and Peter Godfrey-Smith, 'A Modern History Theory of Functions', *Noûs* 28 (1994): 344–62. As noted in Chapter 3, for a more general overview of philosophical analysis of function, see Mark Perlman, 'The Modern Philosophical Resurrection of Teleology', *The Monist* 87 (2004): 3–51.

[23] Although our discussion here focuses on it, 'looking fit' is not the only form of Functional Beauty applicable to animals. Although natural selection often shapes animal parts and traits that have a particular function, its products do not always 'look fit' for that function. Nor do we always find them elegant or streamlined; instead they sometimes appear to us to be, due to constraints in its starting materials, 'odd arrangements and funny solutions', to use Gould's phrase; see 'The Panda's Thumb', in Gould, *The Panda's Thumb*, 19–26; the quotation is on 20. In such cases, Functional Beauty of the third type, as described in Chapter 4, Section 2, may be a more applicable concept.

that we call 'looking fit'. A similar account could be given for the appearance of many animal features, from the broad wingspan of a gliding raptor to the dexterous lankiness of a tree frog's toes.

Furthermore, the appreciation of Functional Beauty can be better defended against the immorality objection than the other ways of aesthetically appreciating living things described in Section 1. For to appreciate the Functional Beauty of an organism requires approaching that organism as a creature with plans, priorities, and projects, insofar as it involves considering the functions of animal traits and parts. This is because the functions of those traits and parts are bound up with the plans, priorities, and projects that animals possess. For example, the functions of the parts and traits of a cheetah reveal just the sorts of plans, priorities, and projects characteristic of that kind of animal: remaining camouflaged in a grassland habitat, quickly running down large prey at high speeds, sighting other animals at long distances, and so on. It is in making such facts about the nature of organisms an essential element of their aesthetic appearance, then, that our conception of Functional Beauty avoids the immorality problem.

Further, this way of avoiding the difficulty is specific to the sense of 'Functional Beauty' that we have advocated. On this sense, 'Functional Beauty' refers to an 'internal' connection between function and aesthetic qualities. In Chapter 1, Section 5, we also described a different sense of 'Functional Beauty', which takes shape in the aesthetic theory of the late eighteenth century, particularly in some strands of Kant's aesthetic views. On this conception, beauty, or aesthetic quality in general, itself does not arise from the application of the concept of function to an object. That is, beauty, or aesthetic quality in general, does not involve function; indeed, it may not involve any concepts at all. The function of the object is, however, related in an 'external' way to the object's beauty, or aesthetic quality, such that its beauty can be described as 'beauty that is functional'. Our knowledge of the function of the object may prevent us from finding certain of its features beautiful, for example, rendering us unable to see an otherwise pleasing arrangement of colours and shapes as beautiful when it is spray-painted on a puppy.[24] Alternatively, we may appreciate the way in which an object's aesthetic quality enhances or facilitates the object's ability to carry out its function, as when we admire the way in which a leopard's pretty spots enable to it to camouflage itself. In cases like this, the beauty of animals is related to their function in ways that enable us to describe it as 'beauty that is functional'.

Although Functional Beauty, understood in this sense, is an interesting notion, and no doubt an important aspect of aesthetic appreciation, it does not provide a potent solution to the immorality problem, nor does it point in a promising direction for the aesthetic appreciation of animals. First, on this conception, the aesthetic quality of the object remains something that is independent of the nature of the object: when an object is beautiful, its function is not here a 'part' of the beauty. In the cheetah example given above, for instance, this conception holds that certain of the cheetah's features are beautiful, or possess other aesthetic qualities. Some of these pleasing features may also contribute to the feature's ability to perform its function. If so, we also admire the way in which the beauty of the animal's features 'lines up with', or makes a contribution to, their function. The cheetah's distinctive 'tear stripes', for example, might simply appear attractive to us. But when we discover that they also serve a function, reducing glare from the sun while the animal pursues its prey, we may also delight in the way that this attractive quality contributes to functionality. But so far as this conception of Functional Beauty goes, the function of the tear stripes is no part of their beauty. It remains the case, therefore, that when we appreciate the aesthetic quality of the animal, we appreciate this apart from an awareness of the function of its parts, and so apart from its nature. The most that can be said in response to the immorality objection, on

[24] This example is adapted from Stephen Davies, 'Aesthetic Judgements, Artworks and Functional Beauty', *Philosophical Quarterly* 56 (2006): 224–41; see 230. In this essay, Davies develops an account of Functional Beauty along these lines.

this conception of Functional Beauty, is that the consideration of beauty, although superficial in itself, is constrained by, or subsumed under, a broader, non-aesthetic appreciation of the organism.

In contrast, our conception of Functional Beauty holds to an 'internal' relationship between function and aesthetic appreciation.[25] It is not merely that certain of the cheetah's features are attractive, and also happen to be functional. Rather, certain of its features are attractive, in part, *because* they possess a particular function. In a species of the great cats where form is not adapted to the function of sustaining high speeds, such as the lion, the cheetah's thin legs and small shoulders would *detract* from the attractiveness of form. It is in this sense that Functional Beauty, in our sense, 'emerges out of' the function of the object. As such, it is this sense that seems to address most squarely the lack of connection between beauty and the nature of the organism that underlies the immorality objection.

This point also suggests a second sense in which our conception of Functional Beauty holds greater promise as a direction for developing an aesthetics of animals than the conception of Functional Beauty as 'beauty that is functional'. For, in holding that the features of living creatures are beautiful, or not, independently of their function, the latter obscures many of their beauties, which are only revealed when we possess an awareness of the functions of these features. For instance, discussing bats, the biologist Richard Dawkins writes that: 'Their faces are often distorted into gargoyle shapes that appear hideous to us until we see them for what they

[25] Malcolm Budd seems to have something like this sense in mind when he discusses aesthetic judgements concerning the pleasing qualitative perfection of an organism '*as being an instance of kind K*'. The aesthetic qualities involved in such judgements, Budd explains, 'depend upon the character of the natural functions of a certain natural kind and the ways in which they are realized in the appearance of something of that kind'. These ways include 'fitness of the parts to perform their natural function' and the 'manifest suitability of the bodily parts to the creature's ability to flourish in its natural environment'; see Malcolm Budd, 'Delight in the Natural World: Kant on the Aesthetic Appreciation of Nature, Part I: Natural Beauty', *British Journal of Aesthetics* 38 (1998): 1–18; reprinted in Malcolm Budd, *The Aesthetic Appreciation of Nature* (Oxford: Oxford University Press, 2002), 24–47; the quotation is on 41–2.

are, exquisitely fashioned instruments for beaming ultrasound in desired directions.'[26] Through an awareness of the way in which animal features have been 'exquisitely fashioned', albeit by the forces of natural selection rather than by a designing intellect, knowledge about those functions alters and enhances our aesthetic appreciation of living creatures, allowing us to delight in the innumerable ways that their forms 'look fit'.

5.4 Function in the Landscape

As we have noted, although the Functional Beauty of organisms has not been given a great deal of attention, one can find endorsement and discussion of it in the aesthetics literature, particularly in the classic writings of the eighteenth-century British aestheticians. But with respect to non-living, inorganic natural things, items such as mountains, clouds, rivers, as well as larger entities such as ecosystems and habitats, the notion has scarcely been broached. And there is good reason for this: although we have strong intuitions that the concept of function must be applicable somehow to the traits and parts of animals, we do not have similar intuitions about the non-living world. Indeed, as we described in Chapter 2, many have thought that the application of teleological concepts, such as function, to the purely physical world can only be a throwback to an outmoded Aristotelian conception of nature.

So it is that we find a number of philosophers explicitly rejecting the idea that Functional Beauty has any application to non-living natural things. Nick Zangwill, for instance, allows that biological organisms can possess aesthetic qualities that are 'relative to function', but holds that non-living things cannot because, he assumes, they have 'no purpose'.[27] Malcolm Budd voices a similar view, noting that 'not every kind of natural thing is, as such, a thing with natural functions. ... Clouds, rivers, valleys,

[26] Richard Dawkins, *The Blind Watchmaker* (New York: W.W. Norton & Company, 1986), 24.

[27] Zangwill, 'Formal Natural Beauty', 116, n. 8.

rainbows, stalactites, and many other natural items do not have natural functions and are not composed of parts that perform such functions.'[28] To better account for the aesthetic appreciation of such items, Budd suggests that we admit 'the possibility that aesthetic pleasure might be derived from the formed matter of an object seen as falling under a *non-purposive, non-functional*, concept, so that its being something of that kind is integral to the pleasure'.[29] And, finally, Holmes Rolston suggests the impossibility of Functional Beauty in non-living nature by his remark that, in contrast to the traits of organisms, 'the scenery cannot fail because nothing is attempted'.[30]

As we will show, there is something correct to be extracted from Rolston's pregnant remark, but it is not the thought that the concept of function is inapplicable to non-living nature. It is true that such things do not have selected functions, since they do not reproduce or undergo natural selection. But, as we have seen in Chapter 3, there are alternative naturalistic analyses of function, such as Robert Cummins's account of causal role function. This analysis identifies a trait or part's having a function with the trait or part in question playing a certain sort of causal role in a larger system of which it is a component. If we understand functions in this sense, even inorganic things that do not reproduce can possess functions, if they play the appropriate sort of causal role in some capacity of a larger system to which they belong.[31] Inorganic things, such as rocks, rivers, and mountains, along with living things, do belong to larger ecosystems. Further, ecologists commonly recognize, and study, the important roles that they play within these systems: estuaries function as filters in the hydrological cycle, sand dunes function as erosion barriers in coastal vegetative systems, savannah grasslands function as habitat for certain animals,

[28] Budd, *The Aesthetic Appreciation of Nature*, 42.

[29] Ibid. (our italics). [30] Rolston, 'Beauty and the Beast', 192.

[31] See the examples of the 'promiscuity' of Cummins functions discussed by Karen Neander, 'Functions as Selected Effects: The Conceptual Analyst's Defense', *Philosophy of Science* 58 (1991a): 168–84, especially 181, and Ruth Millikan, 'In Defense of Proper Functions', *Philosophy of Science* 56 (1989): 288–302, especially 294.

and so forth.[32] These commonplace attributions of function to non-living natural things do not imply that they have been arranged by some intelligence, or that nature is 'attempting' anything, even in the attenuated, Aristotelian sense of that phrase. Rather, they specify some important causal effect that is particularly important in explaining how complex ecosystems operate. In *this* sense, we can, and do, describe non-living nature as functional.

But supposing that there are functions of this kind in inorganic nature, we might still question whether we can take aesthetic pleasure or displeasure in light of this functionality. To address this question, we may consider again the ways in which knowledge of function can alter the aesthetic appearance of an object. One of these is via a functional category causing an object to appear as having no contra-standard or variable features, but only standard ones. This can contribute, often, to functional things having aesthetic qualities like 'appearing elegant' or 'looking streamlined'. These aesthetic qualities, however, do not seem to occur in inorganic natural things: non-living natural things rarely seem elegant or simple in relation to their functional categories, simply because non-living things are not brought into being through a process that aligns their form to their function, as are artefacts and the traits and parts of animals. Rather, inorganic things have the functions they do, not because of their etiology, but because of local circumstances and the action of physical laws. Consequently, although an estuary serves as a water filter, or a glacier as a water source for a running water ecosystem, these hardly appear elegant or simple in relation to these functional categories.

This being said, however, it would be a mistake to infer from this that knowledge of function therefore fails to affect the aesthetic qualities of the natural things in question. For, as we have argued in Chapter 4, it seems possible for our knowledge of an object's function to enhance the perceptual unity of that object to varying

[32] On function in ecology, see Christopher Boorse, 'Wright on Functions', *Philosophical Review* 85 (1976): 70–86.

degrees. Without going so far as to make the object appear simple or elegant, knowledge of causal role functions of the various perceptible elements of an ecosystem may render it less disordered and random-looking, more unified, than it would otherwise appear. It may, in other words, give a different aesthetic appearance to the object.

Consider, for instance, our experience of an environment such as a wetland or swamp. To a first glance, these environments have a significant degree of perceptual disorder. Consisting of clumps of moss and tangles of grass, with insects and birds randomly arranged, and the whole thing drenched in a fetid and mucky standing water, the scene may appear little more than a random jumble of disordered elements. Yet an understanding of the ecological relations between these various elements may allow us to see it as, if not beautiful, at least less aesthetically displeasing. In describing his experience with wetlands, J. B. Callicott reports precisely this phenomenon:

> The sphagnum moss and the chemical regime it imposes constitutes the basis of this small, tight community. The tamaracks are a second major factor. The flora and fauna of the stories between are characteristic of, and some like the pitcher plants are unique to, this sort of community. There is a sensible fittingness, a unity there, not unlike that of a good symphony or tragedy.[33]

Callicott focuses on the living elements of the environment, emphasizing that understanding their coherence with the system as a whole lends to it a visual unity.[34] But the same point can also be made about its non-living elements. For example, the accumulation of sediment and detritus in wetlands, with its attendant microbial activity, plays a key role in sustaining populations of larger animals,

[33] J. Baird Callicott, 'Wetland Gloom and Wetland Glory', *Philosophy and Geography* 6 (2003): 33–45; the quotation is on 42.

[34] Rolston too stresses the 'order that arises spontaneously and systematically' in wetlands, but like Callicott mainly focuses on living organisms rather than non-living factors; see Holmes Rolston, 'Aesthetics in the Swamps', *Perspectives in Biology and Medicine* 43 (2000): 584–97, see especially 594.

and the flooding of wetlands, through the collection of run-off, plays an important role in maintaining the operation of nearby dry ecosystems. An understanding of the roles played by these elements, which at first glance seem to be merely random and anomalous, may help us to see a sensible unity between them and the other elements of the environment. The presence of muck and water as a backdrop for the pitcher plant and the heron may come to seem 'right-looking', in much the way that our understanding of what athletes' motions are 'for' lead us to perceive them as looking graceful and 'right', when otherwise they would appear disordered and random.[35]

The claim that an understanding of causal role function can be relevant to our aesthetic experience of non-living natural things, however, has been challenged recently by Nick Zangwill. He considers a slightly different example raised previously by one of us: that of the periodic flooding of rivers.[36] This behaviour plays an important causal role in the functioning of lotic ecosystems (by distributing nutrients to surrounding floodplains, for example). Given this, we maintain that it is possible for this phenomenon to appear different aesthetically in light of our knowledge of this function. A grasp of the place of this event in the overall ecological scheme of events may cause it to look less disordered and chaotic than it otherwise might. Zangwill challenges this possibility. He asks

> Is the word 'chaotic' being used to name an aesthetic characteristic? Let us assume that Parsons is using it as such, so that he is thinking of chaoticness as a visually appreciable property of the rampaging water. If so, I do not care, aesthetically, if it is aiding life or destroying it. Beauty can be benign and beauty can destroy.[37]

[35] This is not to say that aesthetic pleasure is the only pleasure that one might derive from possessing such knowledge, nor that possessing it is, on its own, sufficient for us to derive this sort of aesthetic pleasure.

[36] Glenn Parsons, 'Natural Functions and the Aesthetic Appreciation of Inorganic Nature', *British Journal of Aesthetics* 44 (2004): 44–56, see especially 51–4.

[37] Nick Zangwill, 'In Defence of Extreme Formalism about Inorganic Nature: Reply to Parsons', *British Journal of Aesthetics* 45 (2005): 185–91; the quotation is on 190.

Zangwill's point is that the chaotic, disordered appearance of flood waters is what he calls a 'formal' aesthetic quality, one that is not affected by our understanding, or lack of understanding, of the waters' function. This point, however, plays on an ambiguity. Zangwill describes the flood waters as 'rampaging', suggesting a torrent of water moving rapidly in many directions at once. Regarding such a scene, Zangwill is perhaps right to say that it is apt to look chaotic and disordered, regardless of one's beliefs about it (though one might note that the players in a football game also move rapidly in many directions at once, without necessarily looking chaotic or disordered at all, at least to those who understand the game). But whatever we say about that case, a flooded river need not be flood*ing*, nor flooding violently. A familiar forest that one day appears submerged beneath standing floodwaters is apt to look visually disordered, chaotic, or disharmonious. But this instance of visual disorder, like that discussed in reference to wetlands above, does seem capable of bending to an understanding of the integral role that such phenomena play in lotic ecosystems: what is contra-standard, in other words, may come to be standard or at least merely variable, given the right knowledge and experience. The acquisition of this knowledge may not be common or easy: most of us, for obvious and culturally entrenched reasons, regard flooded landscapes as highly unnatural, useless, and places to avoid.[38] Be this as it may, Zangwill's point does not vitiate the claim that knowledge of causal role functions, when we have it, can be relevant to the aesthetic appreciation of inanimate nature.

This does not mean that function will play as large a role in the aesthetics of inorganic nature as it does in that of organic nature. It does mean, though, that even here, the notion of Functional Beauty has a place. Further, we think that a consideration of Functional Beauty in the inorganic realm is important for what it reveals about a controversial topic, to which we now turn: ugliness in nature.

[38] Something similar might be true of landscapes that have recently been subject to wildfires, drought, and other natural alterations.

5.5 Looking Dysfunctional and Positive Aesthetics

If natural function can be relevant to the aesthetic appearance of both living and inanimate natural things, it is also apparent that there are important differences between the two cases. For, as we have argued, the sort of function that is applied in each of the two cases is different. We think that a consideration of the differences sheds light on recent debate over a controversial thesis in the aesthetics of nature: Positive Aesthetics.

As mentioned in Chapter 2, Section 6, Positive Aesthetics is, roughly, the thesis that virgin nature, when properly appreciated, is always or usually aesthetically good.[39] Since a parallel thesis concerning artworks—that artworks, when properly appreciated, are always or usually aesthetically good—is highly implausible, Positive Aesthetics, if true, would mark a categorical distinction between the aesthetics of nature and of art (indeed, of artefacts in general). As such, some philosophers have viewed Positive Aesthetics as a foundational, organizing principle for the aesthetics of nature, capturing what is distinctive about the beauty of the natural world.

The categorical distinction between nature and artefacts implicit in Positive Aesthetics has struck some thinkers as plausible because, in general, natural things possess a causal history that is distinct in kind from that possessed by artefacts. Indeed, 'nature'

[39] For discussion of different formulations of positive aesthetics, see Allen Carlson, 'Nature and Positive Aesthetics', *Environmental Ethics* 6 (1984): 5–34; Holmes Rolston, *Environmental Ethics: Duties to and Values in the Natural World* (Philadelphia, PA: Temple University Press, 1988), Chapter 6; Eugene Hargrove, *Foundations of Environmental Ethics* (Englewood Cliffs, NJ: Prentice Hall, 1989), Chapter 6; Stan Godlovitch, 'Valuing Nature and the Autonomy of Natural Aesthetics', *British Journal of Aesthetics* 38 (1998): 180–97; Malcolm Budd, 'The Aesthetics of Nature', *Proceedings of the Aristotelian Society* 100 (2000): 137–57, reprinted in Budd, *The Aesthetic Appreciation of Nature*, 90–109; Glenn Parsons, 'Nature Appreciation, Science and Positive Aesthetics', *British Journal of Aesthetics* 42 (2002): 279–95; Eugene Hargrove, 'Carlson and the Aesthetic Appreciation of Nature', *Philosophy and Geography* 5 (2002): 213–23; and Allen Carlson, 'Hargrove, Positive Aesthetics, and Indifferent Creativity', *Philosophy and Geography* 5 (2002): 224–34.

is often defined in terms of this difference.[40] Eugene Hargrove, for example, builds his defence of Positive Aesthetics around the fact that artefacts, being produced intentionally by human beings, are created in light of pre-existing standards of goodness, whereas natural things, being produced non-intentionally, are not. From this difference regarding the existence of a pre-existing standard in the case of nature and artefacts, Hargrove concludes that there is a categorical difference in their aesthetic character: nature cannot be aesthetically displeasing.[41]

In addition to Hargrove's, there have been several other defences of Positive Aesthetics, but the notion remains controversial. In general, critics have responded to the view by proposing counter-examples to it. Malcolm Budd, for instance, cites plants or animals that are in a condition 'diseased or malformed or indicative of approaching death', and remarks that 'grossly malformed living things will remain grotesque no matter how comprehensible science renders their malformation'.[42] For our purposes, the interesting thing about such counter-examples is that they tend to come from organic, living nature, rather than the inanimate natural world.

[40] See, for example, Budd's definition, which echoes that given by J. S. Mill in the essay 'On Nature' (1874); see Budd, *The Aesthetic Appreciation of Nature*, 2–6.

[41] Hargrove's view is a bit more complicated, since he wants to allow for the case where nature is created by God, but still cannot be evaluated in terms of a pre-existing standard. He writes: 'If nature's existence precedes its essence, the natural product of nature's indifferent creativity, whether through God or through itself, is and has to be good and beautiful, because whatever is so created always brings with it compatible standards of goodness and beauty. Put another way, nature is itself its own standard of goodness and beauty, making ugliness impossible as a product of nature's own creative energy. This takes care of the problem of positive aesthetics.' See Hargrove, *Foundations of Environmental Ethics*, 184. Hargrove's argument fails, for, if the character of nature, simply by existing, sets a standard of beauty that it trivially satisfies, then why does it not also set a standard for ugliness that it trivially satisfies? Hargrove would need to deny that there is any standard of ugliness that nature brings into being or, more plausibly, that although nature introduces a standard of ugliness, no part of nature conforms to that standard. But no reason for believing this is provided. And, in any case, if nature does introduce a standard of ugliness without having to conform to it, why is the same not also true of the standard of beauty? Thus Hargrove's line of thought leaves Positive Aesthetics either unjustified or false.

[42] Budd, *The Aesthetic Appreciation of Nature*, 100, 102. For somewhat different kinds of counter-examples, see Yuriko Saito, 'The Aesthetics of Unscenic Nature', *Journal of Aesthetics and Art Criticism* 56 (1998): 101–11.

Inorganic things tend not to be mentioned in this context, and indeed it seems difficult to provide similarly compelling examples of aesthetically poor things from that realm.

We think that once Functional Beauty is brought into the picture, this fact can be readily explained. Our explanation has two parts. The first part of the explanation is the idea that the aesthetic displeasure that we take in a diseased, malformed, or damaged organism is displeasure in its apparent dysfunctionality: in its 'looking unfit'. Diseased, damaged, and malformed animals often have other displeasing qualities, as well: they may stink, for example, or appear to be suffering in a way that evokes pity and sadness. But if we maintain, as many would insist, the distinction between mere sensory displeasure and aesthetic displeasure, as well as the distinction between what is aesthetically bad and what is morally bad, it appears that what is displeasing *aesthetically* about such creatures is precisely that their parts and limbs appear manifestly incapable of doing what they are supposed to do.[43]

In response to this first component of our explanation, it might be objected that damaged, diseased, or malformed organisms simply display a pattern or arrangement of shapes that is inherently displeasing, so that our finding them ugly does not depend upon any understanding of the function of their parts or traits. Consider the case of a bird, a plover say, with a discernibly broken wing. The suggestion would be that this organism is aesthetically displeasing because the line of its wing is no longer a smooth curve, but some irregular shape instead. Imagine, though, that we discover a new species of bird, just like the plover except that it has floppy appendages that drag on the ground and look just like broken plover wings. Call it the 'splover'. Imagine that we learn further that in splovers these appendages have some function to which they are actually well-suited (allowing the bird to swim underwater effectively, for example). The objection under consideration would entail that splover appendages would be just as ugly, or

[43] On the aesthetic status of smells, see our discussion in Chapter 7.

aesthetically displeasing, as broken plover wings. But this seems implausible. After all, many creatures (the walrus, for instance) have similar floppy appendages used for swimming or other purposes that do not strike us as displeasing in the way that a broken plover wing does. The ugliness of a particular *plover's* appendage seems to come from its appearing incapable of performing what we know to be its function: it just does not look right *for a wing*. Therefore, the objection raised above seems inaccurate. What the standard counter-examples to Positive Aesthetics show is that damaged, diseased, and malformed organisms are aesthetically displeasing in virtue of their apparent unfitness for function.

Thus, ugliness in nature seems to arise when damage or some kind of insult causes an object to appear dysfunctional. However, this alone does not explain why cases of the aesthetically displeasing in nature are drawn only from living things, particularly in light of our earlier argument that non-living things also can possess aesthetic qualities in light of their function. It is here that the distinction between causal role and selected functions becomes crucial, for it is only the latter that admit of *mal*functions due to damage, disease, and so forth.[44]

Philosophers of science describe this difference as a difference in the normativity of these two senses of 'function'. Selected effects functions are normative in the sense that a certain type of trait might have the function of performing X, due to being naturally selected in virtue of performing X, even though a token of that type is currently unable, due to damage or disease for instance, to perform X. In such cases, the entity in question is malfunctioning. In contrast, causal role functions are generally viewed as non-normative, or purely descriptive. Causal role functions are defined in terms of occurrent causal powers: to have one is 'to have certain effects on a containing system'.[45] Thus, when those powers are

[44] On selected malfunctions, see Millikan, 'In Defense of Proper Functions', and Neander, 'Functions as Selected Effects', 180f.

[45] Robert Cummins, 'Functional Analysis', *Journal of Philosophy* 72 (1975): 741–65; the quotation is on 741.

absent so is the causal role function. A particular thing that has the selected effects function of doing X may not actually be doing, or even be capable of doing, X, but if it has X only as a causal role function, and then ceases to do X, it is unintuitive to say that it is no longer 'working', or that it is 'malfunctioning'.

We can illustrate this point using an example of an artefact, adapted from Larry Wright.[46] This provides a case where only Cummins's causal role analysis, but not a selected function analysis, is applicable. Imagine that an engine has a badly adjusted valve that causes it to run poorly. Fortuitously, a small piece of metal falls into the engine and lands in just such a position that it adjusts the valve, allowing the engine to work properly. This piece of metal could have a causal role function (adjusting the valve) in the running of the engine: in the context of an explanation of how the engine is managing to run properly, we would lay out the arrangement of the various components and their contributions to its operation. In this arrangement, the piece of metal must have a place, and its contribution, what it does (namely, adjusting the valve), might be described as its function within this overall arrangement. This is not a function in the 'selected effects' sense, obviously, since adjusting the valve is not the reason that 'ancestors' of the piece of metal flourished and reproduced (or even the reason that they succeeded in the marketplace). If the piece of metal falls out, and the engine stops running again, it seems unintuitive to say that the piece of metal has now 'malfunctioned'.[47] But for all that, while it was in place, it did have a (causal role) function in the particular arrangement of parts that brought about the running of the engine. The causal role analysis, then, admits of attributions of function, but not attributions of malfunction.

[46] Larry Wright, 'Functions', *Philosophical Review* 82 (1973): 139–68, see 152. We have altered the example slightly.

[47] Note that we do want to say, of course, that the valve (as opposed to the piece of metal) is malfunctioning, but this is because it cannot carry out that effect that explains its presence in the first place.

When applied to natural things, this entails that malfunction, apparently the source of natural ugliness, is a possibility for organic things only. Although a particular frog's leg is unable to propel it through the water, for example, this is still the function that it has in light of the selective history of this sort of trait. Hence it possesses a function that it cannot fulfil, and so it malfunctions. Accident, genetic error, or sickness can strip a frog's leg of the power to propel, but it cannot erase its selective history, and so cannot change the fact that it has this as its selected function. However, this is not the case for inorganic things, which have only causal role functions. To have a causal role function is nothing more than to make the right sort of causal contribution to a capacity of a larger system: once this causal contribution is lost, the function is lost along with it. For example, consider a rock formation that acts to divert a river, directing it onto a plain and so functioning as an irrigator for that plain. We would not call a collapse of the rock formation, due to erosion, that rendered it unable to divert the river a 'malfunction' of the rock. This is because the rock's functionality was wholly a matter of its occurrent causal powers and, once eroded, it seems wrong to say that it has a function that it cannot fulfil; rather, it has no function at all.[48]

Thus, the second part of our explanation for the restriction of ugliness to organic nature is that, even when inorganic things do possess functions, damage to those things does not cause them to look incapable of performing those functions. For things with selected functions, such as the parts of animals, change can do this because damage or disease, while it removes a thing's powers, cannot take away its function. But for things with causal role functions, such as inorganic natural things, such damage not only takes away its power to perform its function; it also removes the function itself.

[48] Describing his notion of natural function, Cummins writes 'if the function of something in a system *s* is to pump, then it must be capable of pumping in *s*'; see Cummins, 'Functional Analysis', 757. For concurring views, see Millikan, 'In Defense of Proper Functions', 294, and Neander, 'Functions as Selected Effects', 181. The rock example is an adaptation of an example in Philip Kitcher, 'Function and Design', *Midwest Studies in Philosophy* 18 (1994): 379–97, see 272.

Thus the object never looks incapable of performing its function (since it now has no function at all). This is the truth behind Rolston's remark that 'the scenery cannot fail because nothing is attempted'. Somewhat ironically, the scenery can 'succeed', in the sense that parts of it are able to do certain explanatorily important causal things in the context of an ecosystem. In this sense, they can be functional and we can aesthetically appreciate them as such. But they cannot fail, given the particular kind of 'functioning' that this is.

The counter-examples of damaged, diseased, and malformed living things show that Positive Aesthetics does not hold as a general thesis about the natural world. And yet, there does seem to be a genuine insight manifested in the view. By explaining why the counter-examples to Positive Aesthetics are restricted to organic nature, our analysis shows that Positive Aesthetics does capture something true about the natural beauty of inorganic things. The view fails only when it is applied to everything in nature, without regard for the important differences among natural things.

The inadequacy of taking such a 'coarse-grained' view of objects of aesthetic appreciation ought to be familiar already from the history of aesthetic theory. For, in the case of art, cultural theories of art have taught us the importance of thinking of art-making as a complex and varied social practice that produces a variety of distinct types of things. Yet when we talk about the forces responsible for, and ontologically salient to, natural things, aesthetic theory tends to fall back into simplistic generic descriptions like 'natural processes', or 'physical processes'. By bringing the diverse characters of different natural things and processes to the fore, Functional Beauty more fully illuminates the aesthetic character of the natural world.

6

Architecture and the Built Environment

In the natural world, the acknowledgement of Functional Beauty has been obstructed by the difficulty of accepting functionality in nature. In the case of the built environment, this difficulty, at least, is not a concern. For the built environment is first and foremost a functional one.[1] The elements of this environment—roads, houses, bridges, wharves—are paradigms of functional items. As noted in Chapter 2, Section 3, in the twentieth century, Functional Beauty and ideas related to it gained prominence in thinking about the built environment as central elements in International Modernism, the architectural movement championed by architects such as Walter Gropius, Le Corbusier, and Ludwig Mies van der Rohe. This movement involved abandoning what were seen as parochial and dated traditions in favour of a style that expressed the essence of a modern, industrial society. The influence of International Modernism has been enormous, changing the look of cities across the world in a radical way.

Modernism's legacy, however, has been much disputed. Rather than representing an end to the parade of arbitrary and contingent styles of architecture, some have viewed Modernism itself as an arbitrary style, and one reflective of the worst aspects of bourgeois culture, at that. Rather than cleaving to the essence of modern society, Modernism has been seen as stifling and obstructive to

[1] See Allen Carlson, 'On Aesthetically Appreciating Human Environments', *Philosophy and Geography* 4 (2001): 9–24.

contemporary daily life. And, instead of clarifying the aims of architecture, Modernism has been charged with turning the notion of function into a woolly metaphysical abstraction in an attempt to bestow some sort of cosmic significance on its particular ideal of design.

These criticisms of Functional Beauty, and related ideas, as they have been employed in International Modernism are serious and, in some cases at least, well founded. But, in our view, the difficulties that lead to these criticisms arise not because of defects in the concept of Functional Beauty itself, but because of various mishandlings of this concept. In this chapter, therefore, we will seek to vindicate the idea of aesthetically appreciating the built environment in light of function. We will begin by arguing for the need for such appreciation, and detailing how our conception of Functional Beauty can fulfil this need. We will then address the issues of indeterminacy and translation as they arise in the context of architecture. In doing so, we will attempt to clarify and recover what is correct in the much disputed doctrines that go under the name of 'Functionalism' in architectural theory.

6.1 The Case for Functional Beauty in Architecture

In the previous chapter, we argued that Functional Beauty has an important virtue when considered as an approach to the aesthetic appreciation of living organisms. This consists in its capacity to assuage an important moral qualm about the very idea of extending aesthetic appreciation to such creatures: namely, that it requires treating organisms as a mere 'sensory surface'. Living organisms, of course, are not mere surfaces, and consist in much that is not revealed, and is actually obscured by, their sensuous surfaces. Because of this, we argued that any sound relationship to living creatures ought to take account of these 'hidden aspects', and indeed ought to be based, in part at least, upon them. The advantage of Functional Beauty is that it allows aesthetic appreciation to embody such a relationship, by making these hidden aspects a 'part of' our aesthetic experiences.

This line of thought, we think, also reveals an analogous virtue of Functional Beauty in the context of architecture. First, note that aesthetic appreciation has sometimes given rise to analogous moral qualms with respect to architecture. For when we *aesthetically* appreciate a building, it may be urged, what we evaluate is its sensory surface: the finish or the facade of the building only, and not the building per se. To appreciate buildings in this way, then, is to reduce them to their surface, for the duration of such appreciation at least. But buildings, like animals and people, are more than a surface, consisting of much that is not revealed, and is actually obscured by, their sensuous surfaces. The 'hidden' aspects of buildings, of course, differ from the hidden aspects of organisms, or persons. In the case of buildings, the hidden aspects might include things such as their structural soundness, their commodiousness, their conduciveness to the health and productivity of their occupants, their function, and so forth. But, despite this difference, the hidden aspects of buildings seem vitally relevant to buildings in much the same way that the hidden aspects of organisms are vitally relevant for them. As in the case of animals and people, the hidden aspects of buildings are sufficiently important that any sound relationship to a building ought to take account of them, and indeed ought to be based, in part at least, upon them. Here again, Functional Beauty allows aesthetic appreciation to contribute to such a relationship, by making the hidden functional aspects of buildings a 'part of' our aesthetic experiences.[2]

This sort of moral argument in favour of Functional Beauty in architecture is by no means novel; in fact, it has always been a chief theoretical motivation for the doctrine. Some nineteenth-century thinkers, for example, were drawn to architectural theories that emphasized function as a reaction against what they saw as

[2] Cf. Allen Carlson, 'Existence, Location, and Function: The Appreciation of Architecture', in M. Mitias (ed.), *Philosophy and Architecture* (Amsterdam: Editions Rodopi, 1994), 141–64.

a morally bankrupt appropriation of classical forms by contemporary architects. The American sculptor Horatio Greenough, for instance, lampoons the 'Greek temple jammed in between the brick shops of Wall street or Cornhill, covered with lettered signs, and occupied by groups of money-changers and apple women'.[3] According to Greenough:

> The pile stands a stranger among us, and receives a respect akin to what we should feel for a fellow-citizen in the garb of Greece. It is a make-believe. It is not the real thing. We see the marble capitals; we trace the acanthus leaves of a celebrated model—incredulous; it is not a temple.[4]

The official excuse for this wilful obfuscation of social reality, of course, was beauty. Greenough's critique suggests that, if beauty really entails such frumpery and such a wild distortion of reality, it were better to leave beauty behind. Greenough himself, though, is more sanguine than this about beauty's prospects in architecture, drawing inspiration from the model of nature. Here the forms of animals are beautiful, but always aligned to fit the functions assigned to them by nature. In appreciating the beauty of the animal world, Greenough asserts, we are able to relate to things appropriately, as what they are. But, in appreciating deceptive beauty in buildings, we stray from this ideal: we 'tie up the cameleopard to the rack; we shave the lion, and call him a dog'.[5] Greenough's suggestion for a reorientation of architecture is similar to our own: that we follow the lead of nature and see the beauty of buildings as informed by, as emerging out of, their functions.

An important objection to this suggestion, however, is that our relationships to buildings are here taken too much on the

[3] Horatio Greenough, 'American Architecture' [1853], in Henry T. Tuckerman, *A Memorial of Horatio Greenough* (New York: Benjamin Blom, 1968), 117–30; the quotation is on 126.

[4] Ibid., 121. There are similar moral overtones in other defences of functionalism; note, for example, Loos's famous dictum that 'Ornament is crime'; see Adolf Loos, 'Ornament and Crime' [1908], in *Ornament and Crime: Selected Essays*, ed. Adolf Opel, trans. Michael Mitchell (Riverside, CA: Ariadne Press, 1998), 167–76. See also Ruskin's discussion of the 'Lamp of Truth', in Chapter 10 of John Ruskin, *The Seven Lamps of Architecture*, 2nd edn (London: George Allen, 1880).

[5] Greenough, 'American Architecture', 123.

model of the relationship between persons, or living beings. What Greenough, for example, finds objectionable about the classically styled banks of Wall Street is the deceptiveness of their surfaces: the disconnection between what they appear to be (spiritual retreats) and what they in fact are (houses of usury). Deceptiveness of this kind is objectionable in human relationships, surely, but it is less clear why it ought to be objectionable in the context of architecture. Geoffrey Scott makes this point by way of an analogy:

> If, in discharge of a debt, a man were to give me instead of a sovereign a gilded farthing, he would fail, no doubt, of his promise, which was to give me the value of twenty shillings. To deceive me was essential to his plan and the desire to do so implied in his attempt. But if, when I have lent him nothing, he were to give me a gilt farthing because I wanted something bright, and because he could not afford the sovereign at all, then, though the coin might be a false sovereign, there is evidently neither evil will nor injury. There is no failure of promise because no promise has been made.[6]

Monetary transactions constitute a domain of human relations where honesty and transparency are insisted upon, and deceit rightly rejected. But merely because there are good grounds for rejecting deceit in one domain, we cannot conclude that there are grounds for its rejection *tout court*. According to Scott, when we are taken in by the deceptive facade of a building, no pact between the architect and ourselves has been broken, nor has harm in any substantive sense been done to us. Indeed, Scott goes on to point out that in art, deceit, in the form of illusion, is, and always has been, welcomed and celebrated rather than censured and rejected. That we should be deceived by art is a generally accepted convention that we all willingly endorse, and which brings, not harm, but a positive benefit to us.[7] Nor can we say, as we might in the

[6] Geoffrey Scott, *The Architecture of Humanism: A Study in the History of Taste* [1914], (New York: W.W. Norton & Co., 1999), 117–18.

[7] Ibid., 120.

case of animals, that deception in architecture causes harm to the object of appreciation. To literally 'shave the lion, and call him a dog', for example, may well be to do a real harm, in some moral sense at least, to the lion. But if we are content to pretend, on some level, that a house of usury is something other than what it is—a temple, for instance—whom could we be harming? The insensate heap of marble is not, it would seem, any the worse for our fantasy.

But there is a party harmed here, if only in an indirect way, we think: namely, we the appreciators. To appropriate one of Greenough's metaphors, there would be something undeniably ridiculous, if not defective, about a society that decided to adopt the dress of a past age, such as that of the ancient Greeks, for example. That is, there would be something undeniably ridiculous, if not defective, about a society that engaged in such a massive and pervasive form of self-deception. The life of such a society may even seem to us not to be a form of 'real' life at all, but rather a childish kind of fantasy life (note that this would be the case even if, among the people of that society, it had become a generally accepted convention to accept this perpetual fantasy). The same point holds, we think, for a society that 'dresses' its buildings as things they are not: there is something ridiculous, if not defective, in denying or suppressing reality in such a dramatic and widespread manner. When we consider the case of architecture, the appeal to the harmlessness of deceit in art is somewhat misleading. For art is a discrete part of life, to which we turn at certain times and from which we always return, but architecture is simply not of this nature. We spend much of our lives either in buildings or surrounded by them. Deceptiveness in architecture, consequently, is more pervasive and extreme than the deceptiveness of art, and, in fact, more pervasive and extreme than even the sartorial phoniness considered by Greenough would be. Avoiding this sort of deceptiveness in our aesthetic appreciation of buildings is indeed, therefore, a virtue of Functional Beauty.

6.2 The Function of a Building: The Problem of Indeterminacy

As mentioned above, the suggestion of thinkers such as Greenough is that we follow the lead of nature and construe the aesthetic quality of buildings as informed by, as emerging out of, their functions. The difficulty with this suggestion, of course, is precisely *how* one goes about 'following nature's lead'. For, as we saw in Chapter 3, the functions of buildings are not as easily identifiable as the functions of animal parts and traits; rather, there seems to be a bewildering array of candidates for 'the function' of any given building. Attempts to characterize the functions of built structures in terms of 'the wants of their occupants', in response to which buildings develop 'organically', seem unhelpful here.[8] For the 'wants of the occupants' are often many and various. Which shall determine the function? And why, after all, give the occupant exclusive say? Why not the designer, the builder, the owner, or even the citizens who walk past and view the building? This lack of clarity has led some, in the manner of Scruton, to go so far as to dismiss the idea of 'the function of a building' as meaningless, despite its intuitive appeal.[9] In this way the Problem of Indeterminacy, which we addressed in Chapter 3, perseveres in an especially virulent form for architecture and the built environment.

In contrast to the general solution to the problem that we have suggested, advocates of functionalist doctrines in architecture typically appeal to intentionalist approaches analogous to those considered in Chapter 3. Seemingly influenced by the conviction that architecture is an artform and the architect an artist, together

[8] Greenough, 'American Architecture', 127. Some of the limitations of this kind of approach are illustrated in Allen Carlson, 'The Aesthetic Appreciation of Everyday Architecture', in M. Mitias (ed.), *Architecture and Civilization* (Amsterdam: Editions Rodopi, 1999), 107–21.

[9] For critiques along these lines, see Peter Blake, *Form Follows Fiasco: Why Modern Architecture Hasn't Worked* (Boston, MA: Little Brown, 1974); Brent C. Brolin, *The Failure of Modern Architecture* (New York: Van Nostrand Reinhold, 1976); and Tom Wolfe, *From Bauhaus to Our House* (New York: Farrar, Straus and Giroux, 1981).

with the persistent appeal of various forms of intentionalism concerning art, they have often tried to eliminate the indeterminacy of function by recourse to the view that the architect's intention determines a building's function. The architect decides how the building will be used, thereby determining its function, and then accommodates its structure to his notion. In taking this approach, functionalist theorists, fuelled by Marxist utopianism and an aversion to middle-class tastes, bestowed tremendous power upon the architect.[10] As Gordon Graham puts it, the goal of functionalist architecture, thus construed, was not simply to design buildings, but to 'create a conception of living'.[11] The modernist architect would simply decide, for example, that the facades of office buildings no longer need to be visually interesting, since people would soon be hurtling through the city at speeds too great to permit close scrutiny of any such passing structures.[12] Thus, that building facades henceforth no longer had this function was a fact established by architects' explicit intentions and visions of the future, and given solid form in the physical structures that they delivered.

This intentionalist way of resolving the vexed issue of the indeterminacy of the function of buildings has been thoroughly criticized. The objectionable presumptuousness of this approach was manifest even in the label 'International Style', which suggested that Modernist structures, and their attendant 'conceptions of living', were henceforth applicable to all 'modern people'. In practice, the new conceptions of living determined by the Modernist designers, and given permanent substance in their physical structures, often failed to find mass appeal. The functions for buildings and their parts assigned by designers were often found to be constraining and, in fact, outright afunctional by the people who

[10] On these influences, see: Brolin, *The Failure of Modern Architecture*, 56; Wolfe, *From Bauhaus to Our House*; and Louis Mumford, 'Function and Expression in Architecture' *Architectural Record* 110 (November 1951): 106–12.

[11] Gordon Graham, 'Art and Architecture', *British Journal of Aesthetics* 29 (1989): 248–57; the quotation is on 254.

[12] The example is from Brolin, *The Failure of Modern Architecture*, 27.

ultimately had to use them.[13] Lewis Mumford puts his finger on the fundamental reason for this failure of International Modernism: the functions of its buildings were determined by architects who had an impoverished conception of function.[14] Beguiled by mechanical technology, they thought of function in terms of the engineering functions of buildings, such as airflow, heat exchange, and the like, or else in terms of the most basic physical functions of human occupants, such as sleeping and eating. Modernism, as an architectural theory, settled the indeterminacy of function only at the cost of turning function into something elitist, undemocratic, and, most importantly, detached from the lived experience of most people.

There is much in this critique that is sound. But our response to the failures of International Modernism need not be the abandonment of the very notion of 'the function of a building', and so of the very idea of Functional Beauty. Indeed, although Mumford sees clearly how the concept of function has been mishandled in Modernism, his own recommendation is not to reject Functionalism as an approach to architecture, but to employ a richer notion of function, one that is grounded in people's real lived experience of buildings, rather than the stipulative a priori speculations of social reformers.[15] The conception of proper function that we have outlined in Chapter 3 articulates such a conception. On our view, the intentions of individuals, including designers, are not sufficient to bestow a proper function on an artefact. Rather, in order for a particular effect to become the proper function of an artefact, this

[13] In *From Bauhaus to Our House*, Chapter IV, Wolfe gives an amusing account of the attempts of workers and residents to live with and in the consequences of International Modernism. Asking 'what if you were living in a building that looked like a factory and felt like a factory', he recounts the sad tale of the worker housing project called Pruitt-Igoe in St Louis, which was demolished in 1972, and that of the Oriental Gardens project in New Haven, which met the same fate in 1981; see Wolfe, *From Bauhaus to Our House*, 80–3; the quotation is on 72.

[14] Mumford describes modernist buildings as 'esthetically dull, technically absurd', and modernist architecture itself as 'irrational'; see Louis Mumford, 'The Case Against "Modern Architecture"', in *Highway and the City* (Westport, CT: Greenwood Publishing Group, 1953), 170.

[15] Ibid., 174. See also Mumford, 'Function and Expression in Architecture'.

effect must meet with success in the marketplace, and be selected as a result. In looking for the functions of particular buildings or structures, then, we are directed not to the idealized plans of designers or architects, but to the mass use of similar structures over time. The function of a building is not something that can be willed into being by the architect, but something that is already present when the architect begins her design, a kind of wake trailing from the collective behaviour of past generations.

More specifically, in Chapter 3, Section 3, following Beth Preston's account, we suggested the following selected effects theory of proper function:

> X has a *proper function* F if and only if Xs currently exist because, in the recent past, ancestors of X were successful in meeting some need or want in the marketplace because they performed F, leading to manufacture and distribution of Xs.

On this account, the proper function of a building will be the thing done by such buildings that, in the recent past, has led them to pass muster in the marketplace and thereby be manufactured and distributed. As we argued in Chapter 3, identifying this function may not be an easy task: it will typically involve more than a priori reflection. But determining it does not require an arbitrary selection of one individual's 'wants' over those of others. Neither, on this view, does function become a 'metaphysical monster', originating from some inscrutable source beyond the community's wants and needs. Rather, proper function emerges from, and is a recognition of, our collective treatment of artefacts over time.

We maintain that this analysis of proper function allows a defence of Greenough's (and our) claim that the concept of function can be extended from the natural world to architectural works. That said, certain of the peculiar characteristics of architectural works do require a refinement of the conditions for applying proper function. For example, the account stated above entails that a building's proper function is a part of the explanation for its manufacture and distribution. In the case of animal traits and parts, this generally is the case: to say that a bird's feathers have the proper function of flight implies that flight is a part of the explanation for the manufacture of those particular wings (whether or not this claim is actually true). But, in the case of architectural works, this is sometimes not the case. If an architectural work is very old, it may have acquired a proper function that does not figure, in any way, in the explanation of its manufacture and distribution.

For instance, in Chapter 3 we suggested that, although the Plaza Major in Madrid came into being to serve as a royal courtyard, its proper function *now* seems to be providing a civic space for community events, such as public gatherings and markets. But if facilitating civic events is the proper function of the Plaza Major, then our theory apparently entails that this effect, through passing muster in the marketplace in previous ages and bringing about the manufacture and distribution of city squares, explains the manufacture of the Plaza Major. But the effect of facilitating civic events, insofar as this has affected the manufacture and distribution of city squares, does not seem relevant to explaining the manufacture of the Plaza Major in any way. For the fact that, recently, city squares (Toronto's Yonge-Dundas Square, for example) have been manufactured for this purpose, is no part of the explanation for why the Plaza Major was constructed hundreds of years ago. The construction of a city square due to the need to facilitate city events obviously does not figure in an explanation of the manufacture of the Plaza Major, which occurred hundreds of years before.

This difference in the conditions for attributing proper functions to buildings and animal parts stems from a basic difference in longevity.[16] In both cases, we tend to think of the proper function of the item as 'that recent activity or effect that has caused it to be there'. Since organisms are short-lived, and thus born lately, 'that

[16] This difference, although typical, is contingent—we could imagine animals living thousands of years and buildings disappearing, en masse, every fifty years or so.

recent activity or effect that has caused a trait to be there' usually comes down to 'that recent activity or effect that has caused the trait to be manufactured'. In contrast, architectural works often persist for vast spans of time. Hence, when we speak of their proper functions, we often do not mean 'that recent activity or effect that has caused them to be manufactured'. For, in fact, there is often no such recent effect at all, the causes of their manufacture being ancient. What do we mean, then? In cases like the Plaza Major, in order for an old architectural work to have F as its proper function, its F-ing must explain its existence in a different way, through bringing about its preservation. In this way, a consideration of the built environment prompts us to expand our account of proper function, as follows:

> X has a *proper function* F if and only if Xs currently exist because, in the recent past, ancestors of X were successful in meeting some need or want in the marketplace because they performed F, leading to manufacture and distribution, or preservation, of Xs.[17]

This account is broad enough to make sense of our attribution of proper function to ancient works, such as the Plaza Major. Given the existence of alternative uses for land in Madrid, the Plaza could long ago have been torn up and replaced with something else. It seems reasonable to suggest that it has persisted in recent times because it provides a civic space for community events. If this is true, then the success of public squares in facilitating civic events *does* explain the existence of the Plaza Major, even though it does not explain its manufacture.[18]

[17] Note that Preston's statement of the selected effects theory of artefacts' proper functions does not contain this element. The need for this modification of the theory becomes apparent, we think, when we consider ancient and frequently co-opted artefacts, such as architectural works, rather than the mass-produced artefacts, such as hammers and shovels, on which Preston focuses.

[18] This may seem ad hoc, but similar issues arise concerning biological traits. Bird feathers, for instance, are thought to have been selected originally for thermo-regulation. Later, in warmer climates, they were maintained for their ability to facilitate flight. In this case,

This example supports the view that the concept of proper function can, in fact, be transferred from the natural world to the world of architecture and to the built environment in general. Furthermore, it demonstrates that the concept is flexible enough to do justice to the *distinctive* characteristics of the built environment, allowing us to appreciate its structures and other features as the sorts of thing that they are. These are the key points about Functional Beauty that were grasped by early functionalist thinkers, such as Greenough. Too often these thinkers left the concept of function hazy and ill defined, or saddled it with adventitious and dubious doctrines. But they saw clearly enough that function provides the means for grounding aesthetic character in architecture and the built environment.

6.3 Functional Beauty: a Bourgeois Aesthetic?

In the previous section, we responded to the criticism that 'the function of a building' is an elitist and undemocratic notion by looking to collective behaviour in the marketplace, rather than the oracular visions of architects, as the source of the function of buildings. But this response may prompt the opposite complaint: namely, that the functionality of buildings has become, on our view, unacceptably bourgeois. This charge is not a purely aesthetic criticism and addressing it involves some discussion of social and political issues, but it is still worth considering given the history of Functionalism in twentieth-century architecture. On our view, the proper function of artefacts is determined by the collective behaviour of individuals acting in the marketplace. But why, it might be asked, ought we to be any more content with leaving function hostage to the vicissitudes of market forces than we were with the modernists' decision to consign it to the considered judgement of the elite designer? As a way of pressing this question,

we intuitively think of the latter as the trait's proper function, since facilitating flight is what explains why bird feathers are there *now*, even though facilitating flight did not cause feathers to come into being originally.

it might be urged that here, as in other areas, the appeal to market forces really stultifies so-called 'progressive' criticism and alternative (that is, non-market-based) ways of thinking. This quintessentially left-wing point of view can be illustrated with reference to the case of industrial farms that we introduced in Chapter 3, Section 5. The progressive position on this issue, currently, seems to be opposing these structures, despite, or perhaps even because of, their well-entrenched market success.[19] But when we considered industrial farms in terms of their Functional Beauty, we were led to defend the possibility that they can be aesthetically appealing structures. In this sense Functional Beauty has become, in our hands, something very different from what it was to the Marxist visionaries of the early twentieth century, who sought to sweep away the tired and misguided ways of the multitude. In our hands, it may be charged, Functional Beauty has become a fundamentally conservative, bourgeois notion.

It is accurate to say that there is an element of inherent conservatism in the concept of proper function to which we appeal, but the precise nature and implications of this conservatism need careful consideration. First, although our conception of proper function entails that particular individuals cannot simply change or otherwise determine an artefact's function, this does not mean that proper functions cannot change at all. They can, and do, change over time, insofar as the collective treatment of artefacts in the marketplace changes. The example of the Plaza Major illustrates this, in fact: originally it had the proper function of being a royal courtyard, but now it has the proper function of providing a space for civic events. Similar changes can be gleaned, already accomplished or in progress, in the now widespread phenomenon of 'adaptive re-use' of architectural works. To mention just one additional example, in Europe many churches currently face closure due to declining attendance. As a way of preserving these structures, many of which

[19] See Ned Hettinger, 'Carlson's Environmental Aesthetics and the Protection of the Environment', *Environmental Ethics* 27 (2005): 57–76.

have heritage value, they are being converted into art galleries, shopping centres, bagpiping schools, climbing centres, and night clubs, among other things.[20] If these new uses persist long enough, and serve to keep these churches in existence, these structures will take on new proper functions. Proper function as we conceive it, then, is not hidebound: rather, proper function can be dynamic. Changes in proper function, however, occur only as our collective behaviour changes over time.

One might object, however, that this point only serves to underscore the criticism at issue. If our conception of function justifies the claim that these re-used churches no longer have a spiritual function, and truly *are* no more than shopping malls or climbing centres, surely there could be no clearer evidence of the bourgeois character of that conception. Such a conception would manifest the relentless tendency of capitalist society to melt 'all that is solid' and remake it in its own crass image. Functional Beauty, the criticism continues, is perniciously conservative, not in rendering function eternally static, but in preventing it from ever straying from what the common run of humanity wants. As such, Functional Beauty may be viewed as a handmaiden of capitalist culture, and a fundamentally reactionary, rather than progressive, notion.

We agree that, in some cases, our view ascribes Functional Beauty to built structures that are morally problematic. To return to our example of industrial farms, some of these structures may be functionally beautiful if their form is fitting given their function: providing food cheaply and widely. They also may be morally problematic in polluting the environment and harming human health.[21]

[20] Examples include The Paradiso, on Leidseplein in Amsterdam, which is currently a nightclub, and St Paul's Anglican Church at the Crossing, Walsall, UK, now a shopping and conference centre.

[21] See Allen Carlson, 'On Appreciating Agricultural Landscapes', *Journal of Aesthetics and Art Criticism* 43 (1985): 301–12, and Allen Carlson, 'Viljelysmaisemien Esteettinen Arvo Ja Touttavuus' ('Productivity and the Aesthetic Value of Agricultural Landscapes'), in Y. Sepänmaa, and L. Heikkilä-Palo (eds), *Pellossa Perihopeat* (*Fields: The Family Silver*) (Helsinki: Maahenki Oy, 2005), 52–61, revised and in English as Chapter 6 of Allen Carlson,

However, nothing in our view suggests that the fact that they are functionally beautiful entails that we ought not, or cannot, adopt 'progressive' (that is, left-wing) positions towards them. That is, nothing in our view suggests that we ought not, or cannot, protest the prevalence of industrial farms, or object to their having the particular function that they actually do have, because they are functionally beautiful. We might lament that the function of providing food cheaply and widely has been assigned to such structures, or indeed that any structure has such a function, and we may lobby the masses to change their behaviour so as to eliminate it. Such typically progressive attitudes are not incompatible with finding that entity functionally beautiful, given the function that it has.[22]

What the progressive critic ought not to do, on our view, is base her opposition to the structure in question on the specious claim that the structure does not have that function in the first place. She cannot say that industrial farms are not *really* functionally beautiful, since they do not actually have the function of providing food cheaply and widely. For, if providing food cheaply and widely, is, in fact, the reason that industrial farms exist, then that is their proper function, and the insistence that its 'true' function is something else is just wishful thinking. Once again, this point is clearer in the case of artefacts. Many weapons, guns and swords for example, are both functionally beautiful to a high degree and morally problematic in some sense. Some people view an opposition to the use and even to the possession of weapons, such as handguns, as a progressive and morally justified position. Without attempting to settle this question, we can at least observe that it is plausible to think that there is a case that might be made for this view. It is plausible, for example, that someone could argue persuasively that the function served by handguns is odious and ought not to be countenanced. It is not at all plausible, on the

Nature and Landscape: An Introduction to Environmental Aesthetics (New York: Columbia University Press, 2009), 89–105, as well as Hettinger, 'Carlson's Environmental Aesthetics and the Protection of the Environment'.

[22] Carlson, 'On Appreciating Agricultural Landscapes', 312.

other hand, to say that functionally beautiful handguns actually are not functionally beautiful because they do not have the function of causing death and injury. Obviously, producing death and injury is the reason why the handguns that exist now, by and large, have been produced and distributed, and therefore causing death and injury is the proper function of those guns. Functional Beauty, in other words, is as morally neutral as the functions of artefacts are, and sometimes odious artefacts possess it. We do not need to endorse or support the existence, or use, of any object simply because it is functionally beautiful, but it would be an over-reaction to deny that an object is functionally beautiful simply because the object's function discomfits us.[23]

In fact, the progressive's urge to let moral considerations determine the functions of artefacts ought to be tempered by the recognition that such determinations would then be equally available to his politically conservative opponents. For example, say that Jones despises the open-styled, modernist buildings that dominate today's university campuses. A traditionalist about the university, Jones sees its role as preserving eternal verities for a societal elite. Jones objects to these buildings by calling them functionally ugly: the structures that dominate today's campuses do not look apt, he says, for an institution with the aim of preserving eternal verities for a societal elite. Classical forms, Jones insists, are required here and only such forms could restore Functional Beauty to the university. How are we to respond to Jones's claim that contemporary campuses are functionally ugly? Surely, we ought to reject it as resting on a false assumption. For today's campuses do not have the proper function of preserving eternal verities for a social elite. Their proper function today, more likely, is dispensing the technical knowledge needed by a modern skilled workforce, or something along those lines. Of course, Jones is free to argue that it is a bad thing that the function of the university has changed in this way. He is also welcome to lobby us to abandon our support

[23] Cf. Hume's treatment of this issue, as discussed in Chapter 1, Section 2.

of technical education, and to return to supporting the university's traditional project of imparting timeless verities to a social elite. But he cannot simply appeal to this latter function, in the way that previous generations would have understood it, as if it still adequately described the modern university campus. For, if that notion lingers on today's campuses at all, it is, generally, more as a quaint ideal rather than a reflection of reality. One suspects that the progressive, left-wing thinker would be quick to point this out. But if the progressive opponent of industrial farms is free to ascribe her preferred function to those structures, regardless of their actual history, then conservatives such as Jones ought to be allowed their own flights of fancy.

The moral to draw here is that, although Functional Beauty is constrained by that behaviour of the common mass of humanity that determines function, it does not necessarily line up on the centre-right of the political spectrum. Even when it does, an appreciation of this aesthetic quality need not be viewed as foreclosing criticism on the structure or built environment in question. If, after all this, it still is said that the concept of Functional Beauty remains unacceptably bourgeois, then perhaps it is the culture of late capitalism itself, and not any specific concept articulated within it, that ought to answer for the fault.

6.4 Aesthetic Objections: The Problem of Translation

The notion of 'the function of a building' is not the only source of difficulty for Functional Beauty in the context of architecture. Another important obstacle is Scruton's other problem, the Problem of Translation, which we can now address anew in light of what we have argued above. The problem involves scepticism about function being translatable, somehow, into perceptible architectural form. This scepticism is understandable insofar as the relation between function and aesthetic appearance has often been mishandled in discussions of architecture. In some cases, for instance, proponents of Functional Beauty and related ideas assert that there is one, and only one, form that 'fits' a given function, and that the design of the functionalist architect therefore possesses a kind of necessity and inevitability.[24] Critics have sensibly objected that there is no reason to think that only one form can 'fit' a given function: on the contrary, experience teaches us that many different forms can equally fit a given function (housing religious worshippers, say, or facilitating bureaucracy).[25] There seem to be, in other words, multiple ways for function to 'translate' into perceptible form.

But, beyond this, it seems unclear whether function can truly be said to translate into such form at all. Certainly, some forms can be said to 'fit' a building's function in the sense that they allow that function to be carried out effectively. An office building that allows its occupants to carry out their business efficiently can be said to fit its function, for instance. But how does this fact impact upon, or affect, its perceptible appearance, and hence its aesthetic qualities? As we saw in Chapter 2, in answering this question, proponents of Functional Beauty and similar concepts in architecture have often gestured towards notions like 'sincerity', 'authenticity', and 'structural honesty'.[26] According to such ideas, function is thought to 'show up in', or to alter, a building's perceptible appearance when the building 'honestly' reveals its working parts. The nineteenth-century British architect Augustus Pugin, for example, insisted that 'every building that is treated naturally, without disguise or concealment, cannot fail to look well'.[27] The idea here is that the function of a building is 'inscribed'

[24] For a nicely illustrated criticism of this idea, see Brolin, *The Failure of Modern Architecture*, 36f.

[25] A point made by Graham, 'Art and Architecture', 253–4.

[26] We take the phrase 'structural honesty' from Scruton, who uses it in connection with the 'form of functionalism held up by Ruskin as the "Lamp of Truth" '; see Roger Scruton, *The Aesthetics of Architecture* (London: Methuen and Company, 1979), 41. The Ruskin source is *The Seven Lamps of Architecture*.

[27] Augustus Welby Pugin, *An Apology for the Revival of Christian Architecture in England* (London: John Weale, 1843), 39. Cf. Greenough's remark that buildings ought to 'speak of their use'; see Greenough, 'American Architecture', 125, as well as W. T. Stace's view that

in the look of the building just when there are no non-functional elements to cover up its functional parts.

Buildings that are structurally honest certainly look different from buildings that are not. But it remains unclear how we can understand Functional Beauty in terms of structural honesty. For there seem to be many cases where structural honesty in a building does nothing at all to enhance its aesthetic appeal. Scruton points to air terminals, structures whose functional inner parts are typically left exposed, presumably as a cost-saving measure. These structures are 'structurally honest' but not, thereby, more aesthetically appealing.[28] As noted in Chapter 4, Section 3, Francis Sparshott sums up the more general point in remarking that 'if the demand is simply that the supporting members of a building should be left visible, one is at a loss to see what the aesthetic value of this should be'.[29] He concludes that the admiration of structural honesty ought not to be considered an aesthetic matter at all, but rather 'an almost religious feeling that one should be faithful to the nature of the materials one works with, making bricks look as brickish as possible'.[30] Not only has the aesthetic relevance of structural honesty been seen as dubious; it has also been viewed as setting an absurdly didactic ideal for architecture. For the aim of structural honesty seems to mandate buildings whose function is as obvious as possible. As Pugin puts it: 'the style of a building should so correspond with use that the spectator may at once perceive the purpose for which it was erected'.[31]

when architectural elements appear suited to their function, as when columns look able to bear weight, 'conformity to an end' can be 'fused with a perceptual field to give rise to beauty'; see Walter Terence Stace, *The Meaning of Beauty: A Theory of Aesthetics* (London: Richards and Toulmin, 1929), 192.

[28] Scruton, *The Aesthetics of Architecture*, 42. The classical statement of this objection is Scott, *The Architecture of Humanism*.

[29] Francis Sparshott, *The Structure of Aesthetics* (Toronto, Canada: University of Toronto Press, 1963), 68.

[30] Ibid.

[31] Augustus Welby Pugin, *Contrasts: or A Parallel between the Noble Edifices of the Middle Ages, and corresponding Buildings of the Present Day; Shewing the Present Decay of Taste* [1836]

Difficulties such as these have led other theorists sympathetic to Functional Beauty and related ideas to abandon rather crude notions such as structural honesty for the subtler concept of expression. On this account, a building's function 'translates' into its perceptible form, and so into its aesthetic qualities, when its form expresses the idea of its function.[32] This is an attractive view because it is plausible to construe expressiveness as a matter of the look of the building: a building is expressive of the idea of its function when something about its perceptible form conveys that idea.[33] Since a building can express the idea of its function without having its guts splayed open, an appeal to expression avoids the more risible implications of the call for structural honesty. To illustrate this approach, Gordon Graham uses the familiar example of Gothic churches, whose spires reach upward to the heavens. This perceptible quality is expressive of the church's function of spiritual elevation, insofar as it conveys that idea to the observer.[34]

However, expression, like structural honesty, ultimately seems incapable of capturing the sense in which buildings are functionally beautiful, for there are many ways that a building can express its function without thereby enhancing its aesthetic appeal at all. For instance, imagine a train station that was shaped in the form of—that actually looked like—a train. No doubt such a building would be dramatically expressive of its function, in the sense outlined above. But it would not be functionally beautiful because

(London: Charles Dolman, 1841), 1. Cf. Wolfe's lampooning treatment in *From Bauhaus to Our House*, 65.

[32] Buildings can express things apart from their functions, of course, as has been discussed in Nelson Goodman's writings on architecture and expression; see Nelson Goodman, *Languages of Art* (Indianapolis, IN: Bobbs-Merrill, 1968), 90–1, and 'How Buildings Mean', in Nelson Goodman, *Reconceptions in Philosophy and Other Arts and Sciences* (London: Routledge, 1988), 31–48. Our focus here, however, is on the use of expressiveness to explicate the notion of Functional Beauty.

[33] See Graham, 'Art and Architecture', 256: 'How might the form of a building ... express the function it is intended to serve? It is easy enough to say in the abstract how this is to be done—the most striking architectural features must ... convey to the observer the idea of its function'. A similar idea is pursued in Carlson, 'Viljelysmaisemien Esteettinen Arvo Ja Touttavuus' ('Productivity and the Aesthetic Value of Agricultural Landscapes').

[34] Graham, 'Art and Architecture', 256.

of this. In short, when buildings that are expressive of their function are aesthetically pleasing, as in the case of certain Gothic churches, it is not the mere fact that they are expressive of their function that makes them so. In addition, an account of Functional Beauty based upon expression remains open to the charge of being an overly didactic approach to architecture. For, on that account, a building's form expresses its function by 'conveying ideas' that 'connect' to that function. The architectural work, in other words, should announce its function to the observer. Although this need not involve displaying the innards of buildings, it does involve a certain lack of subtlety.

In our view, the phenomenology of Functional Beauty is richer and subtler than these accounts suggest. In Chapter 4, Section 2, we outlined a number of distinct ways in which function can be translated into aesthetic appearance. The first of these involves aesthetic qualities, such as the traditionally recognized quality of 'looking fit', that things possess when the functional category employed to perceive them causes us to see these things as having no contra-standard features at all and as having, to a high degree, certain variable features that are indicative of functionality. The second includes aesthetic qualities like simplicity, gracefulness, or elegance, which functional things possess when the functional category used to perceive them causes them to appear as having no contra-standard or variable features, but only the essential, standard ones. In the third way in which functional categories can affect aesthetic appearance, things appear able to perform their function, but the functional category that we apply in perceiving them causes them to appear as lacking some standard features. In this event, things, by still looking capable of performing their function, may display a pleasing dissonance in their sensory elements. The resulting aesthetic quality may be described as a surprising, even playful 'visual tension'.

These three forms of 'translation' are all ways in which Functional Beauty is evident in architecture and in the built environment more generally. For example, consider the second way in which function can be translated into aesthetic qualities, which involves the 'streamlined appearance' that is perhaps the most familiar sort of Functional Beauty in the modern built environment. By possessing only perceptible features that are standard or essential for its function, a building's form may take on a unity, or, in more extreme cases of parsimony, a kind of elegance. This austere sort of Functional Beauty had a central role in International Modernism as an architectural style. For example, consider the stark elegance of Mies van der Rohe's and Johnson's classic Seagram Building (1958). A similar kind of Functional Beauty is also exemplified in many of the best-designed structures of industrial agriculture.[35] But a building can also be functionally beautiful in the third way outlined above. It can be functionally beautiful by possessing a surprising deficiency in elements, relative to functional category, that produces a visual tension in the object. This is an effect consciously cultivated by some contemporary architects and sometimes associated with so-called 'postmodern' architecture. For instance, it is a common kind of aesthetic quality found in many present-day churches, which are seemingly intentionally designed to appear very 'unchurch'-like and thereby cause a playful, visually interesting dissonance when they are perceived within their functional categories. Finally, buildings can simply 'look fit' for their function, as a fortified castle looks impregnable, or a stadium looks apt for holding public events. It is worth noting that looking fit is different from being 'structurally honest': a building, such as a castle, could look fit without exposing any of its inner workings. Looking fit for a function is also not the same as expressing that function: a train station's looking like a very good train station is not the same as its suggesting or conveying the idea of train travel. It is a matter of its having, to a high degree, those perceptible properties that are indicative of and standard for the functional category 'train station', and lacking perceptible properties that are contra-standard for it.

[35] See Carlson, 'On Appreciating Agricultural Landscapes'.

Our account has a number of important advantages over other attempts at explaining the translation of function into form in the built environment. First, it accords with the observation that there is more than one way to 'realize' function in the aesthetic qualities of an object. Indeed, our account can explain this insight, insofar as it reveals the different forms that Functional Beauty can take. Any single particular account of how a building's function *must* translate into its form will be too thin an account, missing much of the Functional Beauty of buildings. For Functional Beauty encompasses not only the cold elegance of a modernist office tower, but also the playfulness and drama of a postmodern church and the manifest power of a medieval fortress.

Second, our account avoids the charge of setting an overly didactic ideal for architecture. Structural honesty and expression have been derided for demanding a heavy-handed advertisement of the function of buildings: structures must lay bare, or announce, what they are for. Our view, however, does not entail that buildings must in this way expose or advertise their function. On our view, things are functionally beautiful where their perceptual appearances are altered by our knowledge of their function, in the ways just described. Our knowledge of these functions, however, need not be gained from simply looking at the object. This point is clearer when we look at Functional Beauty beyond the context of architecture. There are many specialized machines, such as the X-ray diffraction detector described in Chapter 4, Section 1, for example, whose function cannot be gleaned from perceptible form alone. Yet such machines clearly can be, and frequently are, seen as functionally beautiful by those who understand how they fulfil that function. There is no obvious reason why the Functional Beauty of buildings, and indeed of the entire built environment, should differ in this respect.

One could insist, of course, that moral considerations demand that Functional Beauty in architecture involve an advertising of function.[36] In the first section of this chapter, we noted that one of the chief motivations for advancing the notion of Functional Beauty is the view that the aesthetic quality of a building ought to be aligned with its true nature, and rooted in its 'hidden aspects', such as its function. It is easy to slide from this moderate moral imperative, that the function of buildings be respected in our aesthetic judgements, to a much more radical imperative that these functions be everywhere highlighted for public display. Perhaps the rash embrace of the latter imperative is, in many cases, a well-meant attempt to remind us of the former. In any case, we ought to reject the latter view, as the critics of more heavy-handed functionalist doctrines have pointed out, for there is something unsatisfyingly earnest and restrictive about this view. But we can do this without abandoning the more sensible moral imperative that we appreciate buildings as the sorts of buildings they are, or the concept of Functional Beauty to which that imperative leads us. The appearance of a building may need to align itself with its function, but it need not don a placard and shill for it.

6.5 The Beauty of Ruins

So far we have demonstrated that Functional Beauty, in the forms we have described, is applicable to architecture and to the built environment in general. As we saw in Chapter 4, Section 5, however, our account allows that, in addition to looking fit, and hence aesthetically good, functional things may sometimes look unfit for their function, and so possess an aesthetically negative quality. In general, this aspect of our account seems to fit well with the built environment. Buildings that have, through damage or neglect, acquired properties that interfere with their ability to

[36] See, for example, Andrew Light and Aurora Wallace, 'Not Out of the Woods: Preserving the Human in Environmental Architecture', *Environmental Values* 14 (2005): 3–20, especially 16.

perform their function seem to look poorer for it. Furthermore, we argued in that chapter that this verdict, in general, does not seem to stem from the practical concern about human welfare that we surely all possess. For example, one might know that an abandoned house is now permanently unusable due to mould, water damage, or what have you. Smashing in one additional window would not render it any less useful than it is, since it is currently of no use at all. Yet one could sensibly object that this modification would make it *look* worse, rendering it even more of an eyesore than it already was.

However, we also noted in Chapter 4 that the built environment seems to provide counter-examples to this general trend in the form of ruins. Ruins have been objects of aesthetic appreciation since the eighteenth century, when they were much in vogue as elements in the burgeoning aesthetic trends of the picturesque and sublime.[37] It is probably safe to say that today ruins are no longer as enthusiastically aesthetically appreciated as they once were, and perhaps are admired more as historical curiosities. Nonetheless, it must also be said that they are not generally viewed as aesthetically poor, or ugly, due to their looking unfit for their functions. A visitor to a classical ruin does not need to suffer a shock to her aesthetic faculties in order to expand her historical knowledge. But this is puzzling if our general claim, that looking unfit for function is a negative aesthetic quality, is true. For ruins, by definition, would seem to look unfit for their function. Missing roofs, punctured or crumbling walls, toppled supports: all bespeak a failure to perform basic architectural functions, such as housing inhabitants from the elements. If they look unfit, why do ruins seem to display no evidence of this negative aesthetic quality?

[37] On the aesthetic appreciation of ruins in general, see Robert Ginsberg, *The Aesthetics of Ruins* (Amsterdam: Editions Rodopi, 2004); Donald Crawford, 'Nature and Art: Some Dialectical Relationships', *Journal of Aesthetics and Art Criticism* 42 (1983): 49–58; and Paul Zucker, 'Ruins—An Aesthetic Hybrid', *Journal of Aesthetics and Art Criticism* 20 (1961): 119–30. On the treatment of ruins in the picturesque tradition, see Christopher Hussey, *The Picturesque: Studies in a Point of View* (London: G. P. Putnam's, 1927), 194 ff.

In Chapter 4 we also discussed an analogous concern in relation to certain obviously impractical items of fashion. The solution that we offered in that case was that, when we aesthetically appreciate these objects, we often treat them as non-functional. That is, we abstract away from or 'bracket' their utilitarian functions and enjoy them solely for their so-called formal qualities, such as their colour, shape, and pattern. This sort of abstraction may sometimes occur in the case of ruins as well. One source of interest in ruins within the early picturesque tradition, for example, was the ability of ruins to offer more variegated and complex patterns of light and colour as a subject for the painter.[38] Through their blending of natural and artificial elements, ruins provide formal qualities not typically available either in pure nature or in the built environment.[39] However, this fact does not explain the puzzle of ruins, for the observer who sees nothing aesthetically negative in a ruin is not always abstracting away from its function, even if he sometimes does this. The tourist taking in a classical ruin, for example, certainly does not abstract away from its function during his entire visit. On the contrary, for most of it, he will be viewing it not as an abstract arrangement of lines and colours, but as a ruined house, temple, or whatever.[40] And yet, generally speaking, the ruined structure's apparent lack of

[38] See, for example, William Gilpin, *Three Essays: On Picturesque Beauty, On Picturesque Travel, and On Sketching Landscape* [1792]; see also Zucker, 'Ruins—An Aesthetic Hybrid', 120.

[39] This point is nicely brought out by Crawford, 'Nature and Art', 53.

[40] Sometimes it is remarked that ruins have lost their functions altogether. Crawford, for example, writes that 'often the partial disintegration brings with it the severance of the functioning of the original. A Roman forum is no longer a forum; a Cistercian abbey is no longer an abbey'; see ibid., 53. If this were true, then our problem would simply dissolve, since a damaged item would simply fail to have a function and so there would be no question of its looking unfit for its function. But this is over-stated: surely a ruined forum *is* still a forum, albeit a ruined one, and not merely a heap of stones. This is shown in the fact that we would appreciate a ruined Roman forum and a heap of stones that fortuitously resembled it exactly in very different ways. We might note the poignancy of the collapsed fountain in the ruined forum, for instance, where an indiscernible pile of rocks in the fortuitous heap would have no such property. Crawford's first sentence does express a sound point, which is that a ruin is a structure that is no longer *able to function*, but, when we are dealing with proper functions, this is logically distinct from the claim that the ruin no longer *has a function*.

fitness will not contribute to a negative aesthetic quality in that structure.

The solution to this puzzle, we think, lies elsewhere, in aspects of ruins that have their sources in Romanticism and the sublime. In particular, the expressiveness of ruins seems to explain why their apparently looking unfit fails to translate into an aesthetic flaw. As Donald Crawford puts it, the Romantic approach to ruins holds that 'the ruin stirs the perceiver's sense of the past and awakens associations of mystery'.[41] In their wild union of the human world and the forces of nature, ruins serve as a visual embodiment of ideas, such as the transience of life and the awesome power of nature, that stir sublime feeling. This visual expressiveness is a quality of ruins that still has the power to charm the eye, if not overawe the mind.

One might appeal to this insight concerning the expressiveness of ruins as the basis for a solution to our puzzle by holding that, in looking unfit, ruins *do* possess a negative aesthetic quality, although this quality is not readily apparent because it coexists with an aesthetically positive quality of expressiveness. By way of analogy, consider a dress that has an aesthetically pleasing cheery quality, but that looks unfit due to a rip or tear. It seems plausible to think that, in such a case, one might not notice the unfit look due to the distraction of the cheery quality. In the case of ruins, a similar kind of distraction, due to the expressive qualities of ruins, might explain our failure to notice the aesthetically negative unfit look of the ruin.

It may be objected, however, that this explanation is not decisive. In the case of the ripped dress, even if we do not attend much to the rip, taken as we are with the cheery quality, we surely *could* attend to it on its own. And, if we did, we would surely see that it is an aesthetic flaw. But in the case of ruins, the situation is not so clear. An appreciator of ruins may be distracted from their apparent lack of fitness by their expressiveness, but imagine

[41] Crawford, 'Nature and Art', 54.

that she brackets that expressive quality, and attends to the ruin's apparent lack of fitness on its own. Would she then see that lack of fitness as a negative aesthetic quality, in the same way that the appreciator of the dress sees its rip to be an aesthetic flaw? If we entertained doubts about the claim that looking unfit is a negative aesthetic quality, then this may be doubted also. In other words, it has not yet been conclusively established that a ruin's apparent lack of fitness is a negative aesthetic quality and, if it is not, then our general claim that looking unfit is a negative aesthetic quality remains in question.

To address this problem, we need to consider more closely the idea of aesthetic appreciation of a ruin that successfully brackets the expressive quality of the structure. In the example of the ripped dress, it may be possible to block out the cheerful look of the item by focusing on one small part of it, rather than the whole. Looking just at the flaw, and not at the overall item's shape, colour, and pattern, we lose sight of its cheerfulness. But this sort of bracketing may be more difficult to do in the case of ruins, which are, as it were, thoroughly flawed. Focusing upon one small part of a ruin, rather than the whole, typically does not enable us to lose sight of its expressive qualities since each piece that is broken, worn, or eroded will tend to exude the same expressive qualities as the whole. Therefore, in order to test the hypothesis that the expressive qualities of ruins mask the coexisting aesthetic quality of looking unfit, we need to imagine a scenario in which a ruin's expressive qualities can truly be bracketed: a ruin that has no expressive quality, but only an apparent lack of fitness.

Imagine, then, that a 'new' Mediterranean island, never before observed or mapped, is discovered. On this island is a lost tribe of ancient Greece. The members of this tribe are modern in most ways, with a few exceptions, the most striking of which is that they continue to live in structures of the kind common in Greece 2,500 years ago. Shortly after being discovered, all members of the tribe decamp to see the world. After their departure, however, a minor earthquake damages many of the structures. It is not hard to imagine that, after the earthquake, the unfortunate isle could be exactly indistinguishable from an actual ancient ruin. The only difference between the two cases is that whereas classical ruins, being ancient artefacts produced by the slow passage of time, are expressive of certain ideas, the wreckage of the lost isle is not. The wreck of a classical ruin would express ideas such as the transience of life and the relentless passage of time, for example, while the wreck of the lost isle would not. Many of the buildings of the lost isle may be no older than the condominium developments in any modern city, and none of the buildings on the lost isle have been destroyed by the passage of time. The lost isle provides us, then, with a case of a ruin that looks unfit but truly lacks expressive qualities typical of ruins.

Now what would a tourist to this city, landing after the earthquake, say of its aesthetic character? Surely he would find the manifest dysfunction of its buildings an aesthetic blight upon them. He would say things like 'I paid all this money to come and see these wonderful buildings; what terrible luck' and 'If only I had come a day or two earlier, I could have viewed these buildings in all their glory'. Such comments seem an entirely reasonable response to the situation, and they suggest that the unfit appearance of these buildings, when considered in itself, is an aesthetic flaw. But this unfit appearance is just the same unfit appearance that a visitor to a classical ruin would have passed over with equanimity, when in the presence of the expressive qualities that a genuine ruin possesses. What this example suggests is that ruins, when they do in fact look unfit, are not an exception to the rule that looking dysfunctional is an aesthetic flaw. This flaw is obscured, however, by their expressiveness, which is sufficiently diverting and pervasive to drive all awareness of it from our minds.

7

Artefacts and Everyday Aesthetics

In the previous two chapters, we have shown some ways in which Functional Beauty can be deployed in the aesthetics of natural and built environments. Although neither environment could be said to rival art as an object of philosophical scrutiny, each of these has been given a good deal of attention by aestheticians. In this chapter, we will turn to a domain that, in contrast, remains largely neglected: the realm of 'everyday aesthetics'.[1]

The idea of developing a theory of everyday aesthetics is typically motivated by the notion that the Western aesthetic tradition, at least at this late stage, has produced a skewed account of aesthetic experience. According to the traditional view, aesthetic experience, in its pure or true form, is to be had either in the art gallery or in wilderness, when we are outside the stream of daily life. But these are rather rare, perhaps increasingly rare, forms of experience for most people. In contrast, almost everyone seems to find some pleasure that is prima facie aesthetic in the midst of 'everyday' activities: cooking meals, driving a car, using tools, and so forth.

[1] Recent overviews of everyday aesthetics include Yuriko Saito, 'Everyday Aesthetics', *Philosophy and Literature* 25 (2001): 87–95; Crispin Sartwell, 'Aesthetics of the Everyday', in Jerrold Levinson (ed.), *The Oxford Handbook of Aesthetics* (Oxford: Oxford University Press, 2003), 761–70; and Tom Leddy, 'The Nature of Everyday Aesthetics', in Andrew Light and Jonathan M. Smith (eds), *The Aesthetics of Everyday Life* (New York: Columbia University Press, 2005), 3–22. A number of other relevant articles are collected in the Light and Smith volume, as well as in Pauline von Bonsdorff and Arto Haapala (eds), *Aesthetics in the Human Environment* (Lahti, Finland: International Institute of Applied Aesthetics, 1999), and Arnold Berleant and Allen Carlson (eds), *The Aesthetics of Human Environments* (Peterborough, Canada: Broadview Press, 2007).

Insofar as the picture of our aesthetic lives painted by theory is belied by reality, then, something has gone awry in our theorizing. This line of thought is reinforced by the fact that the segregation of aesthetic experience from practical, daily activities is a rather late development in the West and is absent altogether in many non-Western cultures.[2]

The project of 'everyday aesthetics', typically, is to redress this situation by providing a conception of aesthetic experience that better reflects its pervasiveness. In this chapter, we will discuss the notion of Functional Beauty as it relates to this project. Historically speaking, the functionality of everyday objects has often been considered a major obstacle to viewing them as objects of aesthetic appreciation. Even in current attempts to analyse the aesthetics of everyday things, functionality has received little attention. As we will argue here, however, the concept of Functional Beauty is not only applicable to everyday things, but offers us a more cogent and defensible framework for understanding everyday aesthetics than other current approaches.

7.1 Five Features of Everyday Aesthetic Objects

As a way of setting the stage for a consideration of current views on everyday aesthetics, it will be useful to try to define the scope of this concept. As Tom Leddy has observed, the category of

[2] On the latter point, see Sartwell 'Aesthetics of The Everyday', 765; Saito, 'Everyday Aesthetics', 88; Stephen Davies, 'Non-Western Art and Art's Definition', in Noël Carroll (ed.), *Theories of Art Today* (Madison, WI: University of Wisconsin, 2000), 199–216, especially 201; and Arnold Berleant, *Aesthetics and Environment: Variations on a Theme* (Aldershot, UK: Ashgate, 2005), 108. For example, Berleant claims that 'most historical societies and present-day non-Western ones value experiences that resemble Western experiences of art but range more broadly ... In the former, aesthetic experiences pervade the many regions of life, from practical activities devoted to food gathering and craftsmanship, to ceremonial observances and other social occasions ... we must abandon the ethnocentric assumptions of modern Western aesthetics that restrict art and the aesthetic to the carefully circumscribed objects and occasions of museums, galleries, and concert halls. Art is more inclusive and aesthetic experience far more pervasive than Western aesthetics has allowed, and their forms and appearances exhibit endless variety' (108).

'everyday aesthetics' is a loose one.[3] A rough way of characterizing it is to take it as including any aesthetic appreciation that falls outside the traditional focus areas of art, nature, and architecture. So defined, everyday aesthetics includes our aesthetic appreciation of furniture, clothes, and machines, such as cars, as well as our appreciation of everyday events, such as baseball games or parades.[4] These kinds of appreciative activities are common, although some of them are more common than others. They deserve to be called instances of aesthetic appreciation because they are, first, aesthetic. That is, they involve the pleasing or displeasing perceptual qualities of things, as when we admire the elegant cut of a good suit, or the lovely shape of a well-designed chair. Second, they are cases of appreciation, in that we sometimes, though not always, attempt to size up those objects with an eye to ascertaining the presence or absence of these aesthetic qualities. Some people pay close attention to the aesthetic features of cars, for example, and these features are an important factor in their decisions about purchasing them. The kinds of activities listed above, then, seem uncontroversial cases of aesthetic appreciation, albeit ones that do not involve art, nature, or architecture. Some writers would also include other activities in the category of everyday aesthetics, such as sexual experiences, experiences of our own bodily movements, appreciation of the weather, and experiences of eating and drinking. These cases, however, are rather controversial. We will discuss some of these later in this chapter, but for now we propose to begin by focusing on the aforementioned uncontroversial cases. Our aim is to uncover some of the characteristic features of everyday aesthetic objects, as opposed to works of art, natural objects, and architectural works.

Despite the diversity of the items on our list, we can extract a number of characteristic, if not universally shared, features of everyday things as objects of aesthetic appreciation. The first of

[3] Leddy, 'The Nature of Everyday Aesthetics', 3.

[4] The baseball game example is discussed by Saito, 'Everyday Aesthetics', 89; see our description in Chapter 2, Section 5.

these consists of having some utilitarian function. Consider some of the kinds of items we have introduced in previous chapters, such as furniture, clothing, and machines. Furniture typically has the practical purpose of creating an immediate environment in which we can easily and comfortably sit, sleep, eat, and so on. Pieces of furniture can sometimes be used for decorative, rather than practical ends, as when we keep the piano that no longer works. But, even in cases like this, the item in question clearly has a utilitarian function, even if it no longer fulfils, or is incapable of fulfilling, that function. Clothes are another example, although the function of at least some clothing may be more complex than that of furniture. At a basic level, most items of clothing function as a protective covering, but some possess important expressive or cultural functions as well. Finally, machines are paradigm cases of items with utilitarian functions, even if the appearance of the machine does not always reveal its function upon casual inspection. And even the sorts of large-scale events that fall into the purview of everyday aesthetics, such as ball games and parades, often seem to possess a function, or be 'for something'.

The prevalence of utilitarian function in the objects of everyday aesthetics, while not universal, is important, since many of the other characteristic features of these objects can be derived from this basic feature. For example, as many authors have noted, the objects of everyday aesthetic experience generally are experienced using multiple senses, including touch, taste, and smell. A contrast with art is evident here. At least for more traditional Western art forms, such as painting, sculpture, and music, our engagement with art tends to be through a single sense modality only. But our intercourse with everyday objects is not so simple: we sit on our furniture, are in tactile contact with our clothes and tools, sit in and smell our cars, and so forth. This fact is not surprising, given the utilitarian nature of these items. It is true that, occasionally, overly fastidious people refuse to sit on their furniture, in effect turning their homes into a sort of 'art gallery' where one may look but not touch.[5] But this is an unusual behaviour, and one that is only possible for a small part of one's furniture: one has to sit *somewhere*, after all, if not on the pristine living-room sofa. For clothes and the machines that we employ in the course of our daily activities, this sort of detachment typically is not possible at all.

The functionality of everyday objects also contributes to a third characteristic feature: the lack of determinate boundaries or foci in the objects of everyday aesthetic experience. The functionality of things such as furniture, clothing, and machines puts these things into a multitude of relations to other things in our environment and to that environment itself. This seems to allow us great latitude in deciding what exactly we ought to appreciate.[6] Consider furniture, for instance. A table can be appreciated on its own, as an individual item. But the fact that tables are used for various things often renders this unnatural, and compels us instead to group them with other artefacts: we appreciate the attractiveness of the table and china, or the table as part of an even larger ensemble of objects (table and china cabinet, table and window, and so on). It does not seem strictly necessary to include any of these additional elements in what we appreciate here, but neither does it seem inappropriate to include them.

Functionality also gives rise to two other important features of the aesthetics of the everyday. First, change and impermanence are typical in the aesthetic objects of this realm. Because furniture, clothes, and machines serve practical purposes, they are often replaced, if this is economically or practically feasible, when they become outworn or substandard. Furniture is, traditionally at least, somewhat more durable than clothing or household machinery. But the widespread availability of more affordable furniture made from cheaper materials is eliminating even this distinction as more and more items become disposable. Second, aesthetic objects in the everyday realm tend not to be highly meaningful, relative to other

[5] Cf., Kevin Melchionne, 'Living in Glass Houses: Domesticity, Interior Decoration, and Environmental Aesthetics', *Journal of Aesthetics and Art Criticism* 56 (1998): 191–200.

[6] See Saito, 'Everyday Aesthetics', 89.

sorts of objects of aesthetic appreciation. Contemporary artworks, in particular, are typically taken to be highly charged with meaning, even if the precise nature of that meaning is somewhat obscure in many particular cases. Some philosophers have even taken this meaningfulness to be a part of what makes something art.[7] Be that as it may, the objects of everyday aesthetics seem, on the whole, not to be highly charged with meaning. Some particular artefacts, of course, are highly significant to us as individuals, such as family heirlooms and personal mementos. And some kinds of everyday item may carry a more general significance, such as a very expensive brand of suit or item of jewellery that conveys power and privilege. But, in general, and perhaps increasingly, the furniture, clothes, and equipment that we employ day-to-day is mass produced and fails to express any definite or substantial idea, emotion, or point of view.[8]

To sum up, then, the paradigm objects of everyday aesthetic experience may be characterized as typically utilitarian in nature, involving us in multi-sensory interactions, and lacking determinate boundaries, permanence, and meaning.

7.2 The Deweyean Approach to Everyday Aesthetics

This characterization of everyday aesthetic objects yields an immediate and sharp contrast with the typical conception of aesthetic appreciation derived from the experience of art. For artworks, characteristically, lack all of these features. When we aesthetically evaluate an artwork, we approach an object that is not used for any practical purpose, such as getting to the office or cutting down

[7] Notably Arthur Danto in *The Transfiguration of the Commonplace: A Philosophy of Art* (Cambridge, MA: Harvard University Press, 1981).

[8] Advocates of semiotics may object to this claim, holding that even the most quotidian everyday objects are full of meaning, constituting a 'language' that we (that is, the semiotician) might learn to read. But this view stretches the concept of 'a language' beyond all recognition: on this issue, see Roger Scruton, *The Aesthetics of Architecture* (London: Methuen and Company, 1979), Chapter 7.

trees. As such, we are able to focus on approaching it visually or aurally, rather than also having to handle it, smell it, and so on. This point seems to hold even when artworks involve, or are constituted by, ordinary functional objects. A classic example of this sort of art is Marcel Duchamp's 'ready-made' work *In Advance of the Broken Arm* (1915), which consists of an actual snow shovel hung in an art gallery. Though the object in question here (the shovel) has a utilitarian function, namely moving snow, this function does not result, as it usually would, in our handling or touching the object, since *In Advance of the Broken Arm* is an artwork on display in a gallery and one is not typically permitted to handle artworks on display in a gallery. Rather, our attention is directed to its visually apparent features only.[9]

Furthermore, the situation of the work in the context of a gallery or collection presents us with more or less clear boundaries and foci of attention for the work. We appreciate *In Advance of the Broken Arm* itself, not the shovel and the security alarm next to it, or the gallery door to the left of it. Situation in the gallery also preserves an artwork in its original state, or, if the artist has allowed it to change, in whatever state of flux was intended by the artist. Finally, as just noted, artworks typically possess a meaning that we can attempt, with greater or lesser success, to uncover or decipher. *In Advance of the Broken Arm*, for example, seems to be *about* something, in that sense of 'about' applicable to artworks. Exactly what it is about, or what it 'says' regarding what it is about, are serious questions for art criticism. But, however these questions are answered, *In Advance of the Broken Arm* seems to be interpretable in a sense in which an indiscernible snow shovel in a hardware store just is not.

In all of these ways, artworks contrast sharply with everyday artefacts. If, then, we base our conception of aesthetic appreciation on the paradigm of art, we are apt to entertain serious doubts about

[9] Art historian H. W. Janson describes Duchamp's ready-mades as 'shifting the context of the objects from the utilitarian to the aesthetic'; see H. W. Janson, *History of Art*, 4th edn (Englewood Cliffs, NJ: Prentice Hall, 1991), 763.

the feasibility of an aesthetics of everyday objects. We may decide that the aesthetic appreciation of everyday objects is, in fact, only possible under certain unusual conditions, such as the 'art-gallery' living room described above, contrived to make everyday objects closely resemble artworks. Even if we are more generous and allow that everyday objects can be aesthetically appreciated outside of such highly artificial situations, we will likely find that aesthetic responses to these objects lack the sophistication and depth found in our aesthetic responses to art. For the everyday must seem too fleeting, too nebulous, and too vapid to sustain the rich sort of aesthetic experience that we find in art or nature. The utilitarian nature of everyday objects, in other words, sets up a serious conflict between traditional aesthetic theory and the realm of the everyday.

Given this conflict, how is an aesthetics of the everyday possible? One important answer to this question is that the traditional, art-centred aesthetic theory that generates the conflict ought to be rejected. Although a radical response, it seems to be the predominant one among philosophers sympathetic to the idea of an everyday aesthetics. In its basic form, this response derives from John Dewey's highly influential book *Art as Experience* (1934).[10] In that book, Dewey attempts to re-orient thinking about art and aesthetics, moving it towards the view that art is a certain sort of experience: namely, experience that is intense, unified, and complete.[11] This sort of experience, Dewey holds, is broader in scope than aesthetic experience as traditionally conceived, since it involves all five of our senses rather than only sight and hearing. Also, aesthetic experience on his account is, Dewey claims, active rather than contemplative, as it is on the traditional account. In fact, Dewey finds value in aesthetic experience precisely for its capacity to fully realize and integrate our various capacities in an active state: as such, an aesthetic experience stands as the paradigm of *an*

[10] John Dewey, *Art as Experience* [1934] (New York: Capricorn Books, 1958).

[11] On the role of these qualities in Dewey's conception of aesthetic experience, see Alan Goldman, 'The Aesthetic', in Berys Gaut and Dominic McIver Lopes (eds), *The Routledge Companion to Aesthetics* (London: Routledge, 2001), 181–92, especially 185–6.

experience. In contrast to more traditional conceptions of aesthetic experience, Dewey's brand *can* be had in daily life, and not only in special places where we are isolated from the practical exigencies of daily life, such as the art gallery or museum. Dewey's main theoretical move, in short, is to overcome the aesthetic tradition's fetishization of art objects by shifting the emphasis away from the object of aesthetic appreciation and towards the subject.[12]

From the perspective of everyday aesthetics, Dewey's is an impressive approach. It turns what appear to be weaknesses of everyday objects, as objects of aesthetic appreciation, into strengths. The impermanence and boundless character of everyday objects, for example, seems ideally suited to producing active experience since these features require us to constantly change our attention and actively mark out the limits of what we are appreciating. Also, the fact that we interact more intimately with the objects of everyday life than we do with artworks, not only looking at and listening to them, but actively using, and hence touching, tasting, and smelling, them, makes those objects more suited to multi-sensory aesthetic appreciation. Finally, by emphasizing the way in which our total sensory involvement in the things of everyday life produces the sort of unified, complete, and intense experience worthy of being called *an experience*, Dewey's account appears to explain why aesthetic experience in the everyday realm should be considered a valuable thing, in the same league as our aesthetic experiences of art and nature.

For these reasons, and perhaps others, the broader (that is, multi-sensory) approach to aesthetic appreciation pioneered by Dewey has been articulated and developed, in different ways and to different degrees, by a number of current writers on everyday aesthetics.[13] Some writers have focused on establishing

[12] Richard Shusterman refers to this as 'perhaps Dewey's most central aesthetic theme'; see Richard Shusterman, 'Pragmatism: Dewey', in Gaut and Lopes (eds), *The Routledge Companion to Aesthetics*, 97–106; the quotation is on 102.

[13] For example, Leddy, 'The Nature of Everyday Aesthetics'; Saito, 'Everyday Aesthetics'; Carolyn Korsmeyer, *Making Sense of Taste: Food and Philosophy* (Ithaca, NY: Cornell

the aesthetic credentials of the 'proximal senses': taste, smell, and touch. Emily Brady, for example, argues for 'the legitimacy and importance of smells and tastes in aesthetic appreciation', holding that smells 'can be appreciated as having aesthetic qualities in themselves'.[14] Likewise Carolyn Korsmeyer takes up the sense of gustation, arguing that our experience of tastes can be aesthetic experiences.[15] Other writers, while pursuing more general matters relevant to everyday aesthetics, explicitly accept the idea that aesthetic experience can involve senses other than sight and hearing. Tom Leddy, for example, argues that the Kantian category of 'the agreeable', which he takes to include smells and tastes, ought to be considered a part of everyday aesthetics.[16] And in her survey of the field, Yuriko Saito looks to traditional Japanese culture for 'rich examples of aesthetic experience facilitated by body and mind'.[17]

Thus, we find that the basic Deweyean move—making room for everyday aesthetics by replacing the traditional concept of the aesthetic with a much broader notion—plays a central role in the most prominent attempts at articulating an aesthetics of the everyday. As we will now argue, however, the advantages of this broader conception are purchased at a significant cost.

University Press, 1999b); and Berleant, *Aesthetics and Environment*. Not all of these thinkers would classify themselves as engaged in, or even as endorsing, the project of developing Deweyean themes in aesthetics; our grouping of them is intended only to indicate the presence of such themes, very broadly defined, in their work. Further, although these themes are evident in their work, they are not necessarily affirmed without reservation. For example, in spite of the similarities between many of Dewey's ideas and Berleant's participatory engagement model of aesthetic appreciation, Berleant associates Dewey more closely with what he calls the 'active model' of appreciation, from which he attempts to somewhat distance his own account; see *Aesthetics and Environment*, 6. Similar themes are developed in David Novitz, *Boundaries of Art* (Christchurch, New Zealand: Cybereditions, 2001).

[14] Emily Brady, 'Sniffing and Savoring: The Aesthetics of Smells and Tastes', in Light and Smith (eds), *The Aesthetics of Everyday Life*, 156–76; the quotation is on 177.

[15] Korsmeyer, *Making Sense of Taste*, see especially 107.

[16] Leddy, 'The Nature of Everyday Aesthetics', 7.

[17] Saito, 'Everyday Aesthetics', 90.

7.3 The Linguistic Practice Argument

One difficulty with the Deweyean approach to the aesthetics of the everyday involves a distinction commonly drawn in aesthetic theory. Traditional aesthetic theories are almost univocal in insisting upon a fundamental difference in kind between aesthetic pleasures and pleasures that are merely 'bodily', such as the pleasure of a warm bath, the pleasure of eating an apple, or sexual gratification. Such theories insist, that is, that there is a difference *in kind* between the aesthetic enjoyment of seeing a lover's face and the bodily enjoyment of engaging in sexual relations with that person, even if these distinct pleasures can sometimes occur in conjunction with one another.[18] In many aesthetic theories, this distinction is secured by the ancient practice of restricting aesthetic experience to the so-called 'distal' senses of sight and hearing.[19] In contrast, the proximal senses of taste, smell, and touch, which register things close to, or in contact with, our bodies, are held to be sources of bodily, but not aesthetic, pleasure.[20]

The traditional distinction between the aesthetic pleasures, associated with the distal senses, and the bodily pleasures of the proximal senses maps on to a fundamental phenomenological difference between the proximal and distal senses: the fact that the pleasures of the proximal senses are typically felt as bodily sensations, whereas the pleasures associated with the distal senses are not. The beauty or elegance of a painted portrait, for example, is

[18] See, for example, Jerrold Levinson's overview in 'What is Aesthetic Pleasure?', in *The Pleasures of Aesthetics: Philosophical Essays* (Ithaca, NY: Cornell University Press, 1996), 3–10. Although aesthetic pleasure is not often a focus in philosophical discussions of pleasure, it is typically classed with the 'higher' pleasures and so distinguished from bodily pleasures on these grounds; see, for example William P. Alston, 'Pleasure', in Paul Edwards (ed.), *The Encyclopedia of Philosophy* (New York: Macmillan, 1964), Vol. 6, 341–7, especially 341.

[19] The *Greater Hippias* considers, as a definition of beauty, 'what we enjoy through our senses of hearing and sight'; see Plato, *Greater Hippias* [approx. 390 BCE], 298a, trans. B. Jowett, in K. Aschenbrenner and A. Isenberg (eds), *Aesthetic Theories: Studies in the Philosophy of Art* (Englewood Cliffs, NJ: Prentice-Hall, 1965), 3–17.

[20] An excellent, albeit ultimately unsympathetic, review of this traditional line of thought can be found in Korsmeyer, *Making Sense of Taste*, Chapter 1.

a quality that appears to the appreciator, phenomenologically, as residing *in* the painting, and the pleasure that is experienced in viewing the painting, whatever the precise nature of that pleasure may be, is not directly felt in any particular region of the appreciator's body.[21] The same is true of pleasure taken in sounds that we hear, as in music. Contrast these cases with the pleasure of taking a warm bath, smelling a pleasant fragrance, tasting a piquant sauce, or engaging in sexual intercourse. In these cases, the pleasure is felt directly in more or less localized regions of the body. This phenomenological difference is one aspect of the traditional distinction between aesthetic and bodily (that is, non-aesthetic) pleasures.[22]

The broad conception of aesthetic experience that serves as the centrepiece of the Deweyean approach to everyday aesthetics, however, seemingly obliterates the distinction between aesthetic and merely bodily pleasures, since on that conception aesthetic pleasure can arise, not only through sight and hearing, but through any of the senses, and, apparently, through any sort of activity whatever (so long, perhaps, as that activity produces experiences with the right features, such as unity and intensity). Thus, the pleasures of exercising, taking a bath, drinking lemonade, or engaging in sexual activity may all count, at least in certain cases, as aesthetic pleasures, on the Deweyean approach.[23]

[21] Santayana, famously, went so far as to define beauty as 'pleasure regarded as the quality of a thing'; see George Santayana, *The Sense of Beauty* [1896] (New York: Collier, 1961), 31.

[22] There have been other suggestions as to the basis of this distinction, notably Scruton's idea that it rests on the fact that pleasures taken in sight and hearing are intentional (that is, directed at an object), whereas pleasures taken in the proximal senses are not; see Scruton, *The Aesthetics of Architecture*, 71–4, 112–14. For a somewhat inconclusive criticism of the second part of Scruton's claim, see Barbara Savedoff, 'Intellectual and Sensuous Pleasure', *Journal of Aesthetics and Art Criticism* 43 (1985): 313–15. See also Korsmeyer, *Making Sense of Taste*, 110; and Richard Shusterman, 'Aesthetic Experience: From Analysis to Eros', *Journal of Aesthetics and Art Criticism* 64 (2006): 217–30, especially 225.

[23] On physical activity, see Barbara Montero, 'Proprioception as an Aesthetic Sense', *Journal of Aesthetics and Art Criticism* 64 (2006): 231–42; as well as the work by Shusterman on what he calls 'somaesthetics': for example, Richard Shusterman, 'The Somatic Turn' and 'Somaesthetics and the Body/Media Issue', in *Performing Live* (Ithaca, NY: Cornell University Press, 2000a), 137–81, as well as 'Somaesthetics and *The Second Sex*: A Pragmatist Reading of a Feminist Classic', *Hypatia* 18 (2003): 106–36, and 'Somaesthetics and Care of

It may be wondered if this is a fair generalization about the views of current writers on everyday aesthetics. It may be thought that these writers differ in the extent to which they are willing to expand the category of the aesthetic to include bodily pleasures. Certainly, some writers openly advocate including all bodily pleasure, including sexual pleasure, in the category of the aesthetic.[24] But others' views are less clear. Some writers, for instance, do not dwell on examples like sexual activity, or taking a warm bath, focusing instead on more plausibly aesthetic cases, such as tasting and smelling. However, the broad conceptions of 'aesthetic' that these writers employ make it difficult to avoid the conclusion that even the pleasures of sex and warmth can be aesthetic. The reason for this is that the characteristics that these theorists offer as justification for the label 'aesthetic' in the cases of taste and smell can easily be found in these other pleasures as well. Brady, for example, argues that taste and smells can be aesthetic because they display an internal complexity or structure, and because 'we can identify, individuate, select and revisit smells and tastes; they can be localized and specified'.[25] Towards a similar conclusion, Korsmeyer asserts that the eating of a tangerine, so meticulously described by author M. F. K. Fisher, 'is classically "aesthetic" because it is pleasurably reflective and gratuitous'.[26] Korsmeyer also argues that gustatory tastes can lay claim to the label 'aesthetic' because, as she argues compellingly, they can have rich and complex meanings associated with them.[27] The characteristics of smell and taste

the Self: The Case of Foucault', *The Monist* 83 (2000b): 530–53. In the latter, he defines somaesthetics as 'the critical, meliorative study of the experience and the use of one's body as a locus of sensory-aesthetic appreciation (aisthesis) and creative self-fashioning' (532). On sexual activity, see Shusterman, 'Aesthetic Experience', as well as Arnold Berleant, 'The Sensuous and the Sensual in Aesthetics', in Arnold Berleant, *Re-thinking Aesthetics: Rogue Essays on Aesthetics and the Arts* (Aldershot, UK: Ashgate, 2004), 73–81, and 'Getting Along Beautifully: Ideas for a Social Aesthetic', in Berleant, *Aesthetics and Environment*, 147–61.

[24] See the relevant work by Shusterman and Berleant cited in the previous note.

[25] Brady, 'Sniffing and Savouring', 184.

[26] Korsmeyer, *Making Sense of Taste*, 107. Fisher describes her experience in M. F. K. Fisher, *Serve it Forth* (San Francisco: North Point Press, 1989), 31–2.

[27] See Korsmeyer's *Making Sense of Taste*, Chapter 4, as well as her 'Food and the Taste of Meaning', in von Bonsdorff and Haapala (eds), *Aesthetics in the Human Environment*,

noted by these authors are important and their discussions certainly illuminate the nature and value of smells and tastes. However, sexual activity can display these very same features: sexual pleasures can be localizable and specifiable, pleasurably reflective, gratuitous, meaningful, and so forth. If so, then the broad conceptions of the aesthetic employed by these authors really entail that any bodily pleasure, including sexual pleasure, can be aesthetic, at least in certain cases.

This, however, seems to us a *reductio ad absurdum* of their conception of the aesthetic, since it is hard to imagine anyone, apart from a diehard adherent to such conceptions, wanting to group together sexual pleasures and the traditionally aesthetic ones (that is, those of sight and hearing). We think it apparent, that is, that current linguistic usage does not classify bodily pleasures, such as those due to warm baths and sexual intercourse, even when those pleasures are complex, specifiable, and meaningful, with the pleasures of listening to Bach or gazing on the *Mona Lisa*. 'Current linguistic usage' is a misleading phrase here, in fact, since the point is an ancient one. In the *Greater Hippias* (390 BCE), Socrates defends the exclusion of the proximal senses from his provisional definition of beauty by saying that:

> everyone would laugh at us if we said that it is not pleasant to eat, but beautiful, or that a pleasant smell is not pleasant, but beautiful; and as to sexual intercourse, everyone would contend against us that it is most pleasant, while admitting that it ought to be enjoyed only where there is none to see because it is a disgraceful and repulsive sight.[28]

Socrates' claim that people find the sight of lovemaking repulsive may seem puritanical to some.[29] In any case, it is irrelevant,

90–105, and 'Delightful, Delicious, Disgusting', *Journal of Aesthetics and Art Criticism* 60 (2002): 217–25. Cf. Levinson, 'What is Aesthetic Pleasure?', 333.

[28] Plato, *Greater Hippias*, 299a. This same point can be found in historical sources as divergent as Aquinas, *Summa Theologiae* [1265–74], Denis Diderot, 'The Beautiful' [1752], and G. W. F., Hegel, *Lectures on Fine Arts* [1835].

[29] As evidence, one may be tempted to point here to Western cultures' widespread indulgence in pornography, or even to the pervasiveness of less explicit lovemaking scenes

since whether the *sight* of lovemaking can be accurately described using 'beautiful' or some other aesthetic term, it seems clear that the pleasurable sensations generated by participating in it cannot. People can and do describe sexual pleasures, though not, conventionally, in polite conversation, but 'beautiful' or 'aesthetically pleasing' are not terms that arise naturally in such contexts. This point of linguistic usage indicates that the 'person on the street' is loath to lump the pleasures of vision and hearing together with the pleasures of the body.

This conclusion about our conceptual framework has been challenged by some writers. Frank Sibley, for example, asserts that our use of the word 'beauty' is a poor guide to how far we extend the concept of the aesthetic. Consequently, 'arguments based on this', Sibley says, 'do not impress'. For:

> They seem to assume that 'beautiful' and 'ugly' are the prime or only terms of aesthetic admiration or condemnation. But unless one stipulates this usage by fiat, it is far from true. Not all aesthetically satisfactory things are beautiful, or all aesthetically unsatisfactory things ugly.[30]

Sibley is willing to concede that we do not apply 'beautiful' and 'ugly' to bodily pleasures. But he insists that we may, and in the case of tastes and smells, do, apply *other* aesthetic terms to the bodily pleasures. Sibley provides a long list of such terms: he maintains that when we say that a smell is fresh or summery, for example, this is an attribution of an aesthetic term to the pleasure. This means that, in applying such a term, we are implicitly grouping it together with pleasures of the eye and ear in the more general category of aesthetic pleasures.

Sibley's point that our aesthetic vocabulary extends far beyond 'beauty' and 'ugliness' is certainly well taken, and no one has

in popular film. These cases do not refute Socrates' claim, however, since these are representations of lovemaking rather than instances of it, and it is clear that representations of repulsive sights sometimes can be beautiful or otherwise aesthetically pleasing.

[30] Frank Sibley, 'Tastes, Smells, and Aesthetics', in *Approach to Aesthetics: Collected Papers on Philosophical Aesthetics*, ed. John Benson, Betty Redfern, and Jeremy Roxbee Cox (Oxford: Oxford University Press, 2001), 207–55; the quotation is on 243.

investigated this extension more comprehensively than he has. But, even taking this insight into account, his denial of the claim that our linguistic practice reveals a conceptual distinction between bodily pleasures and the pleasures of eye and ear is unconvincing. For, even if Sibley is right that 'beautiful' can no longer be viewed as a generic term that applies to anything that is aesthetically pleasing, there are other such generic terms: 'aesthetically pleasing', for one, obviously, or Sibley's own 'aesthetically satisfactory' for another. If the same concept of aesthetic pleasure that we apply in cases of vision and hearing really is being applied in our descriptions of smells, tastes, and other bodily pleasures, as Sibley asserts it is, then the term 'aesthetically pleasing' ought to be applicable to these bodily pleasures, even if 'beauty' is not. But this is not the case. It would be just as awkward to describe a warm bath or a sexual experience as 'aesthetically pleasing' as it would be to call it 'beautiful', if not more so.[31] It seems clear that it would never occur to anyone to employ such a description unless they were in the grip of a philosophical theory aimed at obtaining aesthetic credentials for bodily pleasures. More to the point, even if it *were* to occur to someone to use these descriptions, they would still remain inapt descriptions—ones that could be applied only with a certain amount of linguistic strain or unnaturalness.

7.4 Assessing the Linguistic Practice Argument

The proponent of what we have quite roughly characterized as the 'Deweyean conception of the aesthetic' may respond to the present argument, which we might call the 'linguistic practice argument', in another way. She may accept the argument and

[31] This point seems to indicate that the unusual cases where 'beautiful' is used in connection with the proximal senses are instances of the non-aesthetic sense that we noted in Chapter 1, Section 1. Korsmeyer remarks that some tastes are called 'beautiful', for example; see *Making Sense of Taste*, 106, n. 6. Sibley says the same about some smells, in 'Tastes, Smells, and Aesthetics'. In these cases, it seems that 'beautiful' means no more than 'good' or 'excellent', or is given a non-literal usage similar to that in which scenic natural views are sometimes called 'works of art'.

its conclusion, but remain unmoved. She may ask: why, after all, must we be beholden to the conceptual distinctions of the vulgar, or, as philosophers like to say, the 'folk'?[32] Philosophy, after all, involves more than just the documenting of our conceptual framework. If some parts of that framework turn out, under scrutiny, to be arbitrary or unjustified, then philosophers ought to recommend revising them. Perhaps, this line of thought continues, the distinction between aesthetic and bodily pleasures is one of those parts of our conceptual framework in need of renovation.

Along these lines, Korsmeyer, who recommends that we admit pleasures of gustation as aesthetic, writes that cleaving to the traditional distinction that excludes them is only a 'sort of stubbornness' that 'is immune to argument and simply stipulates sensory limits to aesthetic experience'.[33] Indeed, the proponents of a Deweyean expansion of our conception of the aesthetic suggest potential benefits to be obtained from such a move. Arnold Berleant says that 'instead of making aesthetic experience a "spiritual" communion of "kindred souls", effete and insubstantial', a multi-sensory approach will reveal it to be 'experience perhaps more fundamental, vital, and intrinsically significant than any other'.[34] Brady suggests that recognizing the aesthetic significance of smells and tastes will improve our overall aesthetic sensitivity, opening up 'the possibility of more intimate aesthetic experience of our everyday environment and the possibility of finding more meaning in it'.[35] And Richard Shusterman, embracing the conclusion that sexual

[32] Cf., Plato, *Greater Hippias*: 'When we say this, Hippias, [a hypothetical opponent] would probably rejoin: "I too, understand that you are and have been ashamed to say that these pleasures are beautiful, because that is not the common view; but my question was, what is beautiful, not what the mass of men think it to be"' (299a–b).

[33] Korsmeyer, *Making Sense of Taste*, 107. Cf. Coleman's remark that 'What I need... is a *reason* for not speaking of a beautiful odor or taste. I do not need to be reminded that English-speaking people generally avoid such expressions'; see Francis J. Coleman, 'Can a Smell or a Taste or a Touch be Beautiful?', *American Philosophical Quarterly* 2 (1965): 319–24, the quotation is on 320.

[34] Berleant, 'The Sensuous and the Sensual in Aesthetics', 190.

[35] Brady, 'Sniffing and Savouring', 190.

experience can be aesthetic, holds that his view 'can inspire us to greater aesthetic appreciation of our sexual experience and, consequently, to more artistic and aesthetically rewarding performance in our erotic behaviour'.[36] With such benefits lying in store, we well may conclude that we have nothing to lose, and much to gain, in abandoning the hoary distinction between the aesthetic and bodily pleasures, entrenched as it may be.

But this would be an incorrect assessment. For claims as to the benefits of this conceptual rejigging are highly speculative, as is shown by the fact that its boosters do not make any serious attempt to justify them. In fact, it is an open question whether obliterating this aspect of our conceptual framework would make our experience more vital, render it more meaningful, or improve our 'performance'. Furthermore, we ought to recall that the aspect of our conceptual framework at issue is not an arbitrary or completely unfounded one: it rests on a real phenomenological difference between the pleasures of the distal and proximal senses: namely, the fact that pleasures of the proximal senses are localized in the body in a way that those of the distal senses are not. Most philosophers seem to accept the reality of this difference, although Sibley once again is a notable exception.

Consider, however, Sibley's grounds for rejecting the difference. Sibley concedes that the senses of smell and taste involve some bodily sensations, but restricts these to what he calls 'physical sensations' caused by certain substances that draw attention to the nose or tongue: the stinging due to spicy foods or the itching caused by snuff, for instance.[37] Sibley's view seems to be that tastes and smells 'proper' (the flavour of sugar, or the smell of a rose) are not experienced as localized in the body at all, but are simply apprehended in the same 'disembodied' way that colours and sounds are.[38] But this seems false. The taste of sugar or the smell of a rose may not draw our attention to the tongue or nose

[36] Shusterman, 'Aesthetic Experience', 227.

[37] Sibley, 'Tastes, Smells, and Aesthetics', 214.

[38] Ibid., 220.

in the urgent way that a stinging or an itching does, but these qualities remain localizable in the body in the sense that, if we introspect on those parts of our bodies, the taste or smell becomes clearer and its qualities become more evident. This is not true of colours and sounds: introspecting on one's eyes and ears does not cause colours or sounds to become clearer or more evident: on the contrary, it distracts us from, and obscures, those qualities. Perhaps for reasons such as these, even philosophers who oppose the conceptual distinction between pleasures of the proximal and distal senses seem to acknowledge that this phenomenological difference between them is a real difference.[39]

But if it is a real difference, then the present response to the linguistic practice argument, namely, that the long-standing conceptual distinction between aesthetic and bodily pleasure can simply be ignored in theorizing about aesthetic experience, is cast in a different light. For we might, in that case, view the traditional distinction between aesthetic and bodily pleasure as one that rests on a real feature of lived experience, one sufficiently important to keep that distinction in place across many generations. In other words, the fact that this distinction has formed a part of our common linguistic practice since ancient times speaks for its significance and in favour of our recognizing it in our philosophical theorizing. So, in asking whether we ought to reject or respect the folk distinction between aesthetic and bodily pleasure, we need to weigh this significance against the potential for 'enhanced performance', increased vitality, and the like. When the issue is considered in this context, it is far from clear that there is 'nothing to lose', as it were, in simply disregarding the traditional distinction.

Proponents of the Deweyean conception of the aesthetic do have a response to this line of thought, however. They can respond that

[39] Korsmeyer writes that 'judgments of gustatory taste are reports of how one's body reacts or feels when certain substances are taken into the mouth. This claim refers to the fact that taste qualities are phenomenally subjective. While yellow, loud and square are qualities perceived to be in the objects to which such adjectives are predicated, sweet, lemony, and spicy are qualities perceived to be in the tongue of the taster. This claim is true.' See Korsmeyer, *Making Sense of Taste*, 99, see also 3.

the continued existence of the traditional folk distinction between aesthetic and bodily pleasure does not, in fact, reveal the existence of any significance or meaning in that distinction. Rather, they might maintain, the continued existence of that distinction ought to be explained by something other than significance or meaning in the distinction itself. Supporters of the Deweyean approach have suggested that we ought to explain this persistence of the distinction as the product of the influence of certain philosophical or intellectual traditions. On this view, it is this influence, and not any real significance or importance in the distinction itself, that has caused people to describe and categorize their pleasures in accord with the distinction. In particular, this influence is what has caused them to use different terms for bodily and aesthetic pleasure. We can sum up this response, then, as the view that we ought not to give any weight to the practice of the folk on this matter because these practices do not reflect 'true judgement', on the part of the folk, concerning what concepts or conceptual distinctions are significant or worthy. Rather, these folk practices themselves have arisen only because of the corrupting influence of philosophical tradition.

Along these lines, Korsmeyer remarks 'that smells and tastes are not the contents of "typical" aesthetic judgements is indisputable, indeed overdetermined, for the sense hierarchy pervades our conceptual frameworks'.[40] The 'sense hierarchy', which elevates the distal senses over the proximal, is then traced back to the influential writings of thinkers such as Plato and Aristotle. Shusterman makes a similar point in his comment that 'the aesthetic neglect of sex is not primarily the fault of today's philosophers, whose thinking largely reflects the entrenched presuppositions of our intellectual heritage and our enduring cultural traditions'.[41] If such views as

[40] See Korsmeyer, *Making Sense of Taste*, 106.

[41] Shusterman, 'Aesthetic Experience', 225. Berleant claims that 'the restraining hand of the moral censor, gloved in metaphysical doctrine, is still a powerful force in aesthetic theory, an influence which exhibits itself in this commonly observed distinction'; see Berleant, 'The Sensuous and the Sensual in Aesthetics', 185. And Sibley remarks that 'there

to the true explanation of the folk distinction between aesthetic and bodily pleasure are correct, then, in determining whether we ought to continue to endorse the distinction, we ought to simply disregard the fact that the folk distinction has persisted for so long. For, rather than a true indication of some significance in the distinction itself, its persistence is merely an artefact due to other influences. The contention, in other words, is that the linguistic argument does nothing to justify a continued distinction between the aesthetic and bodily pleasures.

This line of thought is seductive, but it seems to us that the case for it is not persuasive. In fact, it is highly implausible to claim, as these theorists do, that the distinction between aesthetic and bodily pleasure is a product of elements of the Western philosophical or intellectual tradition, rather than a genuine response to lived human experience. The proponents of this claim offer little in the way of empirical support for it. Yet the claim is plainly an empirical one, with observable consequences. One of those observable consequences is that, in cases where philosophical and intellectual traditions vary radically from our own, as they do in non-Western cultures, the distinction between the two sorts of pleasure that is characteristic of Western culture will be absent, or, at least, greatly attenuated. However, inspection of the linguistic practices of non-Western cultures shows little indication that this is the case.

Consider, for example, two cultures very different from our own in philosophical and intellectual traditions, those of China and Turkey. In Chinese, as in English, the term for beauty ('mei') is distinct from the terms commonly applied to pleasures ('kuaiyi', for example): a description of the pleasure of a warm bath using 'mei' is strained in the same way that an English description of the pleasure of a warm bath using 'beautiful' is

has often been a kind of puritanical or high-minded metaphysics or morality at work marking off the so-called higher interests and pleasures from the so-called lower and more animal ones which, as an initial *parti pris*, may have inhibited serious philosophical inquiry in these "baser" matters'; see Sibley, 'Tastes, Smells, and Aesthetics', 212.

strained. In Turkish, the term for beauty, 'guzel', is likewise not naturally applied to bodily pleasures, which are denoted by 'zevk'. If the linguistic practice of distinguishing aesthetic and sensual pleasure 'reflects the entrenched presuppositions of our intellectual heritage and our enduring cultural traditions', as Shusterman puts it, rather than some other causal factor, then one would expect that where those presuppositions are absent their effect—namely, this distinction—ought to be absent also. If it is not, we must conclude that there are some other factors capable of producing this same effect. The fact that the distinction between aesthetic and bodily pleasure persists in cultures, such as those of China and Turkey, where these presuppositions are not in place suggests that it is not, in fact, solely a product of those presuppositions.

Our evidence is selective and anecdotal, of course, which reflects the fact that evidence of this kind, requiring a native speaker's insight into the conceptual distinctions embodied in a language, is difficult to come by. But, at the very least, our examples highlight the fact that empirical evidence is necessary to justify the sweeping claim that cultural or philosophical tradition is wholly responsible for the folk distinction between the pleasures of the proximal and distal senses. In the absence of such evidence, it seems reasonable to conclude that the continued existence of this distinction does, in fact, speak in favour of its significance and utility.

We could go on to ask what precisely it is about human experience that this distinction captures, or what function of the distinction has rendered it significant for people in so many cultures and ages. This is a large question, and an important one.[42] Our purposes, however, do not require us to pursue this issue here. All we have meant to establish is that the distinction is a robust and important one, and as such constitutes part of the 'data' that

[42] A classic attempt to address this question is Friedrich Schiller's claim that the aesthetic occupies a 'middle space' between the wholly selfish pleasures of the body and wholly selfless dictates of duty, a space that Schiller called 'a third joyous realm of play and of appearance'; see Friedrich Schiller, *On the Aesthetic Education of Man* [1794], trans. Reginald Snell (Mineola, NY: Dover, 2004), 137.

any attempt to mark out the scope of aesthetic experience ought to recognize. But, if this is the case, the investigation of everyday aesthetics needs to look away from bodily pleasure, and towards a different direction.

7.5 Functional Beauty as an Everyday Aesthetic

Although the broader conception of the aesthetic suggested by Dewey's approach has its appeal, the flight into sensuality characteristic of so much contemporary writing on the topic of everyday aesthetics seems driven, ultimately, by a particular underlying analysis of the theoretical situation. This analysis was described at the start of Section 2 above, and can be summed up as the view that it is not possible to locate a context or framework for aesthetic appreciation of the everyday that is similar to the kind provided for the aesthetic appreciation of art by the social institution referred to as 'the artworld'. In cultural accounts of the appreciation of art, the conventions, norms, and practices of the artworld provide a rich context in which the sophisticated and complex forms of aesthetic appreciation that we associate with the arts can take shape. To borrow a phrase from George Dickie, the artworld embeds artworks in a determinate 'matrix of conventions' that guides and shapes aesthetic appreciation.[43] Objects in the 'everyday world', in contrast, lack any such matrix of conventions for aesthetic appreciation. Rather, they are left adrift on all of the various currents and eddies of human life. The belief that the project of finding some relatively determinate framework for everyday appreciation is futile makes the turn towards bodily experience compelling.

However, we suggest that this project need not be seen as futile, if we re-orient our thinking about everyday aesthetics towards the notion of function. Despite the prominence of utilitarian functionality as a characteristic feature of the everyday, contemporary

[43] George Dickie, *Art and the Aesthetic: An Institutional Analysis* (Ithaca, NY: Cornell University Press, 1974), 199.

writers on everyday aesthetics have found this concept to be of surprisingly little significance. Often the concept receives no explicit treatment at all. Even when it is considered, it tends to be viewed only as a feature that can facilitate our multi-sensory engagement with artefacts. Yuriko Saito, for example, says that ignoring the utilitarian function of an object such as a knife would 'compromise its aesthetic value by unduly limiting various sensory inputs which are all integrated into our everyday experience of this object'. She writes: 'The aesthetic value of a knife consists not only of its visual qualities and its feel in my hand, determined by its surface texture, weight and balance, but, most importantly, by how smoothly and effortlessly I can cut an object with it.'[44] Functionality here is not viewed as an integral component of aesthetic value, but only as a happy source of additional bodily pleasures that we experience when we use the item: smooth movements of our limbs, pleasing tactile sensations, and so on.

However, if we consider function in its own right, instead of viewing it through the lens of sensualist approaches to the aesthetic, we may find it offers a fresh, and more fruitful, approach to the aesthetic of the everyday. For proper function seems to us a notion that serves to embed virtually all everyday objects in a determinate 'matrix of conventions' that can guide and shape their aesthetic appreciation. We have argued in Chapter 4 that our understanding of the proper function of everyday objects, such as cars, construction cranes, and chairs, allows us to perceive the presence or absence of certain aesthetic qualities, such as elegance, or the quality of looking fit, in those objects. Also, we have shown in Chapter 3 that proper function is a determinate notion: although everyday objects, unlike artworks, are not isolated from the normal course of human life, their proper function is more or less fixed by their history and is not affected by the changing circumstances that swirl around them. In fact, if one were to compare proper functions with 'artworld' conventions, one might argue that the

[44] Saito, 'Everyday Aesthetics', 91–2.

former are the more entrenched and determinate, for, as is well known, the institutionality of the artworld and the stability of its conventions have frequently been called into question.[45] In any event, by providing a relatively determinate context that can ground aesthetic appreciation, the concept of function offers an alternative to the standard Deweyean approaches to everyday aesthetics.

An aesthetics of the everyday oriented around the notion of Functional Beauty also offers a number of important advantages over Deweyean approaches. First, unlike the latter, an approach based on Functional Beauty allows us to maintain the classical distinction between the bodily and aesthetic pleasures. If the linguistic argument presented and defended in the previous two sections is compelling, as we have argued it is, then maintaining this distinction is a constraint upon any acceptable theory of everyday aesthetic appreciation. Functional Beauty, as we have outlined it, involves an object's having aesthetic properties in light of our knowledge of its function. Nothing in this concept of Functional Beauty requires abandoning the traditional restriction of aesthetic pleasure to the distal senses.

A second advantage of a Functional Beauty-based approach is that, like the Deweyean approach, it can also view our use of everyday objects as contributing to and facilitating our aesthetic appreciation of them. As described in Section 2 above, this is one of the chief strengths of the Deweyean view: it describes aesthetic appreciation of everyday objects in such a way that our use of those objects serves to facilitate and stimulate aesthetic appreciation, rather than to obstruct and dampen it. Our account, however, does the same, but in a different way. Where the Deweyean

[45] Discussions of the institutional theory of art concerning the institutional status of the artworld can be found in early critiques such as Monroe Beardsley, 'Is Art Essentially Institutional?', in Lars Aagaard-Mogensen (ed.), *Culture and Art* (Atlantic Highlands, NJ: Humanities Press, 1976), 194–209, and Jeffrey Wieand, 'Can There Be an Institutional Theory of Art?', *Journal of Aesthetics and Art Criticism* 39 (1981): 409–17, as well as in several of the essays in Robert J. Yanal (ed.), *Institutions of Art: Reconsiderations of George Dickie's Philosophy* (University Park, PA: Pennsylvania State University Press, 1994).

approach holds that our use of everyday objects facilitates aesthetic appreciation by getting us to touch, smell, and so on, our approach holds that the use of everyday objects facilitates aesthetic appreciation by drawing our attention to the function of those objects, and so to their Functional Beauty.

Third, an approach to everyday aesthetics based on function is better positioned than Deweyean approaches to address perennial criticisms concerning the lack of depth or substance in aesthetic appreciation of the everyday. As we noted in Chapter 2, Section 5, aesthetic appreciation of everyday objects is often taken to be characterized by a thoroughgoing relativism, in contrast to art appreciation. That is, though it may be intuitive to think of there being better and worse, or more and less correct, judgements about the aesthetic value of portraits or sonatas, it is harder to think of there being better and worse, or more and less correct, judgements when it comes to the aesthetic appeal of toasters or cars. This is manifested, the line of thought continues, in the absence of a substantive critical discourse about the aesthetics of everyday things, and also in the lack of any body of knowledge or expertise that might be brought to bear in justifying particular aesthetic judgements. Whereas there is a body of criticism on the aesthetic value of portraits and sonatas, drawing on disciplines such as art history and art theory, not only is there no analogous criticism or expertise on cranes or cars, it is difficult to conceive of there being such analogues. The idea of someone claiming to be an industrial equipment critic, for instance, in the same sense that one might lay claim to the title 'literary critic' or 'art critic', seems risible. It seems risible at least partly because aesthetic judgements about the everyday do not seem cognitively rich: there seems to be no obvious body of expertise about industrial equipment that one could draw on in supporting judgements like 'this crane is aesthetically excellent'.

This line of thought emerges in the recent overview of everyday aesthetics by Leddy. Considering the application of an analogue of the Scientific Cognitivist position on the aesthetic appreciation of natural things to the sphere of the everyday, Leddy concludes that such an idea is 'somewhat bizarre', since it would require us to aesthetically appreciate 'the home in terms of the science of house management', for example.[46]

The concept of function, however, provides exactly the sort of source of knowledge required to address this criticism. If the aesthetic character of everyday objects is a Functional Beauty, then our knowledge of the functions of those objects, and of how they fulfil those functions, is required for appropriate appreciation of those objects. That is, to the extent that aesthetic judgements of everyday objects are based upon true beliefs about their functions and how they fulfil these functions, they are better or more correct judgements. So the judgement that an object looks bulky and lopsided is less correct than the judgement that it is visually striking, for instance, if the former is based upon the mistaken belief that the object in question is a radio antenna, whereas the latter is based on the true belief that it is an industrial crane. Functional Beauty can at least make a start in addressing the problem of relativism, in other words, by allowing us to take knowledge of function as knowledge that is aesthetically relevant to everyday objects.

This approach also allows one to dispel some of the absurdity thought to attend the idea of serious aesthetic evaluation of the everyday. Consider again Leddy's idea that the science of household management seems unlikely to enrich our aesthetic appreciation of items in the home. Does this case not show that it is misguided to apply a cognitively rich approach to the aesthetics of everyday things? It may be true that much of the science of household management fails to enhance, and perhaps even interferes with, our aesthetic appreciation of everyday items in the home. Tips for doing laundry or cleaning the eavestroughs do seem irrelevant to aesthetic appreciation. However, if the science of household management includes descriptions of the function of household items, and

[46] Leddy, 'The Nature of Everyday Aesthetics', 5.

illuminating accounts of how they function, then it seems to us that appreciating those items in light of these parts of household science would not be bizarre at all, but sensible. It does not seem absurd to think of knowledge and understanding of the *function* of household items enriching and sometimes even constraining our aesthetic appreciation of such items.[47] Deweyean conceptions of everyday aesthetics, in contrast, typically intensify, rather than dispel, the prima facie relativism that attends aesthetic appreciation and evaluation of the everyday. Since such accounts extend the concept of the aesthetic with touch, taste, and smell, turning it into a bodily, multi-sensory engagement with objects, there often seems to be even less of a place for knowledge and criticism in the appreciation of the everyday.

A rejection of the Deweyean direction for everyday aesthetics, however, does not entail an exclusion of the sensual, bodily pleasures of the proximal senses from our aesthetic encounters with the everyday. It does entail that these pleasures, like the pleasures we may take in the feel of a classical sculpture or in the smell of a wild flower, are adjuncts or admixtures to aesthetic appreciation, and not elements of it, strictly speaking. But, although these pleasures are not themselves aesthetic pleasures, they may be compatible with aesthetic pleasures and may add something valuable in their own right, yielding an agreeable and desirable overall experience. This conclusion, of course, is in line with the traditional view, which,

[47] In fact, this point emerges even in Leddy's own discussion. After dismissing an analogue of Scientific Cognitivism for the everyday, Leddy offers the quality of 'looking right' as an aesthetic quality common in everyday things. As examples, Leddy cites the aesthetic satisfaction of a joiner when a wooden joint 'looks right', and that of an electrician when 'all of the wires *look* like they are hooked up right' ('The Nature of Everyday Aesthetics', 8). In these instances of aesthetic appreciation, function seems to be an essential component: one could hardly tell that some wires look like they are hooked up right unless one knows what the wires are for and how they achieve their purpose. Further, Leddy seems willing to grant that expertise on the functionality of objects *does* enrich aesthetic appreciation: he notes that the claim that a carpentry joint that looks right can provide aesthetic satisfaction 'would be especially true for an expert in Japanese joinery'. If this is right, then there is no reason to think it absurd to hold that function is an integral part of our aesthetic appreciation of the everyday, or that some aesthetic judgements of everyday things are better, or more correct, than others.

although it insists on a distinction between bodily pleasures and aesthetic pleasures, does not hold that the two must be completely and at all times isolated from one another. In the case of everyday objects, events, and activities in particular, this conclusion means that the pleasures of the proximal senses, while they ought not to be disregarded, also ought not to be made into something they are not. The motivation for the latter error, however, evaporates when we consider the rich variety of Functional Beauty in the world of everyday artefacts.

In sum, in contrast with Deweyean approaches, a theory that describes our aesthetic appreciation of the everyday as, like that of art, based on a rich body of knowledge, susceptible to better and worse judgement, and even a province for profitable critical dispute, seems better poised to reveal the value that many have sensed in their aesthetic encounters with the things of everyday life. In particular, even if everyday objects in themselves are not, as are works of art, highly charged with meaning, a cognitively rich theory of our everyday aesthetic encounters can help to explain how it is that such experiences are nonetheless highly meaningful. Functional Beauty offers us a start towards such a theory.

8

The Functions of Art

In this chapter, we will consider some implications of our notion of Functional Beauty for art. Prima facie, at least some artworks seem capable of being appreciated in terms of their Functional Beauty. Some works of art seem to have clear functions: much painting in the Western tradition, for example, had the function of inspiring religious or civic feeling in those who viewed it. Awareness of this function plays an important role in shaping our aesthetic appreciation of these works. In appreciating religious painting, for example, we admire not only the skilful rendering of the scene, but also the way in which the work marshals pictorial and symbolic elements to engender the required feelings of awe and devotion.

When it comes to identifying the function of art, however, inspiring religious or civic devotion is by no means the only candidate. On the contrary, philosophers and other art theorists have provided numerous suggestions for the function of art. This point generates a by now familiar difficulty for the notion of Functional Beauty as applied to art, in that it is unclear whether, out of all the various functions that have been attributed to art, any can be picked out as *proper* functions. A particular artwork may function in many ways: it may provide aesthetic experience, express a particular political viewpoint, remind someone of his grandmother, and do much else besides. But which of these 'functions' belongs to the artwork itself, and which are, as it were, merely effects that the artwork happens to have? Given the very wide variation among artworks, one might even suspect that artworks lack a proper function altogether. Perhaps, unlike the shovel and the automobile, art has no function 'in and of itself'. If this is so, then somewhat ironically, rather than being a special problem for non-art, the Problem of Indeterminacy would be, within the context of Functional Beauty, a genuine problem *only for* art.

However, this conclusion ought to be embraced only if, in a final analysis, we cannot apply the notion of the proper function to art. In this chapter, we will argue that a selected effects theory of proper function allows us to apply this concept, and the concept of Functional Beauty, to artworks. We will begin by surveying some prominent attempts to identify the function of art, and critiquing the often tacit theoretical assumptions underwriting these claims. After outlining a selected effects theory of art's proper function, we turn, in the final section, to some implications of the resulting conception of Functional Beauty for works of art.

8.1 Functions of Art: An Overview

If we understand 'function' in a loose way, on which having a function simply means doing something or being used for something or other, then there is no difficulty in identifying functions of art. A particular artwork can cover a hole in the wall, increase the wealth of its owner, offend the ruling class, make someone recall his fifth birthday, and an indefinite number of other things besides. What is at issue in most discussions of art's function, however, is not function in this very loose sense, but something like our notion of proper function: a function that belongs to the artwork itself, as an artwork. Covering a hole in the wall or reminding someone of their fifth birthday might be things that a particular artwork does, but they are not what it is supposed to do: doing those things is not really the function of the work itself. They are, rather, functions that, in some sense, have been imposed upon the object by a user or by circumstance.

As mentioned, there is no paucity of suggestions, from philosophers and other theorists interested in the arts, as to the function or functions of art in this narrower sense of its proper function.[1] These suggestions, however, have emerged almost exclusively as a means to some larger theoretical end. For many theorists, identifying the function of art is a step towards a definition of the term 'art'. For others, it is a way of advancing some substantive thesis about the evaluation of art or about art's value in some general sense. In many cases, these larger projects are subject to well-known and serious criticisms. However, the failure of these larger projects would not, in itself, vitiate their proponents' claims to have uncovered the function of art. In surveying their views, therefore, we will ignore the plausibility of their suggested definitions of 'art' and other theoretical claims, and focus upon their attempts to discern the function of art.

Perhaps the best-known and most intuitively plausible suggestion regarding art's function is the view, sometimes known as 'Aestheticism', that art has an aesthetic function, such as bringing about aesthetic experiences in appreciators. The best-known exponent of such a view, Monroe Beardsley, defines art as '*either* an arrangement of conditions intended to be capable of affording an experience with marked aesthetic character *or* (incidentally) an arrangement belonging to a class or type of arrangements that is typically intended to have this capacity'.[2] We will return to this definition below, but, for the moment, its salient feature is the fact that it is based on the claim that art has an aesthetic function. In defending this definition of art, Beardsley recognizes that art is often used for other things as well, but maintains that 'the main and central (though of course by no means the only notable) function of artworks has *always* been, and remains, the aesthetic function'.[3] A similar emphasis on the special status of the aesthetic function is evident in Nick Zangwill's aestheticist

[1] Our account here draws on David Novitz's review of such attempts in 'Function of Art', in David Cooper (ed.), *A Companion to Aesthetics* (Oxford: Blackwell, 1992), 162–7.

[2] Monroe C. Beardsley, 'Redefining Art', in *The Aesthetic Point of View*, ed. M. J. Wreen and D. M. Callen (Ithaca, NY: Cornell University Press, 1982), 298–315; the quotation is on 299.

[3] Ibid., 312.

approach to art. Drawing an explicit analogy to other functional things, Zangwill writes that 'just as hearts have the function of pumping blood, and spades have the function of enabling us to dig, so works of art have the function of embodying or sustaining aesthetic properties, such as beauty, elegance, delicacy, daintiness, and dumpiness'.[4] Since notions akin to Functional Beauty are usually taken to involve non-aesthetic functions, the claim that art has a predominantly or singularly aesthetic function diminishes the importance of Functional Beauty for art. To say that art has a purely aesthetic function is just to say that nothing art does or is supposed to do, in a utilitarian sense, is relevant to aesthetically appreciating it.

Other theorists have been less sanguine about the supposedly special status of art's aesthetic function, however. These theorists suggest that discussions of the 'true' or 'real' function of art must extend beyond the traditional idea that art serves to give us beauty, or aesthetic pleasure. A famous example of this view is Tolstoy's book *What is Art?* (1898), which mounts an energetic attack on the idea that the function of art is to provide experiences of beauty. 'Just as people who conceive the aim and purpose of food to be pleasure cannot recognize the real meaning of eating,' Tolstoy writes, 'so people who consider the aim of art to be pleasure cannot realize its true meaning and purpose.'[5] The true meaning and purpose of art, according to Tolstoy, is to transmit feeling from the artist to her audience. Tolstoy acknowledges, of course, that art is often used for things other than this function, such as providing experiences of beauty. Nonetheless, doing these other things is not art's 'real' purpose or aim, in the same way that holding a garage door open is not the real purpose or aim of a shovel, but only something that a person might do with one.

[4] Nick Zangwill, 'Aesthetic Functionalism', in E. Brady and J. Levinson (eds), *Aesthetic Concepts: Essays after Sibley* (Oxford: Oxford University Press, 2000), 123–48; the quotation is on 125.

[5] Tolstoy regards beauty as a form of pleasure; Leo N. Tolstoy, *What is Art?*, trans. Alymer Maude (London: Walter Scott, Ltd, 1898), 43–4.

The claim that art's function is aesthetic is also taken to be, if not incorrect then at least overly simplistic, in the views of some psychologists on art. According to Freud, for example, creative writing is 'a continuation of, and a substitute for, what was once the play of childhood'.[6] That is, artistic activity is a sort of wish-fulfilment, 'a correction of unsatisfying reality'.[7] The artist, by creating a fantasy world that differs from the real world, relieves his unhappiness by satisfying his hidden sex or power-oriented desires in the fantasy. Thus, on Freud's view, art, like play more generally, serves as a sort of manifestation of some state of neurosis or psychic discontent.[8] Variations on this psychological approach to art abound, although some of them assign art a more noble station in the mental economy. Jung, for example, tells us that the social significance of art lies in its capacity to reveal the primordial 'archetypes' that stock the recesses of the collective unconscious, 'educating the spirit of the age, conjuring up the forms in which the age is most lacking'.[9] On views such as these, providing aesthetic experience is by no means all that art 'really' does: on the contrary, art's 'real' operation takes place on a much deeper, even unconscious, level.

This is an attitude shared with more socially and politically oriented approaches to the function of art. Marxist approaches, for instance, emphasize art's role in challenging the existing economic and class structures of society.[10] Thus, some Marxist critics criticize art that eschews a political or social message for failing to fulfil its

[6] Sigmund Freud, 'Creative Writers and Day-Dreaming' [1907], trans. Grant Duff, in A. Neill and A. Ridley (eds), *The Philosophy of Art: Readings Ancient and Modern* (New York: McGraw-Hill, 1995), 46–53; the quotation is on 52.

[7] Ibid., 49.

[8] Given that some of these operations, in Freud's case, for example, are supposed to be pathological and hence *dys*functional, it can be awkward to refer to them as art's function. But this awkwardness can be easily removed by saying that art functions as a manifestation of neurosis, or an escape from reality, or whatever. Such redescription is appropriate in light of our treatment of Freud's theory, along with related kinds of accounts, as a causal role theory of art's function in Section 3 of this chapter; see also note 32.

[9] Carl Gustav Jung, 'The Relation of Analytical Psychology to Poetry' [1922], in *The Spirit in Man, Art and Literature*, ed. Gerhard Alder, trans. R. F. C. Hull (Princeton, NJ: Princeton University Press, 1978), 65–83; the quotation is on 82.

[10] For an overview of Marxist (and Marx's) approaches, see Tom Rockmore, 'Marxism and Art', in Cooper (ed.), *A Companion to Aesthetics*, 275–9.

'true' function. For example, concentrating on so-called 'high art', formal and esoteric art that demands a 'certain refinement of mind and temper', David Novitz argues that much art fails to give a voice to individuals and only 'accentuates and reinforces class divisions within capitalist society'.[11] Such critiques are often coupled with proposals for alternative forms of art that serve more socially progressive functions. Social Realism, for example, which bids artists to illustrate the vices of capitalism and virtues of communism, was claimed by some Marxists to be superior art on that account.[12]

The idea that art's function is a social one also emerges, in a different fashion, in some approaches to art in the fields of sociobiology and evolutionary psychology. Such accounts usually attempt to explain art as a kind of adaptive behaviour that originated in our evolutionary pre-history due to its capacity for promoting human survival. The anthropologist Ellen Dissanayake, for instance, views art as an instance of a form of behaviour that she calls 'making special'. This behaviour, she argues, arose as an adaptation during our evolutionary past in virtue of its ability to foster group solidarity.[13] Along similar lines, Noël Carroll suggests that natural selection favoured art making and art appreciation for their capacity to 'promote social cohesion among groups'. Carroll describes this cohesiveness as 'functional' in providing a 'social cement' that helps human groups and individuals survive.[14] Other sociobiological accounts suggest different evolution-based functions for art, such as displaying social status, attracting sexual partners, and developing cognitive abilities.[15]

[11] David Novitz, 'Ways of Artmaking: The High and the Popular in Art', *British Journal of Aesthetics* 29 (1989): 213–29; the quotation is on 224.

[12] For some of the classic writings on Social Realism, see Nicholas Luker (ed.), *From Furmanov to Sholokhov: An Anthology of the Classics of Socialist Realism*, trans. Nicholas Luker (Ann Arbor, MI: Ardis, 1988).

[13] See Ellen Dissanayake, *Homo Aestheticus: Where Art Comes From and Why* (Seattle, WA: University of Washington Press, 1995).

[14] Noël Carroll, 'Art and Human Nature', *Journal of Aesthetics and Art Criticism* 62 (2004): 95–107; the quotation is on 100.

[15] For discussion of the first two, see Jared Diamond, *The Third Chimpanzee: The Evolution and Future of the Human Animal* (New York: Harper Collins, 1992), 168–79. On the latter,

Our brief survey of proposals for the proper function or functions of art is by no means comprehensive. But it is sufficient to impart a sense of the central issue haunting the question of art's proper function: How could one go about adjudicating between these different proposals for the 'real' function of art in any sort of principled fashion? By no means all of the authors mentioned above, it must be admitted, would feel the need to do this. The proponent of the claim that art has some evolutionary function, for example, might be happy to allow that art has other functions as well. If the goal of a claim concerning art's evolutionary function is only to establish that art has a connection with 'human nature', then the existence of other functions need not vitiate this project. More generally, one might be a pluralist about the proper functions of art, holding that art does a number of different things simultaneously: for example, providing aesthetic experience and communicating feeling. This kind of pluralism, in fact, fits naturally with many current cultural approaches to art, which understand 'art' not in terms of the intrinsic qualities of works, but rather in terms of some kind of status a work has within a community of artists, critics, and appreciators. Such approaches often separate function from art status, so that artworks can have all manner of different proper functions. Also, one might further complicate the picture by taking the functions of art to be dynamic, rather than static, changing over time.[16]

However, at least some of our authors would be unhappy with this sort of pluralism. As we have seen, Tolstoy, the Marxist, and the aestheticist all seem committed to some version of the claim that one function (the one each identifies) is the 'real' or 'true' one, the function that we ought to be centrally concerned

see John Tooby and Leda Cosmides, 'Does Beauty Build Adapted Minds? Toward an Evolutionary Theory of Aesthetics, Fiction and the Arts', *SubStance* 30 (2001): 6–27. For an overview of recent evolutionary discussions of art, see Denis Dutton, 'Aesthetics and Evolutionary Psychology', in Jerrold Levinson (ed.), *The Oxford Handbook of Aesthetics* (Oxford: Oxford University Press, 2003), 693–705.

[16] See Robert Stecker, *Artworks: Definition, Meaning, Value* (University Park, PA: Pennsylvania State University Press, 1997a).

with in understanding and evaluating works of art. And all our theorists, including the pluralist, seem committed to the weaker claim that some functions of art are not proper functions. Even the pluralist, presumably, would want to hold that covering a hole in the wall or reminding someone of his fifth birthday are not really functions of a painting in the sense that things such as promoting social cohesion, providing aesthetic experience, or communicating feeling could be functions of that work.[17] When it comes to the proper functions of artworks, then, even if we accept some form of pluralism, we must ultimately provide some theoretical basis for determining those functions.

What this basis could be, however, is not at all clear. As mentioned, the theoretical basis for determining art's proper function or functions is typically given little focused attention, with conclusions as to art's function being driven by more general theoretical considerations, such as deep-seated political commitments or the need to fashion a satisfactory definition of 'art'. Despite this situation, however, there clearly are general accounts of proper function underlying the various proposals discussed above, even though they are not often developed in any explicit way. To evaluate the various proposals for art's proper function, we propose to draw out these accounts and assess their merits as accounts of the proper function. These accounts can be divided into two general categories based on two of the three analyses of 'function' that we distinguished in Chapter 3: intentionalist and causal role analyses.

8.2 Intentionalist Theories of Art Function

An intentionalist approach to the proper functions of artworks would view those proper functions as determined by the use intended for the work by some particular agent. It is natural to take this agent to be the artist, since, typically, the artist has an especially close relationship to the artwork, being both designer

[17] But see the discussion of Richards's view in Section 3 of this chapter.

and maker.[18] An intentionalist approach developed in this way is compatible with particular artworks having a wide range of different functions. For instance, on such an approach, if an artist's intention for her work is that it promote a political viewpoint, then that is its proper function. If another artist intends her work to express grief, then that would be its proper function, and so on. However, for reasons that we will discuss below, intentionalist approaches are perhaps most commonly associated with aestheticist accounts. Consequently, our discussion is focused on such proposals; however, our conclusions are not restricted to such proposals, and apply to any specific suggestion for the function of art that is based on an intentionalist theory of proper function.

In recent aestheticist accounts, the intentionalist approach to art's function has been developed in two ways: for individual artworks and for the social institution of the artworld. To assess the viability of the intentionalist approach in relation to art, we will consider each of these in turn, beginning with the former. In keeping with this more traditional approach, Monroe Beardsley spells out the aesthetic function of art, which he considers its 'main and central' function, in an explicitly intentionalist manner: on his account, being 'an arrangement of conditions intended to be capable of affording an experience with marked aesthetic character' is sufficient to make something an artwork.[19] Nick Zangwill also takes the function of artworks to derive from the intentions of their makers. On his account, the functional properties of an individual artwork are 'bestowed on it by a certain history of production. In particular, the artist's *intentions* are the source of the function.'[20]

[18] Although typical, this is not always the case. A sculptor may design his works by creating the mould, but someone else may cast them. Or a master painter may design a large painting, but leave some parts of it to be completed by apprentices. Even in these cases, however, the makers usually have a limited degree of autonomy, quite unlike the autonomy that the makers of, say, telephones now have from Alexander Graham Bell.

[19] Beardsley, 'Redefining Art', 299. Being so intended is not necessary, however; for further discussion, see Section 3 of this chapter.

[20] Nick Zangwill, 'Feasible Aesthetic Formalism', in *The Metaphysics of Beauty* (Ithaca, NY: Cornell University Press, 2001b), 55–81; the quotation is on 61. See also Zangwill's 'Aesthetic Functionalism', 126. In the latter article, Zangwill says that the artist's intention

Do such theories work? In discussing intentionalist theories of artefact function more generally in Chapter 3, we have already argued that the intentions of designers and makers are not sufficient for determining proper function. As a counter-example, we considered the Plaza Major, which was designed and built to serve as a royal courtyard but which now has the proper function of (something like) providing a space for civic events, such as cultural celebrations and markets. In the case of art, it is difficult to find an analogous counter-example to a theory based on designer/maker intentions because it is controversial just what the proper function of any given artwork is. However, it is possible to address the adequacy of the intentionalist account in a more indirect way. Say that a novelist writes a novel about the impacts of globalization with the primary aim of annoying his father-in-law. Do we want to say, along with intentionalist theories, that the proper function of the artwork, the function that belongs to the work itself, is annoying the author's father-in-law?

Compare this case with a situation involving a non-artwork, an artefact such as a shovel. Say a man makes a shovel with the intention of marking the position of his favourite tulip bulb. He does not just make a garden stake that accidentally turns out to be indiscernible from a shovel; rather, he makes a shovel (imagine that he buys, and follows, carpentry plans for a making a shovel). The man's reasoning is unimportant; perhaps he is just eccentric. At any rate, his primary intention for the object that he is making is that it mark the position of his favourite tulip bulb. In this case, it would seem odd to say that marking the location of tulip bulbs is the function that really belongs to the object made. At the very least, it would seem odd to say that marking the location of tulip bulbs is a function that belongs 'to the object itself' more than the function of moving loose material does. Rather, marking the

that his work have aesthetic property P is not sufficient for that work to have the function of possessing P: if the artist's effort in creating the work is flawed in certain ways, then it might not have this function. Thus, on Zangwill's account, 'how the work in fact turns out' also plays a role in determining its function; see 'Aesthetic Functionalism', 130.

location of tulip bulbs seems a paradigm case of a function that does not belong to the object itself but rather has been imposed upon it. For the object in question is, apparently, a shovel.

If this analysis is correct, then it is tempting to say something similar in the case of the irritating novel—and about artwork in general. If the intentionalist theory of proper function were correct, then we ought to say that irritating the novelist's father-in-law is the function that, more than others, belongs to the novel itself. But this seems odd, in the same way that it seems odd to say that marking the location of tulip bulbs is a function that belongs to the shovel itself more than moving loose material does.[21] It is much less clear that we can isolate the proper function or functions of the novel, in the sense that we can do this for an artefact like a shovel. But whatever those proper functions may be, and howsoever they may be determined, it seems clear that they are not simply whatever the artist intends them to be. If this is the case, then the intentional theory of proper function, as formulated for individual artworks, is false.

As mentioned above, however, the intentionalist approach to the proper function of art could also be developed in a different way, by describing a function for the social institution of the artworld, rather than for individual artworks. This approach is developed in detail by Gary Iseminger in his book *The Aesthetic Function of Art* (2004), wherein he attempts to identify the function of the artworld and practice of art.[22] Iseminger claims that the artworld and practice of art (we will simply refer to 'the artworld' for

[21] One should keep the claim that the *function* of the work is determined by the intentions of the artist distinct from the claim that the *meaning* of the work is determined by the intentions of the artist. In terms of our example, the claim that the novel's meaning is determined by the author's intention to aggrieve his father-in-law is not the same as the claim that the novel's function is to do so. Claims like the former, although the subject of a great deal of debate in the philosophy of criticism, are at least prima facie plausible in a way that claims regarding function, such as the latter, are not.

[22] Gary Iseminger, *The Aesthetic Function of Art* (Ithaca, NY: Cornell University Press, 2004). One of Iseminger's reasons for pursuing this project is to square aestheticist approaches to the evaluation of art with institutional approaches to defining 'art', on which something is an artwork simply in virtue of being related to the artworld in the right way. Iseminger takes his account to support an aesthetic approach to the evaluation of art because he believes that, even if a particular artwork is not produced with aesthetic intentions, it remains the

short) have the function of promoting a particular kind of aesthetic experience that he calls 'aesthetic communication'.[23] Despite the fact that Iseminger seeks to identify the function of an entity (the artworld) that is quite different in kind from the individual artworks that concern theorists such as Beardsley and Zangwill, the notion of function that he employs rests on a similar foundation: namely, the intentions of designer/makers.

Iseminger demurs from analysing the concept of function as it applies to artefacts, and is content to propose and defend a principle of inference for identifying the artefactual function of any given thing. This principle is:

> (AF) If something is good at doing something that it was designed and made to do, then doing that is its (artifactual) function[24]

This principle does not state what it is for an artefact to have a function; rather, it asserts that a certain kind of evidence is sufficient to justify the claim that an artefact has a particular function. This principle, however, is clearly motivated by an intentionalist conception of artefact function. For instance, Iseminger tells us that AF is made reasonable by the fact that the functions of artefacts explain their existence 'in terms of the intentions and actions of a conscious agent—this particular blade is on the knife because someone designed it and someone had it made to be good at cutting'.[25] For Iseminger, then, artefact functions seem to be a matter of the intentions of designers and makers. This would explain why AF asserts that the knowledge that an artefact was designed and made to do X constitutes evidence for the claim that X is the function of that artefact. Further, an intentionalist approach makes sense of AF's assertion that an artefact's being good at X, where X is something that an object was designed and made to do, is evidence that X is the artefact's function. Although being good at doing X is not necessary for having X as a function,

product of an institution with an aesthetic function, and thus is good to the extent that it fulfils this function.

[23] Iseminger, *The Aesthetic Function of Art*, 84. [24] Ibid., 28. [25] Ibid., 80.

it is prima facie evidence that the item's designer meant for it to do X.[26] Artefacts do not typically 'just happen' to be very good at doing things: the chance of a random item from a stationery store being a very good car part, for instance, is essentially nil. As such, the fact that an artefact is good at doing X provides us with good reason to think that the designer of that artefact intended it to do X. In short, if functions are a matter of the intentions of an artefact's designer/maker, then it is eminently reasonable to infer artefact functions in just the way that AF specifies.

Using the principle AF, Iseminger goes on to argue that the function of the artworld is to promote aesthetic communication. He does this by arguing directly that the designers and creators of the artworld intended it to promote aesthetic communication, and also by arguing that the artworld is good at promoting aesthetic communication. The latter claim, on the reasoning just described, lends further support to the claim that the designers and creators of the artworld intended it to promote aesthetic communication. When combined with the principle AF, these considerations yield the conclusion that the artworld's proper function is an aesthetic one: promoting aesthetic communication.

But this conclusion remains insufficiently justified. For, as we have argued, the intentions of makers and designers of artefacts are not sufficient to determine the proper function of those artefacts, even when those artefacts are large-scale items that persist over long periods of time, like the artworld. This vitiates principles such as AF, which take evidence as to the intentions of designers and makers to be sufficient grounds for attributing proper function to artefacts. Consider again the case of the Plaza Major discussed in Chapters 3 and 6: were we to apply AF to this case, we would conclude that its proper function is to serve as a royal courtyard, since it was designed and made to do this, and presumably it is still as good at it as it ever was, even if it is never used for this purpose any more. But this would be a mistake: the proper function of the

[26] Iseminger, *The Aesthetic Function of Art*, 84.

Plaza Major has, over a long stretch of time, drifted away from the intentions of its designers and makers.[27] For all that Iseminger says about the intentions of the artworld's creators, something like this might well be the case with the artworld as well. The artworld, though intended to serve aesthetic ends, and quite capable of serving them, may actually have persisted because of its capacity to reinforce the class structure, for example. Because it might have, Iseminger's conclusion that the artworld's function is to promote aesthetic communication rests on a false principle. Like the related approaches of Beardsley and Zangwill, Iseminger's account goes astray in locating the proper function of artefacts in the intentions of their designers or makers. In doing so, it omits an element crucial to proper function: what artefacts actually do.

8.3 Causal Role Theories of Art Function

In contrast to the approaches discussed in the previous section, other authors seem to base their claims regarding the function of art on what art actually does rather than what its creators intend it to do. In a number of cases, theorists have no real choice on this issue, since the function that they attribute to art (for example, giving vent to unconscious archetypes, expressing neurotic desires, or reinforcing the extant class structure) need play no part whatsoever in the artist's thinking about her work. This being the case, functionality has to be a matter of something other than the artist's intention, at least in the typical sense of that phrase.

The precise sense of 'function' used in these contexts, however, is often left unclear. David Novitz tries to capture the relevant

[27] Iseminger notes cases of change of artefact function, as in the shifting function of college fraternities. In these cases, he acknowledges that the intentions of designers can be 'defeated', and advises that we be alert to such cases in applying AF; see *The Aesthetic Function of Art*, 88. But this renders AF useless: we can now assign function based on designer intent only if we know that designer intentions line up with function in the case at issue. But we can only know *that* if we know already what the artefact's function is.

sense in a general way with his notion of a 'Descriptive view' about the function of art. On such a view, 'by their very nature works of art serve certain metaphysical, psychological, or cultural functions, and do so whether or not the artist knows or intends it'.[28] Descriptive views hold that a function of art is not something that it happens to do in some cases or contexts, but 'a necessary feature of all art'.[29] However, being a necessary feature of all art does not seem sufficient to make something a function of art: increasing the number of artworks is a necessary feature of all art, but no one would argue that the function of an artwork is to increase the number of artworks. Further, being a necessary feature of all art does not seem necessary for being a function of art either: recall Carroll's idea that promoting social cohesion is the function of art. It is at least conceivable that, due to a radical shift in social conditions or human nature, artworks in some place or at some time fail to promote social cohesion (perhaps they promote social fragmentation instead). Be that as it may, it is still possible to ask whether, in general, art has promoting social cohesion as its function, or one of its functions.[30] Novitz's notion of a descriptive function, to be fair, is probably meant only to be a useful rough characterization of a wide class of views (which it is), not to capture the precise sense of function involved in non-intentionalist approaches. Nonetheless, we are still left without an account of what exactly it means to say, in the context of non-intentionalist views like Tolstoy's, Freud's, or the Marxist's, that art has such and such as its function.

In some cases, the relevant sense of 'function' is explicated by an appeal to the metaphor of art's doing something in the 'life' of some larger whole, such as society, or the economy. Thus, on Jung's view, for example, art might be said to serve as a kind of memory organ for human society, keeping it 'healthy' by re-presenting

[28] Novitz, 'Function of Art', 163. [29] Ibid.

[30] Novitz's notion is certainly incompatible with non-intentionalist accounts of art's aesthetic function, some examples of which we discuss below, since providing aesthetic experience is not a necessary feature of all artworks.

the various archetypes. These sorts of appeals to metaphor have a somewhat unsatisfactory vagueness about them, however.[31] They also seem to rule out views such as Freud's, on which art does not help to keep society 'healthy' but, on the contrary, manifests a sort of illness or neurosis. These difficulties can be avoided, however, if we spell out the relevant sense of 'function' using a causal role analysis as developed in Chapter 3. On such an account, X is the function of artefact A when A causally contributes, in a certain sort of way, to the operation of a larger system, of which A is a part, by doing X. As we discussed in that chapter, the paradigmatic application of this sense of function is to physiology, where it is used to explain the operation of complex systems. Thus the heart's function of pumping blood can be thought of as a causal role function in the sense that pumping blood causally contributes, in a certain sort of way, to the circulatory system's capacity for circulating nutrients throughout the body. This account does not depend upon the vague metaphor of society as a living thing: to make the claim that art has a causal role function, we only need specify a larger system of which art is a part, and to which it makes the appropriate sort of causal contribution. Also, this approach allows us to make sense of claims, such as Freud's, that art's function is not a beneficial one: on these accounts, the capacity of the larger system to which art contributes will be one that we consider pathological rather than healthy. As long as art causally contributes, in the proper way, to this capacity, what art does can be called its function in the causal role sense.[32]

The notion of causal role function offers a coherent basis for the more socially oriented, non-aestheticist claims about the function

[31] Iseminger is critical of the vagueness typical in such accounts; see Iseminger, *The Aesthetic Function of Art*, 87.

[32] On non-beneficial causal role functions, see Karen Neander, 'Functions as Selected Effects: The Conceptual Analyst's Defense', *Philosophy of Science* 58 (1991a): 168–84. Neander's example is 'pressing on an artery to the brain': this is something that a tumour might do that helps explain a cancer's capacity to spread throughout the body and cause certain sorts of disruption in an organism. Of this case, she writes, 'this is an actual causal role the tumor has in this pathological process, and one in which we are very interested', even though this is not its proper function; see 181.

of art made by Tolstoy, Marxists, Freudians, and others. However, it can be used to underwrite aestheticist claims about art's function as well. Although many accounts of the aesthetic function of art are primarily intentionalist, some also include a non-intentionalist element. This is the case with the definition from Beardsley discussed earlier: art is '*either* an arrangement of conditions intended to be capable of affording an experience with marked aesthetic character *or* (incidentally) an arrangement belonging to a class or type of arrangements that is typically intended to have this capacity'.[33] The second disjunct in this definition allows something to be art even if its creator lacks the requisite intentions, so long as it actually has a certain sort of effect: namely, that effect typically produced by artistic intentions. Other accounts of the aesthetic function of art reject the intentionalist element completely. Richard Lind holds that 'an "artwork" is any creative arrangement of one or more media whose principal function is to communicate a significant aesthetic object'.[34] Lind is explicit that a thing having a function is not a matter of what it was intended to do, but rather what it does. As he says, 'function is largely determined by *manifest capacity for use*'.[35]

The notion of a causal role function, then, can be used to formulate a variety of cogent claims about art's function. But how do claims based on a causal role conception of function fare as claims

[33] Beardsley, 'Redefining Art', 299.

[34] Richard Lind, 'The Aesthetic Essence of Art', *Journal of Aesthetics and Art Criticism* 50 (1992): 117–29; the quotation is on 124. See also Richard Lind, 'Art as Aesthetic Statement', *Journal of Aesthetic Education* 27 (1993): 1–21.

[35] Lind, 'The Aesthetic Essence of Art', 126 (Lind's italics). James Anderson discusses an approach that, in contrast to other aesthetic definitions of art, 'treats the aesthetic component functionally. The creator of art need not have intended the artefact to have any aesthetic potency. It is a matter of whether the artefact, in fact, rises to some level of aesthetic potency'; see James C. Anderson, 'Aesthetic Concepts of Art', in Noël Carroll (ed.), *Theories of Art Today* (Madison, WI: University of Wisconsin, 2000), 65–92; the quotation is on 66. Stephen Davies's general characterization of functionalist definitions of art is also suggestive of this sense of function. To define something functionally, according to Davies, is for it to 'be the case that what makes a thing an X is its functional efficacy in promoting the point of the concept in question'; see Stephen Davies, *Definitions of Art* (Ithaca, NY: Cornell University Press, 1991), 27. Accordingly, 'a proponent of the functional view of the definition of art holds that only a piece that could serve the point of art could become a work of art'; ibid., 39. See also Stecker, *Artworks*, 31.

regarding art's *proper* function? Does this sense of function provide us with any basis for determining which of the many functions suggested can be correctly described as belonging to the work itself?

We have already considered this claim, in a more general way, in Chapter 3, where we pointed out that a theory of causal role function seems incapable of capturing our notion of proper function. This stems from the fact that a given item can be a component in, and causally contribute to, an indefinite number of systems, giving it an indefinite number of causal role functions. But most of these seem, intuitively, not to be proper functions of the item. In the case of the heart, for example, one could argue that, in addition to pumping blood, it also has the causal role function of making heart sounds. But this seems clearly not to be its proper function, in the sense that pumping blood is.

The same problem of an indefinite proliferation of causal role functions occurs also in the case of artworks: there are an indefinite number of larger systems to which an artwork can be said to belong, and consequently an indefinite number of causal role functions that it can be said to have. This point is exemplified nicely in a recent discussion of 'artistic fitness'. Richard Richards is mainly concerned to argue that art ought to be evaluated in light of its fitness in various contexts. In doing so, however, he develops the notion that artworks 'function' in a variety of contexts. He writes:

> We might listen to music, look at paintings, go to plays and ballets, and see films because of the enjoyment it brings. Or we might experience art to satisfy a psychological need—to escape stressful or unpleasant circumstances through imaginative projection. Art may also serve cultural needs—educating about religious doctrines, or clarifying ethical rules or values. Social needs can be met through art as well. Folkdance, for instance, might function by reinforcing the bonds that hold communities together. Art can also function to make political points, criticizing one view or presenting another in a favourable light. Art can even function relative to philosophical goals.[36]

[36] Richard Richards, 'A Fitness Model of Evaluation', *Journal of Aesthetics and Art Criticism* 62 (2004): 263–75; the quotation is on 266.

Richards does not employ a causal role analysis of function, but his notion of 'functioning well in a context' is a rough analogue. In each of his examples of 'functioning well in a context', we could easily locate a larger system (the context) to whose capacities the artwork can be said to causally contribute: the mind (thought of as a system composed of various psychological parts), a cultural community, a political community, the philosophical profession, and so on. The sheer scope of Richards's notion of 'functioning well in a context' gestures towards the extreme pluralism to which a purely causal role approach to the function of art leads. A painting 'functions well in a context', according to Richards, if it reminds us of a loved one, and this renders it just as 'fit' as the performance of any of the other functions described above. Many will object to this radical pluralism about art's function, but Richards is quite correct to draw out this implication of any view of art's function that goes no further than the causal role notion. For, on such a view, although we can say that art has functions, there simply is no such thing as the *proper* function of art. If we want to retain such a notion, something additional must be brought into our analysis.

In response to this point, the proponent of a causal role approach may be tempted to appeal to differences in importance of the various causal role functions that art has. Much of the beguiling attraction of Freudian and Marxist accounts of art, surely, stems from the fact that they are supposed to pick out not just things that art does, but *the critically important* things that art does.[37] So increasing the number of artworks, while something art does, is unimportant, while reinforcing the class structure is, on the Marxist account, very important. So we might attempt to identify the *proper* function of art, as opposed to its function *simpliciter*, as that characterized by the most important casual role function. However, the important or significant functions of an object and

[37] Iseminger takes critical note of the tendency to accept non-intentionalist accounts of art's function as 'true' simply because they are non-intentional, and so somehow 'deeper'; see Iseminger, *The Aesthetic Function of Art*, 89.

its proper function, or the function that belongs to the object itself, do not always line up. If a shovel is holding open the garage door of a burning house, and thereby happens to represent the only chance of escape for its occupants, holding the garage door open will be its most important and significant function, at least at that moment. But it does not thereby become a function that belongs to the object. The object's proper function is still moving loose material, or whatever the proper function of a shovel is.

Another idea is to define proper function not in terms of the causal role function that is most important, but in terms of the one that the object performs best. Thus one might argue that promoting aesthetic experience in some community of appreciators is the proper function of art because that is the thing that art does better, or to a greater extent, than any of the other things it also happens to do (for example, reinforcing the class structure). But, once again, the function that X carries out best, or to the greatest degree, and the proper function of X do not always line up. Imagine that a public square, like the Plaza Major, which has the proper function of providing a space for civic events, does this very poorly: perhaps it is too small, or is located near a stinking factory, or whatever. In this case, perhaps what it does best remains what it was originally designed to do: serving as a royal courtyard, for example. But, even if that was the case, this would not mean that the proper function of the square now is serving as a royal courtyard.

Ultimately, it seems that the reason that causal role functions are not proper functions, even when they are very important and are well performed, is that they lack an explanatory connection with the object itself. In other words, as we saw in Chapter 6, Section 2, in order for F to be an object's proper function, F must also explain the continued existence, maintenance, or preservation of the object. The reason that the proper function of the Plaza Major is providing a space for civic events is not that this is important (though it probably is), nor that the Plaza Major does this better than it does anything else (which it probably does not), but that providing a space for civic events is the thing that explains why it has been maintained and so currently exists.

This fundamental explanatory limitation of causal role functions is sometimes noted by philosophical critics: Iseminger, for example, puts his finger on just this defect of Marxist and Freudian approaches. However, these critics often fail to see that the very same defect is manifest in the intentionalist accounts of function that they go on to defend. As noted in the previous section, Iseminger, for instance, maintains that the artworld has been maintained for its aesthetic efficacy.[38] But his discussion does not, in fact, justify this claim. His evidence for the function of the artworld, as marshalled under principle AF, is that the artworld's designers intended that it promote aesthetic communication and that the artworld does this better than it does anything else and better than anything else can do it. But, even if these claims are all true, they do not show that the artworld's current existence is explained by its promoting aesthetic communication. The artworld may have been maintained for something else that it does, such that if it ceased to do *this*, it would disappear, despite the fact that the thing it does *best* is promote aesthetic communication. In order to identify the proper function of art, we need to turn to the question: what is it that art does that actually drives its continued production and maintenance?

8.4 A Selected Effects Theory of Art Function

Unlike the intentionalist or causal role accounts that underlie so much contemporary discussion of art's function, a selected effects theory would be capable of underwriting the claim that some of art's functions are proper functions. On such a theory, in line with our findings in Chapters 3 and 6, the proper function of art would be that effect of art that, in the recent past, has caused it to be manufactured, distributed, or maintained in existence.

[38] See Iseminger, *The Aesthetic Function of Art*, 111.

Something along these lines is suggested by George Bailey, who holds that 'Art's proper function is the function it has (if any) that in fact explains why art continues to survive'.[39] Bailey notes that this analysis suggests that the proper function of art could turn out to be 'having aesthetic properties, or being expressive, or being a metaphor for the artist's statement', among other things, and he observes that each of these 'presents interesting possibilities'. However, he then discounts these possibilities out of hand, maintaining that whether or not art actually does these things has no impact on its survival; rather, it is our mere belief that they do these things that explains art's survival. Bailey goes on to claim that 'art's proper function is to make possible and actual the complex social practice that makes art's existence possible and actual. Thus, in a manner of speaking, art's proper function is to exist for its own sake.'[40]

Bailey's handling of the selected effects approach to art's proper function seems to us to suffer from two serious defects. The first is that his description of the specific proper function of art, which we have just cited, seems close to being vacuous. On his view, art's proper function, apparently, is to bring about a social practice that allows art to exist. This means that, on his view, art's existence is to be explained by its doing something that allows it to exist. This is close to being vacuous because saying that art does something that allows it to exist is not much of an explanation of the fact that art exists. Further, even if, as Bailey suggests, art's survival involves people's believing that it does various things, it does not follow that it is this mere belief in itself that constitutes the entire explanation for art's existence: rather, art may still do something specific to engender this belief, and in doing so keep itself in existence. If this

[39] George Bailey, 'Art: Life after Death?', in Carroll (ed.), *Theories of Art Today*, 160–74; the quotation is on 166. Bailey develops his account from Millikan's theory of proper function. See our discussion in Chapter 3, Sections 2 and 3. As noted in that chapter, relevant sources are Ruth Millikan, *Language, Thought, and Other Biological Categories: New Foundations for Realism* (Cambridge, MA: MIT Press, 1984) and Ruth Millikan, 'In Defense of Proper Functions', *Philosophy of Science* 56 (1989): 288–302.

[40] Bailey, 'Art: Life after Death?', 168.

is the case, then this something specific, whatever it is, ought to be included in a determination of the explanation for art's existence, and hence its proper function.[41]

A second and perhaps deeper problem with Bailey's discussion is its a priori character. From his treatment, it seems possible to decide which effects of art are responsible for its survival and continued existence by conceptual reflection alone. For example, he simply dismisses the idea that art's providing aesthetic experience could be responsible for its survival. However, the identity of the effects of art (if any) that are responsible for its survival and continued existence is an empirical issue. Therefore, it is hard to see how this matter could be decided through conceptual reflection alone.

This means that determining the proper function of art may be difficult. Uncovering the causal factors involved in the survival of art seems unlikely to be as straightforward as determining the causal factors involved in the survival of more pedestrian artefacts, such as hammers and shovels. It is fairly clear, for instance, that the shovel has survived because of its ability to move loose material. But, for any of the suggested functions of art, we could find many who would refuse to concede that art does that thing at all, much less that doing that thing explains the survival of art. For instance, aestheticist theories seem to fail to account for the survival of works that apparently have little or no aesthetic dimension, such as some conceptual artworks. Or, one might argue, against Tolstoy, that much art does not facilitate the communication of emotion or, against Marx, that some art has no impact whatever on the preservation or erosion of class structures. The uncertainty that we face in making universal causal claims about the survival of art makes it tempting to simply retreat, as Bailey does, to the view that what art actually does has no role to play in explaining its existence. But this would be an over-reaction, for the simple reason that we cannot rule out, a priori, that what art actually does plays a role

[41] Cf. Preston's account of the bug-zapper that zaps no bugs, in Beth Preston, 'Why is a Wing like a Spoon? A Pluralist Theory of Function', *Journal of Philosophy* 115 (1998): 215–54.

in keeping it in existence. It may not be easy to arrive at accounts of the causal factors involved in keeping art in existence, but this is, after all, commonly the case with empirical matters, and hardly gives us grounds to scotch the very enterprise.

Perhaps the best way in which to approach it, however, is in a pluralist spirit. Given the variation in art and art practices over time and in different cultures and groups, it seems likely that different kinds of artworks have survived for quite different reasons: in different times and places, different capacities of artworks have caused them to be manufactured, reproduced, and kept in existence. Such pluralism would ascribe different proper functions to different kinds of artworks, based on these differing etiologies.

What can we say, then, about the possibility of making such ascriptions of proper function to specific kinds of artworks? A useful way to approach this issue is to ask whether particular artworks can be described as members of functional categories. Many of the artistic categories or kinds that we use in classifying artworks are afunctional in nature. Categories such as 'the Western' or blank verse poetry, for example, are defined not in terms of any function performed by their members, but in terms of content, period or region of production, or structural features.[42] As such, the effects of items falling into those categories will tend to such variety that no very informative proper function can be assigned to them. One might suggest that the symphony form, for example, exists because of its capacity to allow the expression of musical ideas, but this is little more than a short way of saying that the symphony does a multitude of very different things—allow the exploration of melodic themes, produce sustained emotional responses, and so on—all of which make it a valuable medium. To draw an analogy with more utilitarian items, artistic categories at this level of generality resemble not so much our concepts of

[42] This distinction is noted by Noël Carroll, *The Philosophy of Horror, or Paradoxes of the Heart* (New York: Routledge, 1990), 14–15.

dedicated tools like shovels and furnaces as our concepts of very generic instruments such as language. The flexibility and adaptability of such instruments renders the causal histories of their instances so varied and complex that specific claims about the 'proper' function of the instrument itself are probably misguided.

On the other hand, we do also sometimes classify art using explicitly functional categories, which are defined by some effect that works in the category, at least typically, produce. The category of religious art, as we mentioned at the start of this chapter, can be characterized in terms of something that its members do: namely, inspire certain feelings of devotion or awe. In addition to these categories, there are also artistic categories that, while not named with an explicitly functional label, have been characterized in functional terms. The most famous of these is the tragedy, which Aristotle famously speculated to 'through pity and fear... [achieve] purification from such feelings'.[43] What precisely Aristotle meant by 'purification' is unclear from the texts that we possess, and has been the subject of much scholarly debate.[44] But whatever precisely one takes this purification to amount to—a simple expurgation of excessive emotion, or a process of clarifying and understanding certain emotional responses—Aristotle clearly thought not only that the tragedy, when well composed, was especially well suited to engender this response, but that doing so was the essence of the nature of tragedy. This effect is what tragedy is supposed to achieve, even if particular instances of it fail to do so: in our terms, it is the proper function of works in that dramatic genre. More recently, Noël Carroll has offered a similarly functional account of the horror genre. Carroll defines the genre in terms of its production of a particular emotional response, which he calls art-horror. It is this

[43] Aristotle, *Poetics* [approx. 335 BCE], 1449b in *Aristotle: Selections*, ed. and trans. Terence Irwin and Gail Fine (Indianapolis, IN: Hackett, 1995), 544.

[44] For a concise overview of the interpretive issues, see Nickolas Pappas, 'Aristotle', in Berys Gaut and Dominic McIver Lopes (eds), *The Routledge Companion to Aesthetics* (London: Routledge, 2001), 15–26.

response that horror 'characteristically or rather ideally promotes', even if particular instances of the genre fail to do so.[45]

The existence of functional categories, of these kinds, makes it plausible to claim that certain artworks have proper functions. Placing these artworks into functional categories, however, while necessary for establishing a proper function for them, is not sufficient. It is quite easy to slot artworks into categories that are defined in terms of some effect they are 'supposed to produce', but if a selected effects theory of proper function is correct, then this effect must be causally responsible for the production and dissemination of the works in question. In some cases, this seems like a plausible hypothesis. Take the case of religious art, for instance: works in this genre have inspiring religious feeling as their proper function insofar as the production of those sentiments was the causal factor that explains the production of those religious artworks. Although the particular causal history of any given work is an empirical matter, the general features of the systems of artistic production characteristic of much of pre-modern Europe make this a plausible general claim. Church patronage was a powerful and often determinant factor in deciding whether painting, sculpting, or music was pursued, and, if so, how it was pursued. When Renaissance painters produced their depictions of religious scenes, they were employing an artform that had a proper function in much the way that someone who reaches for a shovel is employing a tool that has a proper function (what precisely the individual artist intended to accomplish with that artform, of course, is a separate matter, just as what one intends to accomplish with a shovel is a matter separate from its proper function).

Other attempts to assign proper functions to artworks are more difficult to evaluate, however. Take Aristotle's account of the function of tragedy, for example. To defend Aristotle's view while accepting a selected effects theory of proper function, one needs to

[45] Carroll, *The Philosophy of Horror*, 14 and 31. Carroll cites Aristotle's theory of tragedy as a paradigm for his own theory of horror, 7.

hypothesize that it is the production of the 'purification' response that accounted for the continuing survival of tragedy as an artform: tragedy was produced because it fulfils an important psychological human need. But this claim is a difficult one to evaluate. A preliminary difficulty is that, as noted above, it is somewhat unclear what the purification response is supposed to be. But the deeper difficulty is in finding empirical support for the claim, dealing as it does with the connection between emotional states of the audiences of tragedy and their behaviour. In identifying this response as that characteristic of tragedy, Aristotle was no doubt drawing on both his own experience of tragedy and the reports of the most sophisticated audiences of his day. But the fact that the purification response to tragedy was common and valued would not establish that it is the causal factor behind the survival of that genre. The sight of an aeroplane in flight often lifts our spirits, and baby shoes fill us all with the tenderness that cuteness inspires, but these responses are not what explain the production and continued existence of these items.

This is not to say that we should be overly pessimistic about claims like Aristotle's. The fact that a certain response to a kind of artwork is common and valued makes it a strong prima facie candidate for the causal explanation of its survival. If we demonstrate that it is more likely to be causally efficacious than competing hypotheses, it may be possible to establish it with a good degree of justification.[46] The point, rather, is that we cannot justify a claim to proper function without the latter step.

In sum, a selected effects theory of proper function, properly worked out, points us towards the pluralist conception of art's function that has become familiar from cultural approaches to art. But, unlike cultural approaches, it provides us with a much sharper picture of the functions of art, furnishing the resources for discriminating proper function from function *simpliciter*, and for identifying cases where proper functions are not present.

[46] See Carroll's critical discussion of potential explanations for the existence of the horror genre in *The Philosophy of Horror*, chapter 4.

8.5 Functional Beauty and the Appreciation of Art

In the previous section we outlined a selected effects approach to the Functional Beauty of art. In this final section, we inquire more generally into the significance of Functional Beauty for the appreciation of artworks. Does the notion of Functional Beauty enrich our aesthetic appreciation of art and, if so, how?

In the case of much art, the answer is yes. If certain kinds of artworks, such as religious art and perhaps tragedies, in light of their functional categories, have proper functions, then this is clearly relevant to their aesthetic appreciation. They are properly appreciated in terms of their Functional Beauty. Moreover, the notion of Functional Beauty can do much, for example, to illuminate the appreciation of artworks that have traditionally been located on the margins of art, or outside it altogether in the realm of craft. As discussed in Chapter 2, one of the most enduring legacies of the Distinerestedness-based history of aesthetic theory is the notion that practical considerations ought to be excluded in appreciating art. However, this conception of art appreciation fits awkwardly with a broad conception of art. If we acknowledge the art status of the art of non-Western cultures, much of which is overtly utilitarian in character, and utilitarian crafts such as quilting or textiles, the inapplicability of this notion of appreciation becomes apparent. The role of function is so prominent in these instances that appreciation that neglects their function can hardly be called 'appreciation' at all. The broadening of our conception of art, then, produces a need for a new approach to appreciation.[47]

One response to this situation would be to simply maintain the traditional notion of aesthetic appreciation, and hold that our appreciation of these overtly functional artworks includes also a

[47] See Stephen Davies, 'Aesthetic Judgements, Artworks and Functional Beauty', *Philosophical Quarterly* 56 (2006): 224–41, and Stephen Davies, 'Non-Western Art and Art's Definition', in Carroll (ed.), *Theories of Art Today*, 199–216.

non-aesthetic component. This option is suggested by Nicholas Wolterstorff, whose position we introduced in Chapter 2. In his discussion of the appreciation of so-called 'commemorative art', he writes:

> These memorials do of course have aesthetic qualities; critics have commented on the aesthetic qualities of Maya Lin's Vietnam Memorial. But the people whom I witnessed descending silently into that gash in the earth, caressing the wall where they found a name they recognized, kissing it, and quietly weeping—those people were not engaging the aesthetic qualities of this piece of architectural sculpture. They were doing something else.[48]

Wolterstorff calls for an expansion in our conception of the appreciation of art, to include not only aesthetic responses, but emotional responses as well. This move would, as he puts it, 'break the hegemony of the aesthetic'.[49]

But it is not necessary to take this step in order to do justice to the practical dimension of commemorative art. Given why it is manufactured and maintained, commemorative art has a clear proper function. Thus, rather than placing its practical dimension in 'something else', one might locate it, instead, within the aesthetic response to the work. The concept of Functional Beauty allows us to do just that. For the Functional Beauty of the memorial would not merely involve a consideration of its appearance as an abstract piece of 'architectural sculpture', but as something that aims to evoke, through a visible structure, a specific set of responses to a historical event. An appraisal of the Functional Beauty of the Vietnam Memorial, for instance, might describe its austere, ambivalent appearance. Seeing it as having this aesthetic quality requires seeing it as a war memorial: the very same structure might look elaborate if it were a sidewalk, and overblown and grandiose

[48] Nicholas Wolterstorff, 'Why Philosophy of Art Cannot Handle Kissing, Touching, and Crying', *Journal of Aesthetics and Art Criticism* 61 (2003): 17–27; the quotation is on 26. The work is Maya Ying Lin and Jan Scruggs, Vietnam Veterans Memorial, 1982, Washington, DC.

[49] Ibid., 27.

if it were a public telephone directory. The subterranean path and the simple, repetitive inscription of individual names look austere, given our grasp of the memorial's aim of evoking a response to war and the standard features of war memorials (heroic statuary, elevated architecture, and so on).

Furthermore, employing the notion of Functional Beauty in this way seems a better approach than Wolterstorff's option, since the emotional responses that people have to works such as war memorials surely are not divorced from the visible qualities that they find in the work. That is, viewers do not merely appreciate aesthetic qualities *and* have emotional responses to the work: often they are emotionally moved *by* the aesthetic qualities of the work. This is probably a common response to the Vietnam Memorial, the austerity of which is a profoundly moving sight. But, in order to understand this phenomenon, we need to see the aesthetic qualities of the work as informed by its function. Again, we would have a very different emotional response, if any, to Lin's structure if it were a sidewalk or a telephone directory.

One advantage, then, of Functional Beauty, in the context of art, is its capacity to provide a more comprehensive account of the aesthetic appreciation of art. On the other hand, the notion's applicability to art faces limitations in light of the radical innovation that is characteristic of much contemporary art. On a selected effects theory of proper function, having a proper function requires the existence of what we called 'ancestors', and hence membership in some type that has existed for a certain period. War memorials, horror films, and tragedies meet this requirement, being instances of relatively long-established types, but it is unclear whether some recent artworks do.

Consider some notorious examples of twentieth-century art: Piero Manzoni's *Merde d'Artiste* (1961), Robert Smithson's *Asphalt Rundown* (1969), and *Touch Sanitation* (1980) by the artist Mierle Ukeles. Manzoni's work consisted of ninety tin cans filled (supposedly) with his own excrement. Smithson's work involved dumping a truckload of asphalt down a hill in an abandoned quarry. Ukeles's work, *Touch Sanitation*, consisted of her shaking hands with over 8,000 sanitation workers in New York. There is an obvious difficulty in assigning these works to any sort of established art category that does not arise for a sonata, a portrait, or a war memorial. They are, indeed are intended to be, singular works. If this is the case, it will not be possible to assign a proper function to them. If this is correct, then they are like the truly novel can-opener imagined in Chapter 3 and a novel biological feature generated by a random mutation, in failing to belong to the sort of established type required for proper function.

This issue is significant for the applicability of Functional Beauty to artworks, given the emphasis placed on novelty and innovation in much twentieth-century art. This period was characterized by unease with working in established, defined artforms and by attempts to push the boundaries of what counts as art. This aspect of contemporary art should not be exaggerated, since such experimental work existed alongside continued use of long-established artforms. But it is nonetheless true that many of the most important works in this period are difficult to place in an established artform.

It is tempting to try to avoid this conclusion by appealing to an idea that recurs over and over in the writings of experimental artists and critics: the notion that such art is supposed to prompt meditation on, and often revision of, the concept of art itself. In its severe, modern form, this idea is often traced back to Marcel Duchamp's notorious work *Fountain* (1917), which consisted of a urinal with the inscription 'R. Mutt' painted on it. This object was, arguably, an artwork when it was produced: Duchamp exhibited it in a gallery, after all. But unlike, say, a production of *Oedipus Rex*, it is difficult to say just what *kind* of art it was. Indeed, producing puzzlement about such matters seems to have been part of the point of the work in the first place. Perhaps it is possible to see works such as *Touch Sanitation* and *Merde d'Artiste* as the descendants of *Fountain*, and as having the proper function of stimulating reflection on the concept of art, for, arguably, this explains their continued production and preservation.

The plausibility of this suggestion is a matter for art history to determine. If it is true, then we can at least ascribe a proper function to later experimental artworks. Art of this kind is indeed a tool, albeit one of a very different sort from previous artforms. Perhaps it is best seen, as Arthur Danto argues, as a sort of philosophy.[50] But this may not help us, in the end, to avoid the conclusion that Functional Beauty fails to apply to such works. For the function of producing reflection on the concept of art is so abstract and generic as to render the notion of standard, variable, and contra-standard features nugatory in relation to it. What sort of non-aesthetic perceptual qualities, for instance, would be standard in a work that aims to stimulate thinking about art? If experimental art represents a new sort of tool, then, perhaps because of its newness, it is yet unclear how and to what extent Functional Beauty applies to it.

[50] See Arthur Danto, *The Philosophical Disenfranchisement of Art* (New York: Columbia University Press, 1986).

9

Conclusion

As we said at the outset, the aim of this book is to argue for the cogency and importance of a sort of aesthetic appreciation that accords a central role to function. To achieve this aim, we have developed the notion of Functional Beauty and positioned it within our appreciation of the entire range of things that fall within our aesthetic experience. Indeed, we have attempted to show that Functional Beauty has a role to play in virtually every dimension of aesthetic experience.

Nonetheless, our approach to realizing this goal has been a basically conservative one. In clarifying the logic of the position, for example, we insisted on a weak view of Functional Beauty rather than a strong one. That is, we argued that one ought to assert only that some aesthetic qualities, not all, involve function, or, to put the point another way, that Functional Beauty is one species of beauty, rather than beauty per se. Thus, on our view, the acceptance of Functional Beauty should be viewed, not as a radical revision of the concept of the aesthetic, but rather as a means of rounding out this concept by adding an important dimension to it.

Our approach has also been conservative in another way, namely, in insisting on a traditional definition of the aesthetic, one that excludes the so-called 'bodily pleasures'. Our strategy, therefore, was not to make room for Functional Beauty by expanding the concept of the aesthetic, as some have done, but rather to show that Functional Beauty has a place in the aesthetic even as that concept has been more narrowly understood.

In line with our attempt to fit Functional Beauty into the tradition of aesthetic theory, we have drawn on the insights of various philosophers in that tradition. In Chapter 1, for example, we considered the views of Hume, Alison, and Adam Smith, among others. Although these philosophers have said some insightful things on the subject, this aspect of their thought has been generally neglected. In some cases, that of Smith, for instance, the thinkers themselves have received scant attention in aesthetic theory. In attempting to exhume some of these insights, our project can be seen as an attempt at a reconstruction or rehabilitation of one strand of thought in the history of aesthetics. But our aim was not primarily a historical one, and there are many thinkers whose views on the subject we have not considered. Rather, we have looked to the aesthetic tradition for guidance in trying to find a place for Functional Beauty in contemporary aesthetics.

Accordingly, in Chapters 2 and 4, we have also drawn on some ideas from contemporary aesthetics, such as Kendall Walton's notion of the role of conceptual categories in aesthetic appreciation and, more generally, the idea that aesthetic appreciation of both art and nature must be construed as cognitively rich. Moreover, we found that to do justice to the concept of Functional Beauty it was sometimes necessary to turn away from purely aesthetic concerns altogether. Thus, in Chapter 3, in addressing the Problem of Indeterminacy, we looked to work in the philosophy of science on the nature of function. Our view is that this line of thought provides better answers to the pertinent questions than have previously been on offer in aesthetics. If some find our methods in making the case for Functional Beauty overly eclectic, we can only respond that the nature of the topic itself has demanded an eclectic approach.

Assuming that there is a range of aesthetic qualities of the sort that our account of Functional Beauty describes, what significance does this have? To put the question differently, what do we gain by recognizing these aesthetic qualities? It is true, of course, that any aesthetic quality has an intrinsic interest, from the perspective of aesthetic theory. The intrinsic interest of Functional Beauty is perhaps especially great, given that the idea has often been thought to fall outside of aesthetics altogether. Also, the extent to which questions about the relationship between function and aesthetic appreciation arise in different contexts, from nature to interior design to architecture to art, lends the notion some additional interest.

We have also suggested, however, that a recognition of Functional Beauty may contribute to certain virtues in our aesthetic theory, namely, unity and comprehensiveness. By comprehensiveness, we mean capacity to describe the aesthetic character of all of the diverse sorts of objects of aesthetic appreciation. In Chapters 5 through 8, we tried to show some of the ways in which Functional Beauty arises in these different sorts of objects, and how recognizing it can address and explain various issues arising for each, including the much neglected 'everyday objects'. It seems obvious to us that everyday artefacts—cars, tools, and furniture, for example—are objects of frequent and enthusiastic *aesthetic* appreciation. Aesthetic theory has been relatively silent on the topic, however. By enriching our conception of what is involved in our everyday aesthetic experiences, recognizing Functional Beauty can make our aesthetic theory more comprehensive in its scope of application.

The other virtue that we have claimed for a recognition of Functional Beauty is the ability to enhance the unity of an aesthetic theory. By a more unified aesthetic theory we mean one whose applications to different objects stresses commonalities and continuities rather than sharp differences. Currently, several powerful considerations make a *dis*unified account of aesthetic appreciation attractive. The desire to foster a more positive relationship with the natural environment, for example, makes attractive the thesis of Positive Aesthetics, with its implication that nature possesses an invulnerability to ugliness. Also, the undue restrictiveness that some have felt in the traditional conception of the aesthetic is an impetus for developing, along Deweyean lines, a broader notion of the aesthetic that would apply paradigmatically to everyday artefacts. These moves, however, result in an overall aesthetic theory that lacks unity in the sense of highlighting categorical differences between aesthetic appreciation as it occurs with different sorts of objects.

No one would deny that aesthetic appreciation does differ, to some extent, as it occurs with different sorts of objects. But, pretheoretically, it does not seem that we are engaging in a radically different form of appreciative activity when we go from, say, art to artefacts, or from artefacts to nature. In the latter case, as we discussed in Chapter 5, the thesis of Positive Aesthetics, as it has sometimes been developed, seems overstated. In the former case, it also seems that the difference in appreciation has been exaggerated. The aesthetic appreciation of a wrist watch or a jet fighter does not seem to involve the proximal senses to any greater extent than does, say, the appreciation of an artwork like a statue. Nor does it seem any more 'subjective' than such aesthetic appreciation of a statue would be. The existence of Functional Beauty explains this continuity in aesthetic appreciation by providing a common sort of appreciation applicable to a wide variety of different sorts of things. This brand of appreciation has been neglected, due to certain emphases in aesthetic theory (the focus on various forms of Distinterestedness, for instance) and because of confusion about the concept of function. By bringing Functional Beauty back into the picture, we can obtain a more accurate view of the character of aesthetic experience as a whole.

The philosopher wishing to realize these advantages by rehabilitating the concept of Functional Beauty faces a choice, however. For that phrase, as we have discussed in Chapter 1, Section 5, and in Chapter 5, Section 3, is ambiguous between 'beauty that emerges from function' and 'beauty that is functional'. On the former, the function of a thing is internal to, a part of, its beauty, whereas on the latter, function relates to beauty not as an internal element, but as an external constraint. On the latter view, an object is functionally beautiful when its beauty, a chair's elegant curvature, for instance, fits with or contributes to its function (by making for a comfortable seat, for example).[1] We have chosen to develop Functional Beauty in terms of the former, 'internal', approach. But one might argue that an external account, suitably developed, could make similar claims to comprehensiveness and unity. Why, then, focus on the internal conception?

One reason that we offered for focusing on the internal conception is that if we employ only the external conception, we miss some of the aesthetic quality of functional things. If beauty cannot arise out of function, but only relate to it, then aesthetic qualities such as looking fit will not figure in our aesthetic appreciation and evaluation of functional objects. In this sense, the internal conception enriches our phenomenology of the aesthetic in a way that the external conception does not. Another reason for favouring the internal conception is that it allows for a more forceful response to certain moral qualms about the aesthetic appreciation of certain sorts of things, such as animals and buildings: namely, the feeling that there is something morally suspect in appreciating them primarily on the basis of their 'sensory surface'. On the internal view, although Functional Beauty remains a matter of the object's sensory appearance, it cannot be considered an entirely superficial matter, dependent as it is upon an understanding of the function of the thing in question. This reasoning also suggests a more purely aesthetic reason for focusing on the internal conception of Functional Beauty. This is that Functional Beauty, construed in the 'internal' sense, has a central place in the aesthetic appreciation and evaluation of functional things that its external counterpart lacks. The external sense of Functional Beauty, though a valid notion, understates the importance of Functional Beauty.

This last point can be made evident by more fully explicating the general significance of Functional Beauty in aesthetic appreciation and evaluation. In art, it seems that aesthetic appreciation that is informed by, or that emerges out of, our knowledge of the artwork

[1] The example is from Stephen Davies, 'Aesthetic Judgements, Artworks and Functional Beauty', *Philosophical Quarterly* 56 (2006): 224–41.

is accorded more weight and significance in critical evaluation than appreciation that is not so grounded. Consider a work of sculpture. A casual passer–by, taking in the height and scale of the work, notes that its grandeur is enthralling. Another observer, having some understanding of the work's genesis and background, tells us that through its subtle arrangement of shapes and the skilful interplay of those shapes with the ambient sunlight and shade, the sculpture is a dramatically understated expression of, for example, the tragedy of war. Both judgements may be correct, so far as they go, and each may tell us something about the aesthetic character of the work. But there is also a difference between them, in that the latter judgement not only adds another aesthetic property of the work, namely, its dramatically understated expressiveness, but also identifies one that seems more central to the appreciation and evaluation of the work. The latter aesthetic quality may be less noticeable and impressive than the statue's enthralling grandeur; in fact, it probably is in this case since even a casual passer–by is capable of being struck by the grandeur.[2] But, if we had to choose *one* of these two aesthetic judgements to include in a critical assessment, it would surely be the latter, on the grounds that it tells us something more substantial about the overall aesthetic achievement of the work. Alternatively, consider aesthetic responses to jazz as lively, to rock music as loud, or to poetry as lyrical. These judgements may all be correct so far as they go, but they tell us comparatively little about any particular work's overall aesthetic character. They are, as it were, starting points for appreciation and critical assessment of particular works.

The general aesthetic principle at work in these cases of art appreciation and evaluation seems to be that aesthetic judgements become more weighty, or take on a greater critical significance,

[2] Cf. Noël Carroll's claim that 'if the depth of a response is figured in terms of our intensity of involvement and its "thorough goingness" then there is no reason to suppose that being moved by nature constitutes a shallower form of appreciation than does appreciating nature scientifically'; see his 'On Being Moved By Nature: Between Religion and Natural History', in Salim Kemal and Ivan Gaskell (eds), *Landscape, Natural Beauty and the Arts* (Cambridge: Cambridge University Press, 1993), 244–66; the quotation is on 259.

when they are based on an understanding of the object of appreciation. If this is correct, then Functional Beauty, construed in the 'internal' sense, has a central position in aesthetic appreciation and evaluation. For the proper function of an object, as we have developed the notion here, plays a key *explanatory* role with respect to that object, such that to grasp the function is to grasp something fundamental about the object.[3] Thus, an appreciation of the apparent fitness of a shark, or an aeroplane, or a courthouse captures something more significant about the aesthetic character of that object than does appreciation of its colour, its pattern, its shininess, or its imposing grandeur. If this line of thought is on the right track, then rather than being just one further, and possibly marginal, element in the aesthetic character of functional things, Functional Beauty may occupy a central and primary place in all of our aesthetic experience.

[3] See Glenn Parsons and Allen Carlson, 'New Formalism and the Aesthetic Appreciation of Nature', *Journal of Aesthetics and Art Criticism* 62 (2004): 363–76.

Bibliography

Alison, Archibald (1790) *Essays on the Nature and Principles of Taste* (Dublin: P. Byrne et al.).

Alison, Henry (2001) *Kant's Theory of Taste* (Cambridge: Cambridge University Press).

Allen, Colin, Marc Bekoff, and George Lauder (eds) (1998) *Nature's Purposes: Analyses of Function and Design in Biology* (Cambridge, MA: MIT Press).

Alston, William P. (1964) 'Pleasure', in Paul Edwards (ed.), *The Encyclopedia of Philosophy*, Volume 6 (New York: Macmillan), 341–7.

Amundson, Ronald and George Lauder (1994) 'Function without Purpose: The Uses of Causal Role Function in Evolutionary Biology', *Biology and Philosophy* 9: 443–69.

Anderson, James C. (2000) 'Aesthetic Concepts of Art', in N. Carroll (ed.), *Theories of Art Today* (Madison, WI: University of Wisconsin), 65–92.

Aquinas (1265–74) *Summa Theologiae*.

Ariew, Andrew, Robert Cummins, and Mark Perlman (eds) (2002) *Functions: New Essays in the Philosophy of Psychology and Biology* (Oxford: Oxford University Press).

Aristotle ([approx. 350 BCE] 1941) *Physics*, in *The Basic Works of Aristotle*, ed. Richard Mckeon, trans. R. P. Hardie and R. K. Gale (New York: Random House).

——([approx. 335 BCE] 1995) *Poetics*, in *Aristotle: Selections*, ed. and trans. Terence Irwin and Gail Fine (Indianapolis, IN: Hackett).

Bailey, George (2000) 'Art: Life after Death?', in N. Carroll (ed.), *Theories of Art Today* (Madison, WI: University of Wisconsin), 160–74.

Basalla, George (1988) *The Evolution of Technology* (Cambridge: Cambridge University Press).

Baumgarten, Alexander Gottlieb (1735) *Reflections on Poetry*.

——(1750) *Aesthetica*.

Beardsley, Monroe (1958) *Aesthetics: Problems in the Philosophy of Criticism* (New York: Harcourt Brace).

Beardsley, Monroe (1966) *Aesthetics: From Classical Greece to the Present* (New York: Macmillan).

——(1976) 'Is Art Essentially Institutional?', in Lars Aagaard–Mogensen (ed.), *Culture and Art* (Atlantic Highlands, NJ: Humanities Press), 194–209.

——(1982) *The Aesthetic Point of View*, ed. M. J. Wreen and D. M. Callen (Ithaca, NY: Cornell University Press), 298–315.

Beckner, Morton (1959) *The Biological Way of Thought* (New York: Columbia University Press).

Bell, Clive, ([1913] 1958) *Art* (New York: G. P. Putnam's Sons).

Berkeley, George ([1732] 1993) *Alciphron, or the Minute Philosopher*, in David Berman (ed.), *Alciphron, or the Minute Philosopher in Focus* (London: Routledge).

Berleant, Arnold (1991) *Art and Engagement* (Philadelphia, PA: Temple University Press).

——(1992) *The Aesthetics of Environment* (Philadelphia, PA: Temple University Press).

——(2004) *Re-thinking Aesthetics: Rogue Essays on Aesthetics and the Arts* (Aldershot, UK: Ashgate).

——(2005) *Aesthetics and Environment: Variations on a Theme* (Aldershot, UK: Ashgate).

——and Allen Carlson (eds) (2007) *The Aesthetics of Human Environments* (Peterborough, Canada: Broadview Press).

Berman, David (ed.) (1993) *Alciphron, or the Minute Philosopher in Focus* (London: Routledge).

Best, David (1974) 'The Aesthetic in Sport', *British Journal of Aesthetics* 14: 197–213.

Blake, Peter (1974) *Form Follows Fiasco: Why Modern Architecture Hasn't Worked* (Boston, MA: Little Brown).

Boorse, Christopher (1976) 'Wright on Functions', *Philosophical Review* 85: 70–86.

Borges, Jorge Luis (1964) 'Pierre Menard, Author of the *Quixote*', in *Labyrinths: Selected Stories & Other Writings*, ed. D. A. Yates and J. E. Irby (New York: New Directions Publishing), 36–44.

Brady, Emily (2005) 'Sniffing and Savoring: The Aesthetics of Smells and Tastes', in Andrew Light and Jonathan M. Smith (eds), *The Aesthetics of Everyday Life* (New York: Columbia University Press), 156–76.

Braithwate, Richard (1953) *Scientific Explanation* (Cambridge: Cambridge University Press).

Brand, Margaret and Carolyn Korsmeyer (eds) (1995) *Feminism and Tradition in Aesthetics* (University Park, PA: Pennsylvania State University Press).

Brolin, Brent C. (1976) *The Failure of Modern Architecture* (New York: Van Nostrand Reinhold).

Budd, Malcolm (1998) 'Delight in the Natural World: Kant on the Aesthetic Appreciation of Nature, Part I: Natural Beauty', *British Journal of Aesthetics* 38: 1–18.

—— (2000) 'The Aesthetics of Nature', *Proceedings of the Aristotelian Society* 100: 137–57.

—— (2002) *The Aesthetic Appreciation of Nature* (Oxford: Oxford University Press).

Bullough, Edward (1912) ' "Psychical Distance" as a Factor in Art and as an Aesthetic Principle', *British Journal of Psychology* 5: 87–98.

Burke, Edmund ([1757] 1958) *A Philosophical Enquiry into the Origin of our Ideas of the Sublime and Beautiful*, ed. James T. Boulton (London: Routledge and Kegan Paul).

Callicott, J. Baird (1994) 'The Land Aesthetic', in C. K. Chapple (ed.), *Ecological Prospects: Scientific, Religious, and Aesthetic Perspectives* (Albany, NY: State University of New York Press), 169–83.

—— (2003) 'Wetland Gloom and Wetland Glory', *Philosophy and Geography* 6: 33–45.

Canfield, John (1964) 'Teleological Explanations in Biology', *British Journal for the Philosophy of Science* 14: 285–95.

Carlson, Allen (1979) 'Appreciation and the Natural Environment', *Journal of Aesthetics and Art Criticism* 37: 267–76.

—— (1981) 'Nature, Aesthetic Judgment, and Objectivity', *Journal of Aesthetics and Art Criticism* 40: 15–27.

—— (1984) 'Nature and Positive Aesthetics', *Environmental Ethics* 6: 5–34.

—— (1985) 'On Appreciating Agricultural Landscapes', *Journal of Aesthetics and Art Criticism* 43: 301–12.

—— (1986) 'Reconsidering the Aesthetics of Architecture', *Journal of Aesthetic Education* 20: 21–7.

—— (1993) 'Appreciating Art and Appreciating Nature', in Salim Kemal and Ivan Gaskell (eds), *Landscape, Natural Beauty and the Arts* (Cambridge: Cambridge University Press), 199–227.

Carlson, Allen (1994) 'Existence, Location, and Function: The Appreciation of Architecture', in M. Mitias (ed.), *Philosophy and Architecture* (Amsterdam: Editions Rodopi), 141–64.

——(1999) 'The Aesthetic Appreciation of Everyday Architecture', in M. Mitias (ed.), *Architecture and Civilization* (Amsterdam: Editions Rodopi), 107–21.

——(2000) *Aesthetics and the Environment: The Appreciation of Nature, Art and Architecture* (London: Routledge).

——(2001) 'On Aesthetically Appreciating Human Environments', *Philosophy and Geography* 4: 9–24.

——(2002) 'Hargrove, Positive Aesthetics, and Indifferent Creativity', *Philosophy and Geography* 5: 224–34.

——(2005) 'Viljelysmaisemien Esteettinen Arvo Ja Touttavuus' ('Productivity and the Aesthetic Value of Agricultural Landscapes'), in Y. Sepänmaa, and L. Heikkilä-Palo (eds), *Pellossa Perihopeat (Fields: The Family Silver)* (Helsinki: Maahenki Oy), 52–61.

——(2006) '"We see beauty now where we could not see it before": Rolston's Aesthetics of Nature', in C. Preston and W. Ouderkirk (eds), *Nature, Value, Duty: Life on Earth with Holmes Rolston, III* (Dordrecht, Holland: Springer), 103–24.

——(2007) 'The Requirements for an Adequate Aesthetics of Nature', *Environmental Philosophy* 4: 1–12.

——(2009) *Nature and Landscape: An Introduction to Environmental Aesthetics* (New York: Columbia University Press).

——and Arnold Berleant (eds) (2004) *The Aesthetics of Natural Environments* (Peterborough, Canada: Broadview Press).

——and Sheila Lintott (eds) (2008) *Nature, Aesthetics, and Environmentalism: From Beauty to Duty* (New York: Columbia University Press).

Carritt, Edgar Frederick (1932) *What is Beauty? A First Introduction to the Subject and to Modern Theories* (Oxford: Oxford University Press).

Carroll, Noël (1988) 'Art, Practice and Narrative', *The Monist* 71: 140–56.

——(1990) *The Philosophy of Horror, or Paradoxes of the Heart* (New York: Routledge).

——(1991) 'Beauty and the Genealogy of Art Theory', *Philosophical Forum* 22: 307–34.

Carroll, Noël (1993) 'On Being Moved By Nature: Between Religion and Natural History', in Salim Kemal and Ivan Gaskell (eds), *Landscape, Natural Beauty and the Arts* (Cambridge: Cambridge University Press), 244–66.

____(1994) 'Identifying Art', in Robert J. Yanal (ed.), *Institutions of Art: Reconsiderations of George Dickie's Philosophy* (University Park, PA: Pennsylvania State University Press), 3–38.

____(2004) 'Art and Human Nature', *Journal of Aesthetics and Art Criticism* 62: 95–107.

Clark, Kenneth (1977) *Animals and Men: the Relationship as Reflected in Western Art from Prehistory to the Present Day* (New York: William Morrow and Company, Inc.).

Coleman, Francis J. (1965) 'Can a Smell or a Taste or a Touch be Beautiful?', *American Philosophical Quarterly* 2: 319–24.

Collingwood, Robin George ([1938] 1958) *The Principles of Art* (Oxford: Oxford University Press).

Cooper, Anthony Ashley (third Earl of Shaftesbury) (1711) *Characteristics of Men, Manners, Opinions, Times.*

Crawford, Donald (1983) 'Nature and Art: Some Dialectical Relationships', *Journal of Aesthetics and Art Criticism* 42: 49–58.

Croce, Benedetto ([1909] 1922) *Aesthetic: As Science of Expression and General Linguistic*, trans. Douglas Ainslie (New York: Macmillan).

Cummins, Robert (1975) 'Functional Analysis', *Journal of Philosophy* 72: 741–65.

Danto, Arthur (1964) 'The Artworld', *Journal of Philosophy* 61: 571–84.

____(1981) *The Transfiguration of the Commonplace: A Philosophy of Art* (Cambridge, MA: Harvard University Press).

____(1986) *The Philosophical Disenfranchisement of Art* (New York: Columbia University Press).

Davies, Paul Sheldon (2001) *Norms of Nature: Naturalism and the Nature of Functions* (Cambridge, MA: MIT Press).

Davies, Stephen (1991) *Definitions of Art* (Ithaca, NY: Cornell University Press).

____(2000) 'Non-Western Art and Art's Definition', in N. Carroll (ed.), *Theories of Art Today* (Madison, WI: University of Wisconsin), 199–216.

____(2006) 'Aesthetic Judgements, Artworks and Functional Beauty', *Philosophical Quarterly* 56: 224–41.

Dawkins, Richard (1986) *The Blind Watchmaker* (New York: W.W. Norton & Company).

De Clercq, Rafael (2005) 'The Aesthetic Peculiarity of Multifunctional Artefacts', *British Journal of Aesthetics* 45: 412–25.

De Zurko, Edward R. (1957) *Origins of Functionalist Theory* (New York: Columbia University Press).

Devereaux, Mary (2005) 'The Ugly', *American Society for Aesthetics Newsletter* 24/3, 1–2.

Dewey, John ([1934] 1958) *Art as Experience* (New York: Capricorn Books).

Diamond, Jared (1992) *The Third Chimpanzee: The Evolution and Future of the Human Animal* (New York: Harper Collins).

Dickie, George (1964) 'The Myth of the Aesthetic Attitude', *American Philosophical Quarterly* 1: 56–65.

—— (1974) *Art and the Aesthetic: An Institutional Analysis* (Ithaca, NY: Cornell University Press).

—— (1984) *The Art Circle* (New York: Haven Publications).

—— (1996) *The Century of Taste: The Philosophical Odyssey of Taste in the Eighteenth Century* (Oxford: Oxford University Press).

Diderot, Denis (1752) *The Beautiful.*

Dipert, Randall R. (1993) *Artifacts, Art Works, and Agency* (Philadelphia, PA: Temple University Press).

Dissanayake, Ellen (1995) *Homo Aestheticus: Where Art Comes From and Why* (Seattle, WA: University of Washington Press).

Donaldson, John (1780) *The Elements of Beauty.*

Ducasse, Curt ([1929] 1966) *The Philosophy of Art* (New York: Dover).

—— ([1944] 1955) *Art, the Critics, and You* (Indianapolis, IN: Bobbs–Merrill).

Dutton, Denis (2003) 'Aesthetics and Evolutionary Psychology', in Jerrold Levinson (ed.), *The Oxford Handbook of Aesthetics* (Oxford: Oxford University Press), 693–705.

Eagleton, Terry (1990) *The Ideology of the Aesthetic* (Oxford: Blackwell).

Eaton, Marcia (1998) 'Fact and Fiction in the Aesthetic Appreciation of Nature', *Journal of Aesthetics and Art Criticism* 56: 149–56.

Escobar, Jesús (2004) *The Plaza Mayor and the Shaping of Baroque Madrid* (Cambridge: Cambridge University Press).

Fisher, John Andrew (1998) 'What the Hills Are Alive With: In Defense of the Sounds of Nature', *Journal of Aesthetics and Art Criticism* 56: 167–79.

Fisher, M. F. K. (1989) *Serve it Forth* (San Francisco: North Point Press).

Fox, Charles Philip, and Tom Parkinson (1969) *The Circus in America* (Waukesha, WI: Country Beautiful).

Freud, Sigmund ([1907] 1995) 'Creative Writers and Day-Dreaming', trans. Grant Duff, in A. Neill and A. Ridley (eds), *The Philosophy of Art: Readings Ancient and Modern* (New York: McGraw-Hill), 46–53.

Gerard, Alexander (1759) *Essay on Taste.*

Gilpin, William (1792) *Three Essays: On Picturesque Beauty, On Picturesque Travel, and On Sketching Landscape.*

Ginsberg, Robert (2004) *The Aesthetics of Ruins* (Amsterdam: Editions Rodopi).

Godfrey-Smith, Peter (1994) 'A Modern History Theory of Functions', *Noûs* 28: 344–62.

Godlovitch, Stan (1998) 'Valuing Nature and the Autonomy of Natural Aesthetics', *British Journal of Aesthetics* 38: 180–97.

Goldman, Alan (2001) 'The Aesthetic', in Berys Gaut and Dominic McIver Lopes (eds), *The Routledge Companion to Aesthetics* (London: Routledge), 181–92.

Goodman, Nelson (1955) *Fact, Fiction, and Forecast* (Cambridge, MA: Harvard University Press).

—— (1968) *Languages of Art* (Indianapolis, IN: Bobbs-Merrill).

—— (1988) 'How Buildings Mean', in Nelson Goodman and Catherine Z. Elgin, *Reconceptions in Philosophy and Other Arts and Sciences* (London: Routledge), 31–48.

Gould, Carol (2005) 'Glamour as an Aesthetic Property of Persons', *Journal of Aesthetics and Art Criticism* 63: 237–47.

Gould, Stephen J. (1980) *The Panda's Thumb: More Reflections in Natural History* (New York: W.W. Norton & Company).

Graham, Gordon (1989) 'Art and Architecture', *British Journal of Aesthetics* 29: 248–57.

—— (2003) 'Architecture', in Jerrold Levinson (ed.), *The Oxford Handbook of Aesthetics* (Oxford: Oxford University Press), 555–71.

Greenough, Horatio (1852) *The Travels, Observations and Experiences of a Yankee Stonecutter* (New York: Putnam).

—— ([1853] 1968) 'American Architecture', in Henry T. Tuckerman, *A Memorial of Horatio Greenough* (New York: Benjamin Blom), 117–30.

Guyer, Paul (1997) *Kant and the Claims of Taste*, 2nd edn (Cambridge: Cambridge University Press).

Guyer, Paul (2002a) 'Beauty and Utility in Eighteenth-Century Aesthetics', *Eighteenth-Century Studies* 35: 439–53.

——(2002b) 'Free and Adherent Beauty: A Modest Proposal', *British Journal of Aesthetics* 42: 357–66.

——(2003) 'History of Modern Aesthetics', in Jerrold Levinson (ed.), *The Oxford Handbook of Aesthetics* (Oxford: Oxford University Press), 25–60.

Hargrove, Eugene (1989) *Foundations of Environmental Ethics* (Englewood Cliffs, NJ: Prentice Hall).

——(2002) 'Carlson and the Aesthetic Appreciation of Nature', *Philosophy and Geography* 5: 213–23.

Hegel, Georg Wilhelm Friedrich ([1835] 1975) *Hegel's Aesthetics: Lectures on Fine Arts*, trans. T. M. Knox (Oxford: Oxford University Press).

Hein, Hilda and Carolyn Korsmeyer (1993) *Aesthetics in Feminist Perspective* (Bloomington, IN: Indiana University Press).

Hettinger, Ned (2005) 'Carlson's Environmental Aesthetics and the Protection of the Environment', *Environmental Ethics* 27: 57–76.

Hipple, Walter, J. (1957) *The Beautiful, the Sublime, and the Picturesque in Eighteenth–Century British Aesthetic Theory* (Carbondale, IL: The Southern Illinois University Press).

Hobbes, Thomas ([1651] 1999) *Leviathan or the Matter, Form, and Power of a Commonwealth Ecclesiastical and Civil* (Hamilton, Canada: McMaster University Archive of the History of Economic Thought).

Hogarth, William ([1753] 1997) *Analysis of Beauty*, ed. R. Paulson (New Haven, CN: Yale).

Hospers, John (1946) *Meaning and Truth in the Arts* (Chapel Hill, NC: University of North Carolina Press).

Houkes, Wybo N. and Pieter E. Vermaas (2004) 'Actions versus Functions: A Plea for an Alternative Metaphysics of Artifacts', *The Monist* 87: 52–71.

Hume, Christopher (2006) 'The Opera House We Didn't Build', *Toronto Star*, 16 September.

Hume, David ([1739–40] 1960) *A Treatise of Human Nature*, ed. L. A. Selby-Bigge (Oxford: Oxford University Press).

Hussey, Christopher (1927) *The Picturesque: Studies in a Point of View* (London: G. P. Putnam's).

Hutcheson, Francis ([1738] 1772) *An Inquiry into the Original of Our Ideas of Beauty and Virtue; in Two Treatises*, 4th edn (Glasgow: Robert and Andrew Foulis).

Iseminger, Gary (2004) *The Aesthetic Function of Art* (Ithaca, NY: Cornell University Press).

Janson, Horst Woldemar (Peter) (1991) *History of Art*, 4th edn (Englewood Cliffs, NJ: Prentice Hall).

Jung, Carl Gustav ([1922] 1978) 'The Relation of Analytical Psychology to Poetry', in *The Spirit in Man, Art and Literature*, ed. Gerhard Adler, trans. R. F. C. Hull (Princeton, NJ: Princeton University Press), 65–83.

Kant, Immanuel ([1790] 2000) *Critique of the Power of Judgment*, ed. Paul Guyer, trans. Paul Guyer and Eric Matthews (Cambridge: Cambridge University Press).

Kellert, Stephen (1989) 'Perceptions of Animals in America', in R. J. Hoage (ed.), *Perceptions of Animals in American Culture* (Washington, DC: Smithsonian Institute), 5–24.

Kitcher, Philip (1994) 'Function and Design', *Midwest Studies in Philosophy* 18: 379–97.

Kivy, Peter (2003) *The Seventh Sense: Francis Hutcheson and Eighteenth-Century British Aesthetics*, 2nd edn (Oxford: Oxford University Press).

Korsmeyer, Carolyn (1976) 'Hume and the Foundations of Taste', *Journal of Aesthetics and Art Criticism* 35: 201–15.

____(1999a) 'Food and the Taste of Meaning', in P. von Bonsdorff and A. Haapala (eds), *Aesthetics in the Human Environment* (Lahti, Finland: International Institute of Applied Aesthetics), 90–105.

____(1999b) *Making Sense of Taste: Food and Philosophy* (Ithaca, NY: Cornell University Press).

____(2002) 'Delightful, Delicious, Disgusting', *Journal of Aesthetics and Art Criticism* 60: 217–25.

Kristeller, Paul Oskar (1951) 'The Modern System of the Arts: A Study in the History of Aesthetics I', *Journal of the History of Ideas* 12: 496–527.

____(1952) 'The Modern System of the Arts: A Study in the History of Aesthetics II', *Journal of the History of Ideas* 13: 17–46.

Lageux, Maurice (1999) 'Reconfiguring Four Key "isms" Commonly Used in Architectural Theory', *British Journal of Aesthetics* 39: 179–88.

Landow, George (1971) *The Aesthetic and Critical Theories of John Ruskin* (Princeton, NJ: Princeton University Press).

Lawrence, Elizabeth A. (1989) 'Neoteny in American Perceptions of Animals', in R. J. Hoage (ed.), *Perceptions of Animals in American Culture* (Washington, DC: Smithsonian Institute), 57–76.

Leddy, Thomas (2005) 'The Nature of Everyday Aesthetics', in Andrew Light and Jonathan M. Smith (eds), *The Aesthetics of Everyday Life* (New York: Columbia University Press), 3–22.

Leibniz, Gottfried Wilhelm ([1684] 1989) 'Meditations on Knowledge, Truth, and Ideas', in *Philosophical Essays*, trans. R. Ariew and D. Garber (Indianapolis, IN: Hackett), 23–7.

Levinson, Jerrold (1979) 'Defining Art Historically', *British Journal of Aesthetics* 19: 232–50.

——(1996) 'What is Aesthetic Pleasure?', in *The Pleasures of Aesthetics: Philosophical Essays* (Ithaca, NY: Cornell University Press), 3–10.

Light, Andrew and Aurora Wallace (2005) 'Not Out of the Woods: Preserving the Human in Environmental Architecture', *Environmental Values* 14: 3–20.

Lind, Richard (1992) 'The Aesthetic Essence of Art', *Journal of Aesthetics and Art Criticism* 50: 117–29.

——(1993) 'Art as Aesthetic Statement', *Journal of Aesthetic Education* 27: 1–21.

Loos, Adolf ([1908] 1998) 'Ornament and Crime', in *Ornament and Crime: Selected Essays*, ed. Adolf Opel, trans. Michael Mitchell (Riverside, CA: Ariadne Press), 167–76.

Lorenz, Konrad ([1950] 1971) 'Part and Parcel in Animal and Human Societies', in *Studies in Animal and Human Behaviour*, Volume 2, trans. Robert Martin (Cambridge, MA: Harvard University Press), 115–95.

Luker, Nicholas (ed.) (1988) *From Furmanov to Sholokhov: An Anthology of the Classics of Socialist Realism*, trans. Nicholas Luker (Ann Arbor, MI: Ardis).

Lyell, Charles (1830) *Principles of Geology*.

Macdonald, Graham and David Papineau (eds) (2006) *Teleosemantics* (Oxford: Oxford University Press).

McMahon, Jennifer Anne (2001) 'Beauty', in Berys Gaut and Dominic Lopes (eds), *The Routledge Companion to Aesthetics* (London: Routledge), 227–38.

Matthews, Patricia (2002) 'Scientific Knowledge and the Aesthetic Appreciation of Nature', *Journal of Aesthetics and Art Criticism* 60: 37–48.

Mayr, Ernst (1974) 'Teleological and Telonomic: A New Analysis', *Boston Studies in the Philosophy of Science* 14: 91–117.

——(1988) *Towards a New Philosophy of Biology* (Cambridge, MA: Harvard University Press).

Melchionne, Kevin (1998) 'Living in Glass Houses: Domesticity, Interior Decoration, and Environmental Aesthetics', *Journal of Aesthetics and Art Criticism* 56: 191–200.

Michelfelder, Diane (2003) 'Valuing Wildlife Populations in Urban Environments', *Journal of Social Philosophy* 34: 79–90.

Mill, John Stuart (1874) 'On Nature'.

Millikan, Ruth (1984) *Language, Thought, and Other Biological Categories: New Foundations for Realism* (Cambridge, MA: MIT Press).

——(1989) 'In Defense of Proper Functions', *Philosophy of Science* 56: 288–302.

——(1993) *White Queen Psychology and Other Essays for Alice* (Cambridge, MA: MIT Press).

Montero, Barbara (2006) 'Proprioception as an Aesthetic Sense', *Journal of Aesthetics and Art Criticism* 64: 231–42.

Morreall, John (1991) 'Cuteness', *British Journal of Aesthetics* 31: 39–47.

Mumford, Lewis (1951) 'Function and Expression in Architecture', *Architectural Record* 110 (November): 106–12.

——(1953) *Highway and the City* (Westport, CT: Greenwood Publishing Group).

Nagel, Ernst (1961) *The Structure of Science* (New York: Harcourt).

Neander, Karen (1991a) 'Functions as Selected Effects: The Conceptual Analyst's Defence', *Philosophy of Science* 58: 168–84.

——(1991b) 'The Teleological Notion of "Function"', *Australasian Journal of Philosophy* 69: 454–68.

Novitz, David (1989) 'Ways of Artmaking: The High and the Popular in Art', *British Journal of Aesthetics* 29: 213–29.

——(1992) 'Function of Art', in D. Cooper (ed.), *A Companion to Aesthetics* (Oxford: Blackwell), 162–7.

——(2001) *The Boundaries of Art* (Christchurch, New Zealand: Cybereditions).

Pappas, Nickolas (2001) 'Aristotle', in Berys Gaut and Dominic McIver Lopes (eds), *The Routledge Companion to Aesthetics* (London: Routledge), 15–26.

Parsons, Glenn (2002) 'Nature Appreciation, Science, and Positive Aesthetics', *British Journal of Aesthetics* 42: 279–95.

——(2004) 'Natural Functions and the Aesthetic Appreciation of Inorganic Nature', *British Journal of Aesthetics* 44: 44–56.

——(2006a) 'Freedom and Objectivity in the Aesthetic Appreciation of Nature', *British Journal of Aesthetics* 46: 17–37.

——(2006b) 'Theory, Observation, and the Role of Scientific Understanding in the Aesthetic Appreciation of Nature', *Canadian Journal of Philosophy* 36: 165–86.

——(2007) 'The Aesthetic Value of Animals', *Environmental Ethics* 29: 151–69.

——(2008) *Aesthetics and Nature* (London: Continuum Press).

——and Allen Carlson (2004) 'New Formalism and the Aesthetic Appreciation of Nature', *Journal of Aesthetics and Art Criticism* 62: 363–76.

Perlman, Mark (2004) 'The Modern Philosophical Resurrection of Teleology', *The Monist* 87: 3–51.

Plato ([approx. 390 BCE] 1965) *Greater Hippias*, trans. B. Jowett, in K. Aschenbrenner and A. Isenberg (eds), *Aesthetic Theories: Studies in the Philosophy of Art* (Englewood Cliffs, NJ: Prentice-Hall), 3–17.

Preston, Beth (1998) 'Why is a Wing like a Spoon? A Pluralist Theory of Function', *Journal of Philosophy* 115: 215–54.

——(2003) 'Of Marigold Beer: A Reply to Vermaas and Houkes', *British Journal for the Philosophy of Science* 54: 601–12.

Pugin, Augustus Welby ([1836] 1841) *Contrasts: or A Parallel between the Noble Edifices of the Middle Ages, and corresponding Buildings of the Present Day; Shewing the Present Decay of Taste* (London: Charles Dolman).

——(1843) *An Apology for the Revival of Christian Architecture in England* (London: John Weale).

Rawls, John (1971) *A Theory of Justice* (Cambridge, MA: Harvard University Press).

Regan, Tom (1983) *The Case for Animal Rights* (Berkeley, CA: University of California Press).

Richards, Richard (2004) 'A Fitness Model of Evaluation', *Journal of Aesthetic and Art Criticism* 62: 263–75.

Rockmore, Tom (1992) 'Marxism and Art', in D. Cooper (ed.), *A Companion to Aesthetics* (Oxford: Blackwell), 275–9.

Rogers, David (2001) 'Functionalism', in H. Brigstocke (ed.), *Oxford Companion to Western Art* (Oxford: Oxford University Press), 263–4.

Rolston, Holmes, III (1987) 'Beauty and the Beast: Aesthetic Experience of Wildlife', in Daniel J. Decker and Gary R. Goff (eds), *Valuing Wildlife: Economic and Social Perspectives* (Boulder, CO: Westview Press), 187–207.

____(1988) *Environmental Ethics: Duties to and Values in the Natural World* (Philadelphia, PA: Temple University Press).

____(1995) 'Does Aesthetic Appreciation of Nature Need to be Science Based?', *British Journal of Aesthetics* 35: 374–86.

____(2000) 'Aesthetics in the Swamps', *Perspectives in Biology and Medicine* 43: 584–97.

Rosenblueth, Arturo, Norbert Wiener, and Julian Bigelow (1943) 'Behaviour, Purpose and Teleology', *Philosophy of Science* 10: 18–24.

Ruskin, John ([1843–60] 1907) *Modern Painters* (London: J. M. Dent & Co.).

____(1880) *The Seven Lamps of Architecture*, 2nd edn (London: George Allen).

Sagoff, Mark (1974) 'On Preserving the Natural Environment', *Yale Law Journal* 84: 205–67.

Saito, Yuriko (1998) 'The Aesthetics of Unscenic Nature', *Journal of Aesthetics and Art Criticism* 56: 101–11.

____(2001) 'Everyday Aesthetics', *Philosophy and Literature* 25: 87–95.

Santayana, George ([1896] 1961) *The Sense of Beauty* (New York: Collier).

Sartwell, Crispin (2003) 'Aesthetics of the Everyday', in Jerrold Levinson (ed.), *The Oxford Handbook of Aesthetics* (Oxford: Oxford University Press), 761–70.

Savedoff, Barbara (1985) 'Intellectual and Sensuous Pleasure', *Journal of Aesthetics and Art Criticism* 43: 313–15.

Savile, Anthony (1982) *The Test of Time* (Oxford: Oxford University Press).

Schiller, Friedrich ([1794] 2004) *On the Aesthetic Education of Man*, trans. Reginald Snell (Mineola, NY: Dover).

Scott, Geoffrey ([1914] 1999) *The Architecture of Humanism: A Study in the History of Taste* (New York: W.W. Norton & Co.).

Scruton, Roger (1979) *The Aesthetics of Architecture* (London: Methuen and Company).

Shapin, Steven (1996) *The Scientific Revolution* (Chicago, IL: University of Chicago Press).

Shiner, Larry (2001) *The Invention of Art: A Cultural History* (Chicago, IL: University of Chicago Press).

Shusterman, Richard (2000a) *Performing Live* (Ithaca, NY: Cornell University Press).

——(2000b) 'Somaesthetics and Care of the Self: The Case of Foucault', *The Monist* 83: 530–53.

——(2001) 'Pragmatism; Dewey', in Berys Gaut and Dominic McIver Lopes (eds), *The Routledge Companion to Aesthetics* (London: Routledge), 97–106.

——(2003) 'Somaesthetics and *The Second Sex*: A Pragmatist Reading of a Feminist Classic', *Hypatia* 18: 106–36.

——(2006) 'Aesthetic Experience: From Analysis to Eros', *Journal of Aesthetics and Art Criticism* 64: 217–30.

Sibley, Frank (1959a) 'Aesthetic Concepts', *Philosophical Review* 68: 421–50.

——(1959b) 'Aesthetics and the Look of Things', *The Journal of Philosophy* 56: 905–15.

——(1965) 'Aesthetic and Nonaesthetic', *Philosophical Review* 74: 135–59.

——(2001) *Approach to Aesthetics: Collected Papers on Philosophical Aesthetics*, ed. John Benson, Betty Redfern, and Jeremy Roxbee Cox (Oxford: Oxford University Press).

Smith, Adam ([1759] 1982) *The Theory of Moral Sentiments*, in *The Glasgow Edition of the Works and Correspondence of Adam Smith*, Volume I, ed. D. D. Raphael and A. L. Macfie (Indianapolis, IN: Liberty Fund).

Sparshott, Francis (1963) *The Structure of Aesthetics* (Toronto, Canada: University of Toronto Press).

Speaight, George (1980) *A History of the Circus* (London: Tantivy Press).

Stace, Walter Terence (1929) *The Meaning of Beauty: A Theory of Aesthetics* (London: Richards and Toulmin).

Stecker, Robert (1997a) *Artworks: Definitions, Meaning, Value* (University Park, PA: Pennsylvania State University Press).

——(1997b) 'The Correct and the Appropriate in the Appreciation of Nature', *British Journal of Aesthetics* 37: 393–402.

Stolnitz, Jerome (1960) *Aesthetics and Philosophy of Art Criticism: A Critical Introduction* (Boston, MA: Houghton Mifflin).

Stolnitz, Jerome (1961a) '"Beauty": Some Stages in the History of an Idea', *Journal of the History of Ideas* 22: 185–204.

—— (1961b) 'On the Origins of "Aesthetic Disinterestedness"', *Journal of Aesthetics and Art Criticism* 20: 131–43.

Sullivan, Louis ([1918] 1979) *Kindergarten Chats and Other Writings* (New York: Dover).

Tartarkiewicz, Wladyslaw (1972) 'The Great Theory of Beauty and its Decline', *Journal of Aesthetics and Art Criticism* 31: 165–80.

Thompson, Janna (1995) 'Aesthetics and the Value of Nature', *Environmental Ethics* 17: 291–305.

Tolstoy, Leo N. (1898) *What is Art?*, trans. Alymer Maude (London: Walter Scott, Ltd.).

Tooby, John and Leda Cosmides (2001) 'Does Beauty Build Adapted Minds? Toward an Evolutionary Theory of Aesthetics, Fiction and the Arts', *SubStance* 30: 6–27.

Urmson, James O. (1962) 'What Makes a Situation Aesthetic?', in Joseph Margolis (ed.), *Philosophy Looks at the Arts* (New York: Charles Scribner's Sons), 13–27.

—— (1993) 'Berkeley on Beauty', in David Berman (ed.), *Alciphron in Focus* (London: Routledge), 179–84.

Vermaas, Pieter E. and Wybo N. Houkes (2003) 'Ascribing Functions to Technical Artefacts: A Challenge to Etiological Accounts of Functions', *British Journal for the Philosophy of Science* 54: 261–89.

von Bonsdorff, Pauline and Arto Haapala (eds) (1999) *Aesthetics in the Human Environment* (Lahti, Finland: International Institute of Applied Aesthetics).

Walsh, Denis M. (ed.) (2001) *Naturalism, Evolution and Mind* (Cambridge: Cambridge University Press).

Walton, Kendall (1970) 'Categories of Art', *Philosophical Review* 79: 334–67.

Wicks, Robert (1997) 'Dependent Beauty as the Appreciation of Teleological Style', *Journal of Aesthetics and Art Criticism* 55: 387–400.

Wieand, Jeffrey (1981) 'Can There Be an Institutional Theory of Art?', *Journal of Aesthetics and Art Criticism* 39: 409–17.

Winters, Edward (2001) 'Architecture', in Berys Gaut and Dominic McIver Lopes (eds), *The Routledge Companion to Aesthetics* (London: Routledge), 519–30.

Wolf, Naomi (1992) *The Beauty Myth* (New York: Doubleday).

Wolfe, Tom (1981) *From Bauhaus to Our House* (New York: Farrar, Straus and Giroux).

Wolterstorff, Nicholas (2003) 'Why Philosophy of Art Cannot Handle Kissing, Touching, and Crying', *Journal of Aesthetics and Art Criticism* 61: 17–27.

Wright, Larry (1968) 'The Case against Teleological Reductionism', *British Journal for the Philosophy of Science* 19: 211–23.

—— (1973) 'Functions', *Philosophical Review* 82: 139–68.

Xenophon ([approx. 370 BCE] 1970–4; 2005) *Memorabilia*, trans. E. C. Marchant, in Wladyslaw Tatarkiewicz, *History of Aesthetics*, Volume 1 (London: Continuum), 109–10.

—— ([approx. 360 BCE] 1998) *Symposium*, ed. and trans. A. J. Bowen (Warminster: Aris and Phillips).

Yanal, Robert J. (ed.) (1994) *Institutions of Art: Reconsiderations of George Dickie's Philosophy* (University Park, PA: Pennsylvania State University Press).

Zangwill, Nick (2000) 'Aesthetic Functionalism', in E. Brady and J. Levinson (eds), *Aesthetic Concepts: Essays after Sibley* (Oxford: Oxford University Press), 123–48.

—— (2001a) 'Formal Natural Beauty', *Proceedings of the Aristotelian Society* 101: 209–24.

—— (2001b) *The Metaphysics of Beauty* (Ithaca, NY: Cornell University Press).

—— (2003) 'Beauty', in Jerrold Levinson (ed.), *Oxford Handbook of Aesthetics* (Oxford: Oxford University Press), 325–43.

—— (2005) 'In Defence of Extreme Formalism about Inorganic Nature: Reply to Parsons', *British Journal of Aesthetics* 45: 185–91.

Ziman, John (ed.) (2000) *Technological Innovation as an Evolutionary Process* (Cambridge: Cambridge University Press).

Zucker, Paul (1961) 'Ruins—An Aesthetic Hybrid', *Journal of Aesthetics and Art Criticism* 20: 119–30.

Index

adherent beauty 22–3, 27
aesthetic appreciation
  of animals 112–124
  cognitively rich 35, 37–40, 58–9, 61, 91–2, 95, 192–5 *see also* Functional Beauty
  cultural theories of 32–8, 57–9, 91–2
  and feminism 116–7
'Aesthetic Concepts' (Sibley) 32
aesthetic attitude 24–6, 32
aesthetic pleasure 46, 102–3, 105–6, 125–6, 177–8, 183–8, 194–5
  concept of 4–5
  and disinterestedness 24–6, 32–7, 104–5
  and function *see* Functional Beauty
  immediate experience of 18–20
  and proximal vs. distal senses 175–89, 194–5
  and utility 8–11, 102–6
aesthetic qualities
  function-dependent 95–100 *see also* Functional Beauty
  negative 107–10, 161–6
aesthetic theory
  comprehensiveness of 12, 57–60
  unity of 38, 57–60
Alciphron (Berkeley) 7–8
Alison, Archibald 11–12, 16
Alsop, Will 99
The Analysis of Beauty (Hogarth) 11
Anderson, James 212 n. 35
animals
  aesthetic appreciation of 112–24
  as counterexamples to Functional Beauty 13–17
architecture
  deception in 140–2
  and Functional Beauty 138–42, 158–61
  and Functionalism 42–5
  see also buildings
Aristotle 40, 220, 221–2
art
  aesthetic appreciation of 12, 55–60, 110, 152–3, 171–2, 189–95, 222–7
  autonomy of 24–30
  and craft 29–30, 36–7
  cultural theories of 32–7, 57–60
  commemorative 36, 224–5
  and Functional Beauty 222–7
  functions of 197–203
  Institutional theory of 34–5, 190–1, 206–9
  proper function of 216–22
artefacts: everyday 12, 55–60, 168–172
  and Functional Beauty 189–195
  novel 79–84
  proper functions of 72–7
Asphalt Rundown (Smithson) 225–6

Bailey, George 217–18
Bauhaus movement 44
Baumgarten, Alexander 7
Beardsley, Monroe 27 n. 73, 198, 204, 212
beauty
  adherent 22–3, 27
  as aesthetic appeal in general, xii–xiii *see also* aesthetic pleasure, aesthetic qualities, Functional Beauty
  non-aesthetic sense of 4
  as a particular aesthetic quality 17–8
Bell, Clive 26–7
Berkeley, George 7–8, 11 n. 27
Berleant, Arnold 59, 168 n., 175 n. 13, 183, 186 n. 41
Best, David 97–8
Beverley Hills lawn chair: aesthetics of 99, 104
biology, philosophy of 69–73
bodily pleasures 177–89, 194–5
Boorse, Christopher 65 n.
Brady, Emily 176, 179, 183

Budd, Malcolm 123 n., 124–5, 131
buildings
  and expression 157–8, 160
  functions of 143–9
  proper functions of 146–9, 150–1
  structural honesty of 155–7, 159, 160
  see also architecture, ruins
Bullough, Edward 24
Burke, Edmund 12–14, 17, 18–19, 21–2

Callicott, J. B. 127
can openers 83–4
Carritt, E. F. 28 n. 75
Carroll, Noël 27, 34, 201, 210, 233 n.
  on horror genre 220–1
cars: aesthetics of 96, 101–2
causal role functions
  defined 70–1
  and positive aesthetics 130–6
  and proper functions 71
Cervantes, Miguel de: *Don Quixote* 51
Clark, Kenneth 115
cognitively rich aesthetic appreciation *see* aesthetic appreciation, cognitively rich
Coleman, Francis J. 183 n. 33
Collingwood, R. G. 29–30
commemorative art 36, 224–5
comprehensiveness: in aesthetic theory 12, 57–60
craft: and art 29–30, 36–7
cranes: aesthetics of 99–100
Crawford, Donald 163 n. 40, 164
Critique of the Power of Judgment (Kant) xi, 21
Croce, Benedetto 28–9, 30 n.
Cummins, Robert 70–2, 75 n., 125, 135 n.

Danto, Arthur 32–3, 227
Darwin, Charles 41
Davies, Paul Sheldon 75 n.
Davies, Stephen 212 n. 35
Dawkins, Richard 123–4
De Clercq, Rafael 52–3, 54
deception in architecture 140–2
dependent beauty *see* beauty, adherent
Dewey, John 174–6, 191–2, 194
Dickie, George 32, 33, 101, 189
  on Institutional theory of art 34–5
  on natural objects 37
disinterestedness
  two senses of 24–6
  as appreciating things non-conceptually 32–7
  as appreciating things for their own sake 104–5
Dissanayake, Ellen 201
distal senses *see* aesthetic pleasure and proximal vs. distal senses
Don Quixote (Cervantes) 51
Donaldson, John 14 n. 37
Duchamp, Marcel 173, 226
dysfunction: aesthetics of 107–10

Eaton, Marcia 119 n. 21
ecosystems: and causal role functions 125–9
elegance *see* Functional Beauty, phenomenology of
Essay on Taste (Gerard) 11
everyday aesthetics
  Deweyean approach 174–6, 177–8, 182–6, 191–2, 194
  features of 168–72
  and Functional Beauty 189–95
  and functionality 170–1
  and the linguistic practice argument 177–82
  and meaningfulness 171–2
evolutionary psychology 201
expression 28–30, 219, 233
  and buildings 43, 157–8, 159, 160
  and ruins 164–6
Expressionism: as a theory of art 28–30

fashion: aesthetics of 109–10, 163
feminism
  and aesthetic appreciation 116–17
  and disinterestedness 33
fine arts 26
fitness for function *see* Functional Beauty, looking fit for function as
flak towers, Vienna 64–5
Formalism: and aesthetic appreciation 26–7, 118
Fountain (Duchamp) 226

Four Seasons Centre, Toronto 49–50, 85–6
Freud, Sigmund 200, 211
function
knowledge of 91–4
naturalization of 69–73
theories of *see* casual role functions, intentionalist theories of function, selected effects theory of proper function
see also proper function
Functional Beauty
as bourgeois aesthetic 149–54
as central in aesthetic experience 232–4
concept of xii–iiii, 2–5
and everyday aesthetics 189–95
and Formalism 26–8
and looking dysfunctional 107–10
internal/external senses of 23–4, 121–4, 231–2
looking fit for function as 17–18, 95–6, 100–6
in classical thought 2–5, 55
criticism of 12–18
and Kant 21–4
in 17th/18th centuries 6–12
moral neutrality of 152–4
phenomenology of 94–100
and relativism 51–6, 84–9, 192–4
weak/strong senses of 3–4, 15
see also Problem of Indeterminacy, Problem of Translation
Functionalism: and architecture 42–5

Gerard, Alexander 11
Goodman, Nelson 32–3, 81 n. 37
Gould, Stephen J. 114, 119, 120 n. 23
Graham, Gordon 144, 156 n. 33, 157 n. 33
The Greater Hippias (Plato) 2–3, 180, 183 n. 32
Greenough, Horatio 140–1
Guyer, Paul 6, 15 n. 41, 22, 108

Hargrove, Eugene 131
hearing *see* distal senses
Hegel, G. W. F. 112
Hettinger, Ned 87–8
Hobbes, Thomas 11 n. 29
Hogarth, William 11
horror genre 220–1
Hospers, John 28 n. 75, 100
Houkes, Wybo N. 67 n. 8
criticisms of selected effects theories 80, 82
intentionalist theory of artefact function 78–9
Hume, Christopher 50, 86
Hume, David: on beauty and utility 8–11, 102–3, 108
Hutcheson, Francis 14, 17, 18, 97 n. 6

In Advance of the Broken Arm (Duchamp) 173
Indeterminacy, Problem of 49–57, 84–9
industrial farms: proper function of 88, 150–4
intentionalist theories of function 63–5, 75 n.
and proper functions 67–9, 78–9, 203–9
and novel artefacts 84–9
Institutional theory of art 34–5, 190–1, 206–9
International Modernism 44, 137–8, 144–5, 159
Iseminger, Gary 206–9, 214 n., 216

Janson, H. W. 173 n.
Johnson, Philip 159
Jung, Carl Gustav 200, 210–11

Kant, Immanuel xi, 21–4
Kellert, Stephen 114 n. 11
knowledge *see* aesthetic appreciation, coginitively rich
Korsmeyer, Carolyn 103 n., 176, 179,182 n., 183, 185 n., 186

landscape *see* nature, aesthetic appreciation of
Landow, George 15 n. 41
Le Corbusier (Charles- 'Edouard Jeanneret) 44
Leddy, Tom 168–9, 176, 192–4
Leibniz, Gottfried 6
Lin, Maya Ying 224–5

Lind, Richard 212
linguistic practice argument 177–89
Loos, Adolf 140 n. 4
Lorenz, Konrad 114
Lyell, Charles 41

Manzoni, Piero 225–6
Marxism 33, 200–1, 214
Mayr, Ernst 69–70
meaningfulness: and everyday aesthetics 171–2
Memorabilia (Xenophon) 2, 3–4, 15
Merde d'Artiste (Manzoni) 225–6
Michelfelder, Diane 113
Mies van der Rohe, Ludwig 159
Millikan, Ruth 66 n. 6
Modernism *see* International Modernism
Mumford, Lewis 145
muscle cars: aesthetics of 96, 101–2

natural environmental model of nature appreciation 39
natural theology 40–1
nature: aesthetic appreciation of
  criticism of 116–20
  living 112–16
  and neglect of Functional Beauty, 37–42
  non-living 124–9
  see also animals
nature: and concept of function 40–2, 69–73
nature: Functional Beauty of
  living 120–4
  non-living 124–9
  and positive aesthetics 130–6
Neander, Karen 211 n. 32
novel artefacts
  can openers 83–4
  and proper functions 80–4
  teletypewriters 80, 82
Novitz, David 201, 209–10

organisms: and Functional Beauty 120–4; *see also* nature, aesthetic appreciation of

perception: and beauty 5, 18–20
perceptual qualities 91–4
phenomenology of Functional Beauty 94–100
A Philosophical Enquiry into the Origin of our Ideas of the Sublime and Beautiful (Burke) 13–14
Plato 2–3, 180, 183 n. 32
Plaza Major, Madrid: proper function of 64, 147, 150–1, 208–9, 215–16
Positive Aesthetics 59–60, 130–6
Preston, Beth 67–8, 74, 75 n., 81
proper function 65–7
  and causal role functions 70–1
  intentionalist theories of 67–9, 78–9, 203–9
  and novel artefacts 80–4
  selected effects theories of 72–7, 146–9
proportion: and beauty 8
proximal senses, *see* aesthetic pleasure and proximal vs. distal senses
Pugin, Augustus 155, 156

Rationalism 6–7
Rawls, John 81 n. 37
ready-mades 173, 226
reflective equilibrium 81 n. 37
relativism: in aesthetics 51–6, 85, 89, 192–4
Richards, Richard 213–14
Rogers, David 19 n. 53
Rolston, Holmes 113, 125, 127 n. 34, 136
ruins: aesthetics of 161–6
Ruskin, John 112

Sagoff, Mark 114–15
Saito, Yuriko 55–6, 176, 190
Santayana, George 29 n. 75
Schiller, Friedrich 188 n.
Schreckengost, Viktor 99
Scientific Cognitivism 39–40, 57, 58, 192–4
Scott, Geoffrey 141
Scruton, Roger 45, 62, 90, 156, 178 n. 22
  on the aesthetics of architecture 47–51
sculpture 36
Seagram Building 159

selected effects theory of proper function 72–3
applied to artefacts 73–84, 146–9
Sharp Centre for Design, Ontario College of Art and Design: aesthetics of 99
Shusterman, Richard 178 n. 23, 183–4, 186, 188
Sibley, Frank 32, 181–2 & n., 184
sight *see* distal senses
simplicity *see* Functional Beauty, phenomenology of
smell *see* proximal senses
Smith, Adam 11, 12, 105, 106, 229
Smithson, Robert 225–6
Social Realism 201
sociobiology 201
Socrates 2, 3–4, 15, 55, 180
somaesthetics 178 n. 23
Sparshott, Francis 100–1, 156
Stace, W. T. 155 n. 27
Stolnitz, Jerome 24–6, 32–4
strainer arch 47–8, 90
structural honesty 155–7, 158, 160
Sullivan, Louis 43
sympathy: beauty and 10
Symposium (Xenophon) 15

'The Tall Office Building Artistically Considered' (Sullivan) 43
taste (gustation) *see* proximal senses
taste, judgements of 21, 23
Tatarkiewicz, Wladyslaw 4 n. 9
teletypewriters 80, 82
The Theory of Moral Sentiments (Smith) 11, 12
Tolstoy, Leo N. 199
Touch Sanitation (Ukeles) 225–6
tragedy 220, 221–2
Translation, Problem of 45–9, 90–100, 154–61
A Treatise of Human Nature (D. Hume) 8–9

ugliness 2–3, 130–6, 181
and functionality 50, 109, 132–3, 153, 162
Ukeles, Mierle 225–6
unity in aesthetic theory 38, 57–60, 230–2
utility
and aesthetic pleasure 102–6
as beauty 8–11

Vermaas, Pieter E. 67 n. 8
criticisms of selected effects theories 80, 82
intentionalist theory of artefact function 78–9
Vietnam Memorial 224–5
visual tension *see* Functional Beauty, phenomenology of

Walton, Kendall 32–3, 37–8, 91–2
What is Art? (Tolstoy) 199
Winters, Edward 53, 64
Wolfe, Tom 145 n. 13
Wolterstorff, Nicholas 35, 224
Wright, Larry 41

Xenophon 2, 3–4, 15

Zangwill, Nick
on aesthetic function of art 198–9, 204
on animals, aesthetic appreciation of 115–16, 118
on organisms, aesthetic appreciation of 124
on non-living natural things 128–9

Lightning Source UK Ltd.
Milton Keynes UK
UKOW06f1424240717
305945UK00001B/18/P

9 780199 659319